The Romantic Virtuoso

THE
ROMANTIC
VIRTUOSO

Morse Peckham

Wesleyan University Press

Published by University Press of New England

Hanover and London

Wesleyan University Press
Published by University Press of New England, Hanover, NH 03755
© 1995 by Robert Peckham
All rights reserved
Printed in the United States of America
5   4   3   2   1
CIP data appear at the end of the book

This book has been supported by a grant from the
National Endowment for the Humanities,
an independent federal agency.

Contents

DEDICATED

TO

DAVID L. POWELL

Introduction

L E O D A U G H E R T Y

Morse Peckham was both a great skeptic and a dazzlingly original social and literary theorist. After first getting interested in nineteenth-century culture, he became obsessed with Romanticism. Where had it come from? How had it happened? What, in the end, had happened to it? And most important of all: what *was* it? Peckham's skepticism extended to all previous answers to those questions, especially the last, and it was not driven solely by his frustration at those answers' historical and explanatory inadequacies. It was also driven by his puzzlement over why such answers didn't account for what had come, to him, to seem so obvious about Romanticism: that it was easily the most significant, as well as the most bafflingly anomalous, phenomenon in Western culture for which we possess an adequate historical record from beginning to end. So part of his life's work—the part which this, his last book, brings to a close—was devoted to figuring all this out.

As Peckham worked on Romanticism over the years, he gently (but, for those who disagreed with his findings, maddeningly) put most of the previous theory and history of it to shame—and, for many of us who read him carefully and thought about him deeply, to rest. But he also developed his own new and powerful theories and historical explanations, breathtaking in their erudition and brilliance, to account for various pieces of the puzzle of Romanticism—and, ultimately, for the thing itself. For most people, that would be quite enough for one life of the mind. But for any account of Morse Peckham's work and its significance, it is only one piece of the story.

Citations in the Introduction are to editions listed in section VIII of the Bibliography.

The reason lies in those two words *erudition* and *brilliance*. Peckham self-deprecatingly joked about his "dilettantism"; but dilettantes are people who know a little about a lot of things, whereas he knew more about a lot of things than many specialists know about those same things. In fact, he was a person so deeply erudite, and so brilliant in his ability to think originally about what he knew, that talks with him struck a good many people, knowledgeable in their own right, as being like dreams, science fiction (as in "close encounters"), or marginally supernatural experiences. But they were nothing of the sort. Those talks were with a person who had worked hard for years to learn what he knew and what he thought about it. (He was forty-eight, for example, when he felt he knew enough to publish his first real book.) The bright flash of his thought—especially when it came in a moment of typically lucid out-loud musing about a new problem one had brought him—was a shock one but gradually got used to. And it was this erudition and brilliance, when applied to the enigma of Romanticism, that many years later led Peckham (or, as he felt, *threw* him) into the outlandish step of creating his own original theory of human behavior.

For Peckham felt that one could not understand Romanticism in isolation. It was not enough to know, for example, "where it came from." One needed to know *why* it came as it *did*—since, for him, it was *sui generis* as a piece of culture history. It was literally unlike any other cultural response to previous events and states of affairs, and unlike any other cultural innovation—in general structure, in the extremity of its innovations, and in the protean forms it took. He agreed with others that there were arguably "several Romanticisms," but he also felt that there was a central core of *most deeply innovative* Romanticism, to which its variants stood as weaker relations. He could not at first explain to himself how such an unprecedented innovation could have occurred. But he gradually became convinced that the right question to ask was, "what were those few central and seminal people at the forward edge of the cultural response we call Romanticism *doing*?" He decided that the only chance for an adequate answer lay in pursuing Romanticism across all the cultures in which it emerged—and in doing this in terms of its foundational documents and artifacts, as well as across all the arts and other cultural genres (for example, the disciplines of anthropology and psychology) in which it emerged. And this, unbelievably, he actually did.

But he still remained unsatisfied, feeling that he had not yet touched anything very near bottom. His reasoning over the years went something as follows. In order to understand a particular work of literature (as representative of, say, a "movement" as problematic as

Romanticism), one needed a good critical and historical theory of literature in general. But the theoretical paradigms that were part of his own "received culture" as a young literary critic were woefully inadequate, partly because they were crypto-religious, partly because they were provincial, partly because they were frighteningly anti-intellectual, but *mainly* because they were not solidly based on a good critical and historical theory of aesthetics in general. Looking around, Peckham found no such good theory, so he worked hard to create one of his own. But it didn't take him too long to see that since works of art (no matter how defined) are made of signs and perceived as signs, a good theory of aesthetics would really require a good theory of (at the very least) verbal and visual semiotics.

After first trying to base such a semiotic theory on the work of Charles Morris, he threw up his hands and once more decided to make his own. But, since verbal and visual signs are made by people, one would need a good general theory of human behavior (in order to go back and explain, in any really adequate way, such a behavioral innovation as Romanticism), and once more he looked high and low and could find none good enough. ("My objection to academic behaviorism," he said in both seriousness and jest, "is that it is not nearly behaviorist enough" [*Romanticism and Behavior* vi].) And so he again created his own. But (going still further in search of something to premise things on), he created it out of his longstanding bedrock conviction that any reliable theory of human behavior would have to be based in turn on a reliable theory of human evolution, itself solidly based on the theory of general evolution.[1]

And so it was that Peckham, cheerfully (as always) working his way up the subsumption ladder, terminated his own "explanatory regress" (a late rhetorical term of his own coinage) by ultimately explaining the Romantics in terms of his own early (but unwavering) interest in Charles Darwin. He had done the standard variorum of the *Origin*, and his often-reprinted essay "Darwin and Darwinisticism" remains a minor classic in the history of science.[2] (The conclusion is inescapable, according to Peckham's theory, that Darwin turned out to be one of the central and most significant of all the nineteenth-century Romantics.) In any event, the byproducts of Peckham's work on Romanticism over the years—especially his theory of human behavior, which he finally managed to articulate in his most difficult book, the luminous *Explanation and Power: The Control of Human Behavior*—were every bit as important as the work itself, arguably even more so, and Peckham knew it.[3]

After all, if your obsessions had led you to have and to hold two pivotal and generative intellectual interests during your long working life, and if those interests happened to be Romanticism and human behavior (and even if you thought the two inextricably linked, as Peckham did), you would most likely conclude that your work on the larger subject of behavior was probably more important than the smaller subject that in special and fascinating ways exemplified it. Still, though, you might find that Romanticism wouldn't go away, simply because it struck you as the *most interesting* single behavioral response a small group of people (followed in various ways by millions of others) ever made. You might, then, like Peckham, end up in staying with both. And you might also eventually find yourself at seventy, as he did, with no academic field of your own at all. But you might not feel as good about it as he did on most days; the occasional grumble about *anomie* and all that aside, he loved it. After all, he *approved* of *anomie*.

Peckham's theory of Romanticism grew and changed through the years, along with all the rest of his social, literary, and language theory. " 'I used to think . . . , but now I think . . .' is a figure so frequent in Peckham's conversation that his friends sometimes needle him about its occurrences," writes one former student (Matalene xix). But a good basic primer of that theory, which could also serve as the history of its development, could be made up of only eight lucid essays that take it from the beginning to the end: "Toward a Theory of Romanticism" (1950); "Toward a Theory of Romanticism: II. Reconsiderations" (1960); "The Dilemma of a Century: The Four Stages of Romanticism" (1964); "Romanticism: The Present State of Theory" (1965); "Romanticism and Behavior" (1974); "Literature and Behavior" (1980); "Cultural Transcendence: The Task of the Romantics" (1981); and the Introduction to *Romanticism and Ideology* (1985).[4] And all of these are included in Peckham's three collections of essays (*The Triumph of Romanticism, Romanticism and Behavior*, and *Romanticism and Ideology*). The late novelist and historian Rudolph von Abele once said roughly this to me: "My God, on top of the fact that Peckham's always talking about Darwin and behaviorism and Wagner and Nietzsche and Caspar David Friedrich in his stuff on Romanticism, he's constantly *building the theory*. And he's always warning that any and all of his conclusions are only tentative, only provisional, only 'probes.' Everybody I know *wants* to be able to follow it, but they say they just don't know enough and just can't keep up and just can't grasp it."

But it's actually much easier to follow Peckham through the years than one might think. One reason is that he always tells you, in so many words, "I used to think . . . , but now I think. . . ." A second reason is that, like many other notable intellectual and artistic figures, he did his very best work toward the end—thus making it fairly simple to see what he "really thought" about Romanticism (or anything else he'd developed during his lifetime) by looking at what he said about it in the late seventies and then throughout the eighties. A third reason is that he pushed his thinking so far that it eventually generated conclusions he could at last feel reasonably happy to *stand by*—conclusions stemming from both his theoretical and historical work—some of which he got to only with the present book.[5]

The center of Peckham's theory of Romanticism (from which one can work backward and outward as far as one likes or needs) is this. A few very innovative people in Western culture discovered, and then established within that culture, what Peckham calls "the basic behavior pattern of culture transcendence" (*Romanticism and Ideology* 8). This discovery was the result of those people's judgment that "explanatory collapse—the failure of powerful implicit and explicit language-based ideologies—had occurred. (Peckham's definition of "ideology" is "regnant platitude" [22].) In these people's case, what had collapsed on them was precisely the foundational language of that explanatory house of cards, the Enlightenment. Peckham believed that such explanatory collapses actually happen all the time; but, for him, the uniqueness of Romanticism was caused by the immensity of the crash and the resultant immensity of its effects upon these few people, taken together with the unparalleled innovativeness of their individual and collective cultural responses—some stylistic, some substantive.

In addition to the collapse of Enlightenment explanations, the Romantics' "basic behavior pattern of cultural transcendence" was also caused by their resultant "alienation from the culture and the society's institutions" (8). It came to be characterized by, and soon thereafter strategized through, several other factors: (a) "cultural vandalism"; (b) "social withdrawal"; (c) "reducing the [individual's social] interaction rate to the minimum"; (d) "randomizing behavior"; (e) "selecting a promising emergent innovation"; (f) "collecting a little group of supporters"; (g) "propagandizing the [resultant] cultural emergent or innovation or 'creativity.'"[6] But by far the most important consequence of the Romantic's cultural transcendence (and innovative Romanticism's most defining characteristic as well) was that the person underwent "a deconversion from hypostatized redemptionism . . . [which in turn] led to a conversion into a *permanent deconversion*" (italics mine) (8).

This state of permanent deconversion led the Romantic to feel free enough for (or to be driven to) "the acceptance of an irresolvable tension between subject and object, between mind and nature, between theory and empirical data, between language and the world"—and this acceptance Peckham believes to be "the heart of the Romantic position" (40). But the position includes a related claim that is crucial to understanding where Peckham was coming from and where he was going: that this same acceptance is "identical with the heuristic conception of scientific explanation, or theory," because in fact "the epistemology of Romanticism is congruent with the epistemology of the more sophisticated philosophies of science" (40). For Peckham, it was obvious that the people who managed this acceptance best were those who proved best able to transcend their cultures and those cultures' various (but always present in some form or another) power-serving ideologies—and, in particular, those ideologies that were redemptively unity based and (hence) stasis based.

In a nutshell, then, the innovative Romantic was a person who responded to the collapse of the Enlightenment by deciding, or somehow coming to feel, that not only the explanatory cultures of the past must be dismissed and transcended, but also the explanatory cultures of the present. Such a person therefore stopped moving from one ideological conversion to another (especially religious conversion) and simply came to rest (although it could never be a comfortable rest) in the "permanent conversion to deconversion." And the reason the most interesting Romantics did that, Peckham felt, lay in their discovery that (in his words, although not in their own) "all language is fictive and normative."[7] In partial consequence, these same people were enabled (whether in joy or resigned melancholy) to "accept the tensions." Thus, the stage was set: such people, having so concluded (whether consciously or not), were ready to do serious innovation—and indeed, if they were going to do anything, could do nothing else.

In holding that language is "normative," Peckham means simply that instances of it are always attempts—whether masked or not—to get the hearer or reader to do as the utterer wishes. In holding that language is "fictive," he means only that it is what other theorists past and present might call "purely imaginative"—liberated from all actual real-world referents. (The claim that language is "fictive" is not far from anticipating, and is fairly close to, slightly later "nonreferential" claims about language by such philosophers as Donald Davidson and Richard Rorty.[8])

Thus, since they are made up solely of normative language, all ideologies are attempts to control human beings by verbal power—or, that failing, by force. And Peckham's pivotal argument about the Romantics concludes that the most interesting ones were simply the first people to understand this, to transcend the cultural attempt to do it (and, thereby, to transcend the cultures making the attempt), to "just say no" to it—and to all the "its." Peckham's Romantic "permanent conversion to deconversion" thus means just what its words say: a person "decides"—because of finding out that the language of the "received" ideology is merely fictive and normative (but especially, when it comes to ideology, normative)—to become permanently separated from any ideologies he or she might hold, and to become permanently committed to never again becoming converted to any.

Does this mean that Peckham was, in the postmodern and post-structuralist sense, "antifoundational"? Yes and no. In most ways, yes. But Peckham hoped for a different kind of intellectual future than the one we now have (though I think we will yet get something like his). In Peckham's version of the future, the best scientific work should play a central role—particularly theoretical work—and should be central to the social and intellectual lives of all people everywhere. Because "appropriate" response to ideological control "can ultimately be maintained only by the application of force in the form of economic deprivation, imprisonment, torture, and execution," he saw the main hope for the future resting with "the capacity of science to exploit ideological instability" (6).[9] His skepticism thus did not extend all the way to the best work done by the best scientific workers, although he certainly thought such workers should know more about the history and theory of their work (including their own invested social roles). He also thought they should know more about the serious problems caused for their work by its unavoidably rhetorical nature, by the fact that it is in large part just more "discourse" in service to ideologies, themselves in service to stasis-based power. He thought the only way out lay in a science of the future which would carry forward the work of the Romantics in "undermining the ideological superstructure of Western culture, and of culture itself." In fact, Peckham saw this as "an undermining which, it may be, is the only human hope" (24).

He pinned this hope on the science of the future turning out, literally, to be (in his sense) "Romantic" science. The scientific workers of the future, if permanently converted to deconversionism, would have a chance of being free from the controls laid down by ideological explanations, or for any (psychological) need for them in the future; hence, they might turn out to be accepting of, and maybe even committed to, the same "irresolvable tensions" necessary for true Romanticism—and for true innovation. The result would not be that such people could, in their work, achieve "disinterestedness" and "objectivity"—for achieving them, or even coming close, is obviously impossible for humans (a fact which has too long served the neoluddites too well as a red herring). Rather, such people would merely *want* them enough, and *try* for them enough, to innovate their way freely toward them, thus helping to bring about the destabilization of stasis-based cultural power and the "regnant platitudes" that ever explain and justify its continuance.

It is important to recognize that Peckham's ideas on Romanticism and science are flatly opposed to the ideas of such theorists as Rorty (in *Contingency, Irony, and Solidarity*) and Donna Haraway (in *Simians, Cyborgs, and Women*), who respectively argue that science can provide no such foundation, or, even if it could, that its workers should not want to try for objectivity and disinterestedness. Rorty believes the former, arguing that Kuhnian "scientific revolutions" are merely "metaphoric redescriptions," and thus that "we must resist the temptation to think that the redescriptions of reality offered by contemporary physical or biological science are somehow closer to 'the things themselves,' less 'mind-dependent,' than the redescriptions . . . offered by contemporary culture criticism" (Rorty 16). With "foundations" cleared out of the way, Rorty has freed himself up to advocate the kind of communitarian authority he wants (since authority of some kind is obviously needed, and since there is, on his account, no other kind possible than those which communities make up). Haraway, meanwhile, believes the latter, and in consequence makes a passionate argument for a future that is the direct opposite of Peckham's. She believes the real hope lies in replacing scientific objectivity and disinterestedness and (ideological) "innocence" with subjectivity, interestedness, and "guilt," because she believes that science should be brought into the service of the (ideological, then social) agenda she wants (Haraway 72–124). She thus seems to hope for something Peckham truly dreaded: a cultural future governed largely by an ideology-driven scientific foundation in service to well-intentioned, high-minded, and otherwise idealistic politics. (I can hear him now, ticking off the historical precedents, starting of course with science under Hitler.)

The underlying question, assuming that one wants a future liberated from ideology-justified power establishments, is simply, Where do you place your strategic bets? Most other contemporary social theorists place them on either the denial of scientific (or any) foundations or the advocacy of competing ideological foundations for science and its methods (for example, that it must serve "justice," or "the community," or "the earth-goddess Gaia")—and that the scientific endeavor should otherwise be opposed. But Peckham's bet is that the destabilization of ideology-based power structures can only be achieved through demonstrating, with a "Romantic" science we don't even have yet (and which by its very nature can never be fully realized), that the self-interested, justificatory explanations of power structures are falsely premised, poorly argued, and erroneously concluded because they don't match the best data.

Which data can be explained in better ways.

Which explanations, if good enough, will redound to the ultimate betterment of people and their world.

The best and most promising example from the past and present: Darwin's theory and its revisions by those neo-Darwinists most faithful to its methods and spirit.

Yet if one sets the disagreement about science aside, what remains is mostly agreement between Peckham and the postmodernist/poststructuralist theorists as to what to be skeptical about (that is, virtually everything, including most of science as currently practiced), and why. Part of the reason is their shared love of, and reliance upon, Nietzsche—who was certainly one of the two or three major influences on Peckham. This consonance can appear odd on the surface, however, because Peckham also traced his intellectual lineage back through George Herbert Mead, John Dewey, and William James to C. S. Pierce, saying explicitly that he was working in the tradition of American Pragmatism (he refined Mead's theory of meaning but stayed pretty much with it, while eventually rejecting Pierce's theory of signs). And it is hard to think of many postmodernists and poststructuralists who have much affinity for, or even interest in, Pragmatism—until one thinks of Rorty, who is a neopragmatist (although one who, like Peckham, traces back to what Rorty calls "Nietzschean Pragmatism"), and whose ideas about language (for example, its "nonreferentiality" and "contingency") are close to their own and to Peckham's. Yet they are suspicious of Rorty (in a way that those who know about Peckham are not), and rightly so.

The reason lies in the disagreement between Rorty and Peckham (and themselves) about the goodness of innovation and its role in the undermining of regnant communitarian ideologies—a disagreement that goes back to the fact that Rorty dislikes those aspects of Nietzsche which Peckham (and the postmodernists/poststructuralists) love, and vice versa. In particular, Rorty's (uncharacteristically) cobwebby talk about the distinction between public and private behavior makes it clear that he has little use for the Nietzsche who publicly advocated the sort of public innovation which might undermine liberally established communitarian consensus. For Peckham, however, it is precisely *that* deathly cultural reality—as experienced in the real, power-based-relations world lived in by real people—that needs to be forever transcended, forever opposed. And in thinking so, he is joined by some of the more prominent poststructuralists.

Two such theorists are Gilles Deleuze and Jacques Derrida. Peckham's theory of what the Romantics were up to is in fact very near Deleuze's idea that "language is not made to be believed but to be obeyed" and with his long corollary obsession with the (then) obvious question: How do you get something new? (Deleuze 22). In the case of Derrida, the resemblances are, if anything, even more obvious because his and Peckham's respective theories, albeit couched in different rhetorics, are nearly identical. When he talks about "deconstructing," he means the destabilizing of ideological foundations—and, equally as important, the building-back-up of new (but, as with Peckham, always provisional) foundations. If Peckham is a "foundationist," then, he is one in Derridaean terms: his foundation is his belief in, and commitment to, the continual reaffirmation of deconstruction/innovation. He differs from Deleuze and Derrida only in his claim that scientific research at its best—"Romantic science"—doesn't merely contribute to that work, but does in fact constitute the major hope for its successful continuance.

Peckham's theory of Romanticism (and of its cultural usefulness in the past, present, and future) is also consonant with the underlying positions of several other formidable figures in contemporary arts and letters. A short (if initially surprising) list would include Jean Baudrillard, William S. Burroughs, and Noam Chomsky. What these figures share is a passionate social and intellectual libertarianism (which is the direct opposite of the rather naive communitarianism of such theorists as Rorty and Haraway). This core position leads them, by means of their various rhetorics, to posit, and then to participate in, something of a Manichean high drama in which a "sons of light" power of infinitely various, innovative, and (hence) culturally destabilizing "speech" (interpreted broadly) is pitted against an oppressive "sons of darkness" cultural power establishment (endlessly imperialistic and hegemonizing, albeit inherently unstable because of its inner contradictions), itself armored in ideological explanations/justifications of stasis and unity ultimately backed up by force. (All four, in their various gentle and even pacifistic ways, counsel war.) Moreover, this same libertarian (and hence dualistic) drama is also what connects up, *internally*, Peckham's own theories of Romanticism, aesthetics, language, and human behavior itself. Much less obviously, however, it provides the same internal linkage for Chomsky's theories of syntax and politics; for Baudrillard's social theory, media, and travel writing; and for the whole of Burroughs' narrative work from the late 1950s through the present.[10]

Granted that the attempt to make "histories of ideas" is still thought worth doing, I would argue for the usefulness of considering Peckham's theory of Romanticism within the context of both the deconstructionist work of Derrida and Deleuze and the libertarian/dualist "Romantic Manicheanism" of Baudrillard, Burroughs, and Chomsky. These figures premise virtually everything on the (relative) goodness of continuous, culturally destabilizing innovation, and they committedly advocate the social "right" to such innovation. Although their connectedness has not been obvious, they have nonetheless separately worked the same shared territory at the same time, for the same underlying reasons and in the same passionate hopes. As we come to the end of the century, it seems appropriate to try to see those deep affiliations between our major figures which will likely seem obvious after the small stuff fades away and the broader outlines emerge.

What remains to be discussed here is Peckham's historical work on Romanticism and the circumstances of its publication. From the beginning, his ideas on the subject had drawn fire—sometimes from the most eminent scholars and critics of their day—because he did not, they said, provide sufficient examples. "Who *are* these 'central' cultural transcenders and innovators Peckham is always talking about?" they asked. Since he was usually being quite clear about who they were (albeit arguably in piecemeal fashion resulting from scattered publication, some of it in ephemeral journals), and since his arguments about Romanticism were usually models of lucidity (at least for people knowing the history and willing to take on the complexity and subtlety of his thought), this question amounted to something of a rationalization for disliking (and in some cases despising) the ideas and arguments themselves.

I think it fair to say that Peckham was a bit troubled and irritated by the complaint. After all, he had early on done an anthology of what he considered the seminal Romantic texts, *Romanticism: The Culture of the Nineteenth Century*, which, although greatly neglected, remains the best such anthology ever published in English. But at the same time he was aware that a thoroughgoing history of Romanticism was in fact badly needed—one that would take it from its beginnings in the late eighteenth century up to its end (in Peckham's nearly solitary recognition) in about 1912. Such a history would trace Romanticism's development across the fine arts, humanities, social sciences, and natural sciences. It would especially stress the point that Romanticism's high-water mark was Nietzsche, of whom Peckham wrote as early as 1965: "The whole Romantic tradition moves irresistibly towards Nietzsche.... And it is Nietzsche who was the great liberator and releaser for almost every creator of modern art and culture" (325). Such a history would also foreground significant relationships and patterns as they moved through time, especially those not generally recognized. And . . . it would at last name all the names.

And so it came to pass that, at some point in the early 1980s, when he was around seventy and at the very top of his game, Morse Peckham signed a contract with a small publisher to write a multivolume history of Romanticism titled *Romanticism and its Consequences: Emergent Culture in the Nineteenth Century, 1790–1912*. The first volume, *The Birth of Romanticism: 1790–1815*, appeared in 1986. Arguably the most distinguished cultural history of Romanticism ever written, it went generally unreviewed, undistributed, and unread, although a few key ads did appear (most notably some full-page ones in *PMLA*). Peckham appeared oblivious, and indeed he probably was; always something of the reverse snob, and unusually enamored (for the fiercely careerist 1980s) with the antiprofessional pleasures of casual (and even desultory-seeming) publication, he struck me as taking a certain delight in the disparity between the book's excellence and its (lack of) reception. He simply sat down and started writing the second volume in the series, which bore the working title *The Romantic Virtuoso, 1815–1825*.

*   *   *

At some point in the summer of 1990, I found in my mailbox a big package from Peckham. It contained a typescript of the book, in two major sections, retitled *The Romantic Virtuoso, 1815–1825, and Meditations on the Consequences of Romanticism*. A covering note said that he had tired of the entire project and was sending me the one book he had made out of all that remained to be done. He implied that he was not at that time interested in publishing it—he had evidently decided to write and publish no more—but was sending it along because he knew I was interested in its progress (which he had kept me up on in his letters of the late 1980s[11]), and because he thought I might enjoy it. Which I did.

A few months later, Peckham suffered the first of a series of debilitating strokes, and for nearly three years afterward the typescript of his last book sat on my shelf. I did not quite know what, if anything, to do about it. Finally, in the early summer of 1993, I decided that it was too valuable a book (in general terms, but also because of its status as Peckham's last word on Romanticism at the end of some forty-five years) to go unpublished. I also felt responsible for doing something about it through learning that the typescript in my possession had turned out, apparently, to be the sole surviving copy (although others had read the book, at least in draft). I consulted with two of Peckham's oldest and dearest friends—Bill Matalene (who came to write the Biographical Afterword for the book) and David L. Powell (to whom Peckham dedicates it)—and they encouraged me to pursue publication. So, sometime in the middle of the summer I offered it to Wesleyan University Press, whose editors and readers were enthusiastically receptive. In September, Morse Peckham died in his eightieth year.

Manuscript corrections in the author's hand indicate that he had originally meant to do a few more pages on the first section (that is, *The Romantic Virtuoso* proper) but had decided they would be unnecessary to concluding it as he wished. Other notes and changes indicate that at about this same time he did definitely replan the volume so as to make it into the present book in nearly its present form, and that this new plan was for a "real book," albeit one somewhat unconventional in form. I provide this information because I think it important to know that Peckham planned out, radically restructured at midcourse, and then completed this work—that it is not a fragment or "notes toward" a book—and that he revised the entire manuscript. As much, at least, as he ever revised anything.

* * *

The book's first two chapters trace Romanticism from Scott to Schubert. What is now a Coda (a word Peckham himself used in discussing the section entitled "Meditations on the Consequences of Romanticism") provides a synoptic account of the rest of the projected volumes in the series, but its narrative line is centered, as its title implies, directly on the theme of "consequences." (Readers of Peckham's three volumes of collected essays will be familiar with his dependence on the word; he thought of many of his shorter pieces as being "consequences" essays—for example, "The Deplorable Consequences of the Idea of Creativity" [in *Romanticism and Behavior*]—and hence grouped them under "Consequences" in his tables of contents.) The "Meditations" section begins with Goya, Beethoven, and the young painter Richard Parkes Bonington; it ends with Freud, Joyce, Picasso, and a stunning summary account of Modernism itself, in which Peckham tells how some of the central Modernists brought Romanticism proper to a close:

What the Moderns did was to refuse so completely the cultural controls over both the form and semantic content of art that only a few individuals could at first ascribe value to them and to their works. What they did was to create their own cultural controls, a behavior made possible by alienation and also by the culture that made it value-laden to disobey certain cultural controls. That creation of one's own cultural controls is the "self." One may say, therefore, that only with the Moderns did the self emerge fully from the matrix of Romanticism. (210)

For Peckham, then, this was the end of the whole long story of Romanticism, and of the other long story of his attempt to tell it. It was how things had finally come out—with the creation of the twentieth-century notion of the self. But he should not be misunderstood on the point, for in fact his immense skepticism had always extended to the whole idea of the self (along with just about every other muddled idea), and he had early on cast *it* overboard too, writing as early as 1965: [The self] is not a metaphysical entity, something that really exists, but is only the sense of identity. . . . Thus value is not something that the self creates. *Value is the self.* The mere feeling that life is worth the trouble it takes to live it is what we are talking about when we use the word 'self.' "[12] Moreover,

The solution to the Romantic problem lies not in attempting the impossible, not in trying to stabilize the Self, but in continuous self-transformation, in continuously transcending tragedy, and comedy, and good, and evil. . . . With Nietzsche, Romanticism got to the root of its problem and found a stable solution to its difficulty in instability itself, in conceiving of life as the eternal possibility for continuous self-transformation. (*Romanticism: The Culture of the Nineteenth Century* 323)

In these 1965 statements about the self, we find Peckham, as ever, leading the way with an idea, albeit with few (knowing) followers. The congruence of this position with the positions of Lacan, Foucault, and Rorty—not to mention the myriad of postmodernists and poststructuralists who now hold it—will be obvious to people familiar with recent social and literary theory. It will be equally obvious that all of them, Peckham included, trace back to Nietzsche. But what will not be obvious to most such people is that Peckham's position (as I have tried to stress here, and have perhaps belabored) traces straight back to Darwin, too—and that Darwin's primacy for Peckham's theories (of the self and everything else) may in the end keep him in the field after they have all gone the eternal way of fashion. For it is Darwin as well as Nietzsche who leads Peckham to the exit line at the end of *The Romantic Virtuoso* that sums up everything he most deeply believed, taught, and lived by: "Readiness is all." Future biographers of Morse Peckham, in casting about for book titles, could do worse.

N O T E S

1. I note that my recounting of Peckham's theory-building follows the logic of its development rather than strict year-by-year chronology.

2. See the Bibliography for publication specifics regarding both Peckham's edition of the *Origin of Species* and the essay "Darwin and Darwinisticism," reprinted in his first collection of essays, *The Triumph of Romanticism*.

3. One of the most formidable works of social theory to appear in the last twenty years, *Explanation and Power* (1979; 1988) has met with unfathomable neglect and is now virtually forgotten (though still in print). For those seriously working along Peckham's lines, it is yet-to-be-discovered treasure, while for those seriously working along opposed lines it will prove more of a deeply buried yet unavoidable mine.

4. Peckham's Introduction to *Romanticism and Ideology* is a synopsis of the argument of *Explanation and Power*; it also appears as Appendix II of *The Birth of Romanticism 1790–1815*.

5. Still, Peckham did not believe at the end that the question (in his own self-parodying words), "What was Romanticism, really?" is a good one. In carrying his thinking as far as he could, he explicitly resisted (even his own) reductionist impulses, believing them to be (quite literally) atavistic. Late in his life, he wrote: "I believe in the inherent instability of theory construction, and I have endeavored to practice it" (*Romanticism and Ideology* 33).

6. Peckham helpfully provides this list in the introduction to *Romanticism and Ideology* (8); he also provides careful analyses of these topics in the eight essays on Romanticism listed above, all contained in his three volumes of collected essays, as well as in *Explanation and Power*. The best advice for readers wishing to go further is to consult the indexes to those works.

7. Peckham explains this point in several places. The briefest late discussion is *Romanticism and Ideology* 1–9; and with particular reference to literary language, 348), although the only thorough analysis is *Explanation and Power*, *passim*.

8. As others have correctly pointed out, however, Davidson and Rorty are themselves not nearly as close as Rorty thinks.

9. Peckham most succinctly presents his ideas on science in two essays, "Romanticism, Science, and Gossip" and "Literature and Behavior," both in *Romanticism and Ideology*.

10. Baudrillard is quite candid about his own affinities with the kind of "Romantic Manicheanism" posited here (see, for example, *Baudrillard Live* 139–40, 176, and *The Ecstasy of Communication*, *passim*. Raphael Salkie is helpful in showing how Chomsky's dualistic social libertarianism both links up

his work in syntax theory and political theory and helps place him within the intellectual context discussed here (*The Chomsky Update* 201–219). Deleuze's relatedness to this position may be easily derived from much of his writing, but an accessible source is the book of interviews *Dialogues* (124–147, and, with particular reference to his dualism, 132). I presume (perhaps wrongly) that Burroughs' longstanding advocacy of this general position (specific theories of "what language is" aside) will be self-evident to students of his work.

11. As an example of his adventures in doing the book, Peckham wrote to me in a letter of 1 September 1986: "I was just about to finish Chapter I by writing about Schopenhauer when a truck hit me as I was walking along Bull Street [in Columbia, S.C.]. After Medicare had been repaid and the lawyer had his cut, I got $20,808.00 as a settlement. If it had been $30,000.00 I would have gotten myself hit again."

12. Peckham reaffirmed this same position with respect to the self in his later writings on the subject. See, for example, *Romanticism and Ideology* 30–31.

The Romantic Virtuoso

CHAPTER ONE

1815–1820
The Aftermath
of Waterloo

Waterloo. The exile of Napoleon to St. Helena. After twenty-five years of revolutionary turmoil, the effects of which spread to every corner of Europe, and of the Napoleonic wars, during which much of Europe lost for a time its national independence, Europe was faced with coming to terms with the consequences. European political life had before it the tremendous problem of restoring the old political systems, with the full knowledge that those systems could not possibly be restored. The awakening of Europe to politics in its modern sense was a fact that could not be ignored or defeated. It was obvious to all but a few political leaders—those who could not bear to contemplate what had happened—that the age of the dynasts was over and that the age of the peoples had begun. Together the Revolution and Napoleon had created the first national armies, and in doing so had created the modern nation, the nation not of a monarch but of a people. After the French Revolution of 1830 there was no longer a King of France; there was a King of the French. So the rulers of Europe, those restored to their thrones or those who barely held on to them, needed to reckon with popular feelings and demands, even if their only strategy was to attempt by means of censorship and a police modeled on Napoleon's to suppress at least the expression of those feelings and to circumvent the manifestation of those demands. Indeed, in much of Europe the new age was the Age of a New Censorship, a bureaucratic censorship, which was yet another piece of the Revolutionary-Napoleonic bequest.

Europe was faced with the political dilemma it is still faced with, the diremption, as Hegel called it, the splitting in two, the pulling apart, of political and much of cultural life into the liberal and the conservative, the reactionary and the radical. Both capitalism and socialism were Enlightenment ideas, for there was a conservative (and reactionary) Enlightenment as well as a liberal (and radical) Enlightenment. Yet at a profounder level this opposition revealed the fundamental incoherence of Western culture—and very possibly of all cultures that can be called advanced. Perhaps that diremption, that splitting, that pulling apart, that incoherence is the inescapable condition of the human enterprise.

On the one hand, the brain's capacity for random response to any stimulus means that if interaction is to occur with any success and smoothness, controls (that is, culture) must be imposed upon human behavior, so that predictability of behavior may result, a predictability essential above all for economic activity and interaction. Nevertheless, it is equally the condition that those controls, being primarily linguistic constructs, must be more or less inadequate and that innovation is as essential to the human enterprise as are controls. Human beings desperately need both innovation and defenses against innovation. The profoundest revelation of the Enlightenment failure was to uncover precisely this inexorable incoherence in human affairs. Ever since the Revolution there have been laments for what has mistakenly and sentimentally been believed to have been a lost unity, and likewise apocalyptic cries for the restoration of that unity which never existed. The revelation of that incoherence was the problem the Romantics had to struggle with. It is the problem that makes their struggles still relevant today.

The individual's sense of his own value, his experience and judgment of his own value, the value of others, and the value of human existence itself depend in equal measure both on his capacity for validating innovation when he judges it to be creative and for rejecting and invalidating innovation when he judges it to be error. What made that judgment in the nineteenth century so difficult and still makes it so difficult was what the French Revolution revealed to a few individuals. To repeat the conclusion of *The Birth of Romanticism*, what it taught was "liberty that yields oppression, equality that yields tyranny, brotherhood that yields murder," a terrible bequest "made even more terrible by the fact that that bequest did indeed yield liberty, equality, fraternity as well as oppression, tyranny, and murder." Thus the ensuing century after the defeat of Napoleon was to see superficial Romanticisms that had the political overtones either of the radical-liberal or of the conservative-reactionary. Yet the essence of Romanticism was to analyze and, in necessary consequence, to dismantle what Marx was to call the cultural superstructure, which Hegel had already called *Geist*. It was an effort that at first and for a long time meant and to a certain extent still means the fundamentally futile effort to reconcile and synthesize control and creativity, culture and innovation, to attempt to heal that diremption in human behavior which the Enlightenment had revealed and which it was the task of Romanticism to struggle with. We can see this in both of the two figures who were to dominate European culture for at least a quarter of a century after Waterloo, Walter Scott and Lord Byron. Thus the ten years which it is the aim of the first part of this volume to examine can be called with equal confidence either the Age of Byron or the Age of Scott. With the older of these two writers, Walter Scott, we shall begin.

WALTER SCOTT (1771–1832)

Scott's impact and fame were tremendous, yet the Waverley Novels present certain problems. Can they justly be called Romantic? Politically, Scott was a typical liberal-conservative, a product of the Enlightenment. On the surface, at least, the Waverley Novels offer little to indicate that Scott was affected by the diremption of European culture that was the result of the Revolutionary-Napoleonic period. There is little in Scott's biography or in the novels to suggest that he felt the post-Waterloo tension. A second problem is Scott's indifference, it would seem, to plot. It is almost as if he felt that any plot complication that he could improvise would do. As a result he often used even wornout plot devices, such as the long-lost heir to the great estate. A third problem is the hero of the Waverley Novels, usually a young man almost without character, respectable, to be sure, but that is all, a figure Scott himself called "imbecile." A fourth problem is that there is little evidence that Scott saw himself to be engaged in a serious artistic undertaking. In the early nineteenth century the novel was by no means a high-ranking genre, and Scott seems hardly interested in giving it greater dignity. Unlike his earlier poems, the Waverley Novels were published anonymously. He has been called a machine for manufacturing fictions, and there is just enough truth in that accusation to be disconcerting.

And yet with all that can be said against the Waverley Novels— and particularly today in a time of sophisticated and demanding fictional criticism—the fact remains that he was not merely popular, he was idolized, from one end of Europe to the other, and translated into almost every European language. There is no doubt that almost in spite of himself he raised the novel to a higher cultural level than it had yet occupied, since it was, after all, in comparison with other literary genres, of fairly recent origin. There is no doubt also that he is rightly called a great figure of Romanticism whose fictions spread, in a subtle way, the problems Romanticism struggled with to every corner of Europe and affected every aspect of high culture. He was called "the great unknown" and "the Wizard of the North." His works and those of his followers were turned into plays and operas and ballets, and became the source of innumerable paintings, as well as the inspiration and model for works in all the arts not derived specifically from historical novels but illustrative of historical incidents. Indeed the tradition of the historical novel, as created by Scott, continues to this day in popular fiction and even in fiction of a high cultural level. Some of the most ambitious novels in the 1980s have been historical novels. Moreover, the nineteenth century was the great age of historical narrative, multivolume histories of such immense popularity that hardly a western country was not busy discovering its past and defining itself and understanding itself in terms of its past. And these historians reaching for a wide public found that audience in a readership created for them by the Waverley Novels from Spain to Russia and from Norway to Italy, and in the new United States of America. There the first novelists to be popular were direct imitators of Scott, James Fenimore Cooper in the North and William Gilmore Simms in the South.

The result was that more than anyone else, far more, Scott was responsible for one of the most profound consequences of Romanticism, the historicization of European culture. Furthermore, from the Waverley Novels was born a new kind of history, social history, first practiced by the historian Thomas Babington Macaulay. Deliberately and with full self-consciousness he set out, several decades after Scott's death, to reach with pure history the public Scott had reached and indeed had created with historical fiction. In the Waverley Novels the particularity of detail, of every kind of detail, from food to clothing to furnishing to architecture to customs to church ritual to smuggling and so on almost endlessly, gave the readers of the time and can still give the reader of today the sense of what it was like to have lived at some moment in the past. To be sure Scott was at his best when writing about the late seventeenth and eighteenth centuries, when Scotland was little different from the country and the society Scott had encountered in his youth. Now this particularity was not merely antiquarian, in the limited sense, nor merely picturesque. It was intimately and directly illustrative and produced by the life of people, and above all of ordinary people, peasants, fishermen, soldiers. So true is this that possibly the greatest cultural achievement and consequence of Scott is that in the Waverley Novels for the first time the common people step forth on the stage of history.

The common folk in Scott are not stereotypes or even national types. They are as individually realized and as individually real as any of the characters from the upper classes. In fact—and it is one of the puzzles of Scott—his upper-class types, particularly his protagonists, tend to be less individualized, more stock characters, than his ordinary people, his peasants, fishers, and farmers. Among his most passionate and noble characters are women of the people, women who have suffered, who have seen their men drowned or killed in war and who have responded by revealing a grandeur of spirit that more than once has been called Shakespearian, though not very accurately. No novelist before Scott, or poet or dramatist, and few since, have so revealed and explored the strangeness of human beings, their capacity for transcending the platitudinous conceptions of human behavior by means of which we all live. Yet he was not alone in his generation in discerning and bringing forth the concealed grandeur of the apparently ordinary. As we have seen, Wordsworth also could do something of the sort, and perhaps Scott learned it from him or at least learned it was a fit subject for literature. At any rate that human strangeness and that nobility were passed by Scott to Balzac, to Zola, to Faulkner.

To understand how and why this could have been so, to comprehend why it is just to rank Scott the novelist not merely among the Romantics but among the major Romantics, it is useful to look in two directions, one at the underlying pattern of the plot of many of the Waverley Novels, and the other at the novels not merely as a sequence of stories but as a great interlocking structure. The series of the Waverley Novels, as they came to be called after the title of the first one, *Waverley*, extended in publication from 1814 to 1831 and in historical time from 1098 to 1812, if we include in the series *St. Ronan's Well*, published in 1823, and *The Antiquary*, which takes place in 1795, only twenty-one years before it was published. The settings of the series extend as far as India, but all but a few are in the British Isles, and of the thirty-two titles, four of which are short stories, twenty-one take place in Scotland, though a few of these are only partly in Scott's own country. Just half of them take place between 1679 and 1795.

It is necessary to recognize that the conception of a cycle of interrelated fictions, no matter how imperfectly and fragmentarily executed, was Scott's other bequest to Balzac, Zola, and Faulkner, to the

Spaniard Perez y Galdos and the Frenchman Jules Romains, and to Thomas Mann when he wrote his Joseph cycle. The value of looking at the Waverley Novels from these two points of view is that it enables us to discern how Scott's Romantic particularity was brought into literary actuality. And that examination will also enable us to understand his immense popularity.

To Scott the plot of a novel was of little importance, just so much machinery, the only purpose of which was to keep the reader interested by means of the usual plot device of presenting problems and postponing their solutions. But the underlying pattern which the plot exemplified, what we might effectively call the explanatory structure of the Scott novel, was the matter of central importance. It was what Scott as a Romantic and as a writer relevant to the Romantic problem is all about. That pattern first appears in the first novel of the series, *Waverley*, conceived in 1810 or 1811, partly written then, put aside as unpromising, and then taken up and finished and published in 1814. A young man of what Scott himself called "imbecility," a word by which he meant not of subnormal intelligence but of subnormal interest to the reader, has been brought up by a Jacobite uncle and a Hanoverian father, two opposing political positions, though both fundamentally conservative. These loyalties have, as it were, canceled each other out. Waverley is, in short, a typical proper upper middle-class Englishman who, in default of anything better to do, obtains an army commission. Joining his regiment in Scotland, he enters by a series of incidents of only trivial and plot interest from the normal modern world of 1745 (not too different from the world of 1814 in its superficial character) into the world of the Highland clans, a Catholic, not a Protestant, culture, a medieval culture, a rival social system, a world committed to the restoration of the Stuarts, a devotion that had nothing to do with the quality of any given Stuart but simply had to do with the ancient quasi-religious devotion to the king. That Waverley joins the Jacobite party, that he fights in the battles of the incursion of the Pretender into England and his defeat, and that he is eventually pardoned is merely a matter of storytelling, of plot. The real power of the work, its fascination and its appeal, lies first in the very featureless personality of the hero, with whom any reader can therefore categorize himself and with whom he can experience the entry into a different world, a world presented with all of Scott's masterly particularity, a particularity derived from Scott's endless explorations into the documents and artifacts of a Scotland no longer in existence.

This pattern is repeated in quite a different way in Scott's next novel, *Guy Mannering*, published in 1815. The plot, a complex web of unresolved and evidently unresolvable mysteries and problems, is little more than the ancient tale of the stolen, lost, recovered, restored, heir. Scott, of course, has been condemned for his failure to provide more than the most commonplace stories, for his, as it is often called, carelessness. But this criticism is to miss the point. The clichés of the plot left Scott free to devote himself to what interested him, the exploration of an alternative society and culture—and the same carelessness and indifference leaves the reader free. In *Guy Mannering* a very proper retired officer, Colonel Mannering, encounters in the southwest corner of Scotland a world of gypsies, smugglers, and Border farmers, and also Scotch lawyers in the Edinburgh of 1765. Colonel Mannering is again a personality almost as uninteresting as Waverley, and the purpose of the Scott hero or protagonist becomes even clearer, since Harry Bertram, the youthful and alternate hero, is equally pallid. All three of these figures come from the same class as Scott himself, the class in which his readers, he anticipated correctly, would be found. Bertram is also an army officer, and so is the hero of the next novel, *The Antiquary*, published in 1816.

This recurrence of army officers is a consequence, of course, of the Revolutionary and Napoleonic wars. In the background of *The Antiquary*, set in 1795 on the northeast coast of Scotland, are the French Revolution and the threat of a French invasion. In the figure of Jonathan Oldbuck, Scott dramatizes his own interest in the past and shows how the exploration of the past can reveal the concealed meaning of the present. But at the same time he also dramatizes how a false past can be created by deceit and forgery. And these themes emerge from Scott's shameless use again of the plot device of the lost heir. In addition, a profound Scott theme emerges even more forcefully than in the previous works, the passion and the intelligence of representatives of the common people. All this is played against a background of a wild seacoast, an ancient provincial town, and old houses and castles. Thus, by setting the novel at a time only a couple of decades before it was written, Scott dramatizes what he had done in the first two novels, history not as past events but history as the exploration of the past, history as discovery of alternative meanings to win an understanding of the present.

It is probable, indeed one might almost say it is evident, that this consideration of the nature of history enabled Scott in his next two novels to reach farther back into the past of Scotland. *The Black Dwarf* was set in the Border country in 1706 and *Old Mortality* in the hills southeast of Glasgow in 1679. The events of the first are linked to a failed Jacobite rebellion, and the central activity of the second is the religious rebellion of the extreme Calvinist Covenantors against the attempt to impose English episcopacy on Scotland. What emerges most powerfully is the moral grandeur of the Covenantors, as well as their passionate and bitter determination and fanaticism. In this work the common people not only step forth on the stage of history; they take an active and compelling and aggressive part of the struggle over the central cultural issues of seventeenth-century Scotland.

The term "culture" now becomes of crucial importance in understanding what Scott was doing. It was proposed in *The Birth of Romanticism* that Hegel, of the same generation as Scott and a few months older, in giving his special meaning to the term *Geist* was creating an idea virtually identical with the modern, anthropological or behavioral meaning of "culture." *Old Mortality* is centered on a culture conflict, one to be found in the very home and family of the hero. Scott's next novel was *Rob Roy*, published in 1817 and placed in 1715, the year of the first major Jacobite rebellion against the Hanoverian monarchy, the first large-scale effort to abrogate the union of the Scottish and English crowns in 1707. Again we find the ordinary young man faced with a different, even antithetical culture, and the culture conflicts of the work are several: Protestant versus Catholic, merchant class versus aristocracy, English culture versus Scots culture, Lowland Scots versus Highland Scots. The most intense cultural conflict is the latter, with Rob Roy, a proscribed and once famous Highland clan chieftain, revealing in his troubled life the inability of non-Highlanders to understand his culture. Scott is beginning to see as clearly as Hegel that the individual is the product of his culture, the unique traditions of learned behavior into which he is born and which he spends his life expressing.

The very title of his next fiction, *The Heart of Midlothian, set in* 1736 and published in 1818, shows his sharper conception of what he was doing, for the title means simply the town of Edinburgh, the world which formed the heroine Effie Deans, the girl of common origin who in order to save her sister from execution evinces a moral grandeur found in almost no other of Scott's characters, a moral beauty rarely found or even attempted in fiction. She is the true heart of everything that Scott believed to be worthy in the culture and history of his country and his city. The next novel, *The Bride of Lammermoor*, set in 1695 and published in 1819, is very different, concerned almost exclusively with the landed gentry of southeast Scotland. In this, as in *Rob Roy*, which is not only a political novel but more importantly the first novel centered upon a business problem ever written, the impact of economics as well as politics upon the individual's capacity to act out his culture is brought out in the murderous insanity of the heroine. Now Scott turned to English history, and his second foray into that field yielded one of his most popular works, *Ivanhoe* (1819), a work which would be hard to take seriously, so typical is it of historical fiction of no seriousness of intent, were it not for the telling exhibition of what he had discovered to be a central theme of his thought and his writing, the conflict between cultures, here between Saxon and Norman and between Christian and Jew.

Nevertheless, as important as the theme of culture conflict is the theme of cultural transcendence. To be the full realization of one's own culture, to encounter another culture, to feel powerfully the conflict between the two, and yet to be able to transcend the difference, to rise above the limitations of one's own culture, to be able to realize the merits and the historical justification of an antithetical culture and to enter into it sympathetically, even temporarily to ally oneself politically with it—all this is in fact the achievement of those featureless imbecilic heroes of Scott's novels. These characters are a trap and a seduction for the reader. Precisely because they are so pallid, so featureless, so without (in the ordinary sense) character, they represent no barrier to the reader's experiencing the events and above all the particularity, the cultural identifying signs which the hero encounters and to the way he encounters them and responds to them. Thus the reader finds no hindrance to the central experience of those heroes, cultural transcendence. As was proposed in *The Birth of Romanticism*, the search for cultural transcendence is indeed the central task of Romanticism.

That is one direction in which to look for Scott's place among the major Romantics. The other is to see the novels we have looked at, the Waverley Novels from 1814 to 1819, as a cycle of novels. To review briefly, these Waverley Novels, the works which made Scott famous and made him known (so long as he remained the "great unknown") as the Wizard of the North, take place in 1679, 1695, 1706, 1715, 1736, 1745, 1765, and 1795. They form a series in which every important political turmoil of Scotland during the late seventeenth and the eighteenth centuries is used. They are a true cycle, even if they may have been unplanned as a cycle (though indeed it is hard to believe that Scott did not realize what he was doing). The cycle is a peculiarly Romantic form or device in that it recognizes that the encounter with a work of art is as much a creative act as the making of it. The cycle forces the reader to be creative. The author offers the reader the material for a structure, for developing an understanding, in this case, of

Scottish history and Scottish cultures, but he does not complete that structure. That is the task, the opportunity, and the pleasure of the individual reader. And in thus becoming creative himself the reader transcends his own cultural limitations of comprehension and intellectual perception. Thus the two directions in which we look for Scott's Romanticism and his greatness come finally together in a single focus. And that is also the basis for his immense appeal.

The French Revolution and the French conquest under Napoleon of nearly all of Europe, or at least the subjection of Europe to French hegemony, meant an utter dislocation and disturbance of educated and uneducated Europeans in their culture and in their political systems. Whether one was a conservative or a liberal, a reactionary or a radical, one experienced that loss of confidence that has become endemic today, that loss of belief in the stability or, more important, the rightness or the justification of both culture and political system. That loss was intensified by the economic dislocations brought about by the events of the period from 1790 to 1815. The industrialization of England had, of course, already begun before this period, but it was given an immense, an enormous impetus by the fact that in order to defeat Napoleon, England armed Europe, and to do so industrialized itself far sooner than would otherwise have happened.

Not the least of these industrializations, and indeed in the long run perhaps the most important, was the industrialization of papermaking, which for centuries had been a handicraft, ever since it had been introduced into Europe in the fourteenth and fifteenth centuries. This enormous increase in the availability of paper, not to speak of its new cheapness, depended in great part upon the new supply of rags produced by the industrialization of cotton spinning and weaving in England and what might be best understood as the slave labor industrialization of cotton growing and processing in the United States. This new supply of paper meant not only the proliferation of government and business bureaucracies, and thus the interchangeability of individuals in analogous behavior patterns and situations. It also meant that there was now some point and purpose in the development of literacy, for the poor now had something to read. By 1830 in England, for the first time in history, books, magazines, and newspapers became cheap. The knowledge industry was born; and above all the social and political ideals of the liberal and radical Enlightenment tradition could for the first time be easily disseminated to a rapidly growing literate and politically and socially self-conscious proletariat. Thus it is not too much to say that the industrialization of papermaking created the proletariat, created class-consciousness. The workingman autodidact became a new human type.

All this accounts for the immense success and vast dissemination of the Waverley Novels. Dissatisfaction with one's culture and one's political systems, exacerbated by both the futile post-Napoleonic effort to restore the prerevolutionary world and the economic disturbances of spreading industrialization, became endemic from top to bottom of society. A violent reactionism is as expressive of dissatisfaction as an equally violent radicalism. What Scott's novels offered was on the one hand a basic pattern, too subtle to be obvious and blatant, too powerful to be missed, of cultural transcendence; and on the other hand in the cycle of the Waverley Novels the opportunity to create a world. Once learned, that power to create imaginatively a world could then be applied to the world one lived in. Scott was so popular because no other writer met so completely, and yet so subtly, the primary cultural need of his age.

LORD BYRON (1788–1824)

It was proposed in *The Birth of Romanticism* that what made Byron so popular was his powerful revelation of the loss of the efficacy of the culture's traditional sources and modes and institutions of value ascription, and that the task of value creation was the isolated individual's—with, as yet, no notion of how to go about it. Most crucial, most critical, absolutely central in this loss was the disappearance of a valid and reliable mode whereby the individual might ascribe value to himself. That was the significance of the fact that Byron's Turkish Tales were organized, if such a word can justly be applied to works so loosely constructed, around the notion of guilt. In his next two works, both composed in the autumn of 1815 and, significantly, after Waterloo and the defeat of Napoleon, that guilt takes a different turn. These are *The Siege of Corinth* and *Parisina,* published together in February 1816. The earlier tales, *The Giaour, The Bride of Abydos, The Corsair,* and *Lara,* evidently take place at a time contemporary with their writing and publication, Turkey and Greece as they were in the second decade of the nineteenth century. But the next two poems are historical. Although the setting and the conflict are respectively still Greece and the enmity of Turk and Christian (that is, Venetian), *The Siege of Corinth* takes place in 1715. *Parisina,* moreover, not only takes place in a remote past, 1425, but is set in Ferrara, in Italy, which in the autumn of 1816 was to become Byron's home until shortly before his death in Greece in 1824. This shift to historicism was not to be isolated in Byron's work. On the contrary the vast majority of his poetry written from 1816 on was to be historicist. Most of Canto III and almost all of Canto IV of *Childe Harold's Pilgrimage* consists of meditations on the past. *Manfred* by implication is medieval. *Beppo* and *Don Juan* are set in the eighteenth century. (Byron planned the latter to end in Paris during the French Revolution.) And the series of dramas begun in 1820 were all historical. The first was *Marino Faliero,* set in Venice in 1355. It is possible that the success of the first two of the Waverley Novels, all of which Byron admired and read as soon as possible after their publication, had turned his attention to the possibilities of historical narrative. That would have been fair enough, since Scott had given up poetry and taken to the novel because Byron was so much more successful that Scott felt his poetry could not compete with Byron's. But it is possible that Byron's turning to the past was also a response to Waterloo and the fall of Napoleon, a recognition that a period of history had come to an end, that "the present" no longer could subsume the Revolutionary-Napoleonic period.

A further development or at least change was to be found in the two new poems. Alp, the hero of *The Siege of Corinth,* can only be said to be guilty of pride and hate in refusing the pleas of his beloved, Francesca Minotti, to return to the religion and the country he had rejected. For he had left Christianity and his native Venice simply because he had been falsely and anonymously accused of treason. He fled, in fact, to preserve his life. He is now a leader in the Turkish forces besieging Corinth, then a Venetian possession. The governor is Francesca's father. Alp is killed in the attack on Corinth, having learned from Minotti that Francesca is dead. And the poem concludes with Minotti's blowing up a mine that destroys both besiegers and besieged. This gratuitous violence is a further attack upon the social order which has expelled Alp with utter injustice. So the prime source of viciousness is not some mysterious crime by the protagonist, as in the preceding poems, but is the consequence of the activity of the state, of society itself.

In *Parisina* that brutality emanates from the ruler of Ferrara, the Marquis of Este, and the Estes claimed to be the most ancient noble family of Europe. Byron took the story from Edward Gibbon's *Miscellaneous Works,* which had been reprinted in 1814 and again in 1815 with additions from the original edition of 1796. A note to *The Corsair,* sent to Byron's publisher John Murray in January 1815, though not added until the Tenth Edition of 1818, is further indication of his reading of Gibbon and his interest in history. The story of *Parisina* tells how the Marquis of Este discovered that his son and his second wife were lovers. He had both of them beheaded. Technically, of course, they were guilty of incest, but only technically, since there was no consanguinity involved. (It is hardly necessary to add that Byron himself almost certainly was a lover of his half sister Augusta Leigh). But the incest was only the Marquis' excuse. What Byron brings out powerfully and what is his real subject is the tyrannical brutality of the representative of society and social and political power. It is of some interest that in 1815 the Italian poet Silvio Pellico had made the same point in his drama of the story of Francesca de Rimini and Paolo, and that in 1820 Byron made a *terza rima* translation of that episode in Dante's *Inferno*. Byron's comprehension of the cultural situation had deepened; his attention was moved from the failure of the individual to the failure of society.

There is little doubt that if such was his perception, it was intensified by what happened to him in the opening months of 1816. His wife left, he thought, on a visit to her parents, taking their daughter with her; and shortly thereafter he received from her lawyers notice that she wished a separation, that she could never again live with him. His current financial difficulties, the result of his lordly carelessness and his indifference to the financial rewards of his poems, only made the situation worse. London, and soon all Europe, boiled with rumors. The scandal was tremendous. But the upshot was that in April Byron left London and England forever, traveling through the low countries and up the Rhine to Switzerland, and in the following autumn to Milan and then to Venice, where for a time he settled down.

While on his journey he began Canto III of *Childe Harold*, finishing it in June 1816 and publishing it the following November. It has been said often enough that it was only a fiction that the poem was about Harold; clearly it was about himself. But actually neither the notion that Harold is a fictional creation nor the notion that the poem is really autobiographical is at all adequate to explain what Byron was actually doing in Canto III. In Stanza VI he proposes with great subtlety both a theory of poetic creation and a theory of personality. Why he should have arrived at this crisis (for crisis it was, since no individual forces from himself a radical and innovative theory of personality unless some personal crisis forces him to it, forces him to seek a new mode of valid survival) can be understood by grasping the destructive effect of the separation, an effect above all shattering to his self-esteem, that is, to his capacity to ascribe value to himself.

What he realized was, "What am I? Nothing." And he seized on the notion that the fundamental task of thought is precisely a self-creation by means of creating an imagined personality, and that this creative activity is a continuous process. It seems clear that he means that the creating of poetry or of a personality in poetry is but one means of such, as it must be called, continuous self-creation. So the most accurate and certainly the most descriptive subtitle for Canto III would be something like, "An Experiment in the Ongoing Reconstruction of a Valid and Acceptable Self-Perception and Self-Interpretation." This is what makes Canto III of *Childe Harold's Pilgrimage* so central to the development of Romanticism. It was the first widely available and easily accessible setting forth of the central Romantic problem, the creation of a convincing sense of one's own value solely from one's own resources, without submissive recourse to social institutions or cultural traditions. Moreover, it seems more than probable that Byron could not have accomplished this new step without experiencing the rejection of society he had achieved in *The Siege of Corinth* and *Parisina*, as well as *The Prisoner of Chillon*, the tale of a victim of tyrannical sociopolitical power, written in June and published in December 1816.

The strategies Byron employed for this difficult step were two, introspection and history. The journey to Switzerland is paced by three successively deeper excursions in the past: the field of Waterloo, where Napoleon was defeated less than a year before Byron visited it; the fortress on the Rhine of Ehrenbreitstein, captured and dismantled by the French Revolutionary armies; and the field of Morat, where in the fifteenth century the free men of Switzerland defeated and killed Charles the Bold, Duke of Burgundy. This historical strategy reveals the link between Romantic self-creation and historical comprehension. Here Byron begins what he was to continue in Canto IV, the attempt to understand himself by discovering in the past specific situations analogous to his own, events analogous to his own experiences. In doing so he has penetrated to the foundation of thought, for fundamentally all we have to think with is analogy: two or more events or other configurations are sufficiently similar so that we judge it to be appropriate to respond to both in the same way. And since nothing has meaning in itself, meaning can be constructed only by analogy, by transferring to a new event a meaning already established. Nor does Byron propose simplistic "lessons from history." Rather, in all three instances, and perhaps most forcefully in the meditation on Waterloo and Napoleon, he presents the equivocal, the ambiguous character of these events. The tone to the rest is given by the recognition of the greatness of Napoleon and also of his base failure in that he destroyed the freedom which had brought him to power, the result of which (Byron predicts) will be the reimposition of that tyranny which Napoleon and his armies did away with, at tremendous human cost, but only to impose his own version of unrestricted and tyrannous social and political power.

The theme is failure, the failure of Napoleon at Waterloo, even the failure of the famous Brussels ball on the evening before Waterloo; the failure of Ehrenbreitstein to withstand its country's enemies; the failure of Charles the Bold to overcome the apparently far inferior Swiss forces. Byron's own failure, with which the poem begins and which is restated in various ways throughout the poem—his failure, for example, to tolerate other humans—is not justified but explained by the fact that failure is almost the norm of human effort. Thus the shattering effect of the separation is eased of its uniqueness and Byron is eased of self-recrimination.

So it is not surprising that when the poem reaches Switzerland Byron tries another strategy to achieve a viable self-ascription of value. Since alienation from mankind is justified or at least explained by human violence, cruelty, and moral failure "in wretched interchange of wrong for wrong," it may be, he thinks, that in nature or in some interaction with or relation to nature may be discovered a source of value. The rest of Canto III is for the most part devoted to his experiences on and around Lake Geneva, in actual fact made more pleasant by his new friendship with Shelley, who with Mary Godwin and Claire Clairmont lived nearby, and in time by his friendship with Madame de Staël, who lived across the lake from Byron's villa. (Claire Clairmont, a kind of stepsister to Mary, had succeeded in becoming Byron's mistress before he left London, and was soon to be the mother of his second daughter, Allegra, who died as a child.) But these friendships are not to be thought of as inconsistent with his alienation from humanity and his turning to nature. Rather his identification with nature made those friendships possible. He describes himself as feeling one with nature, but it was more of a cognitive than an emotional interchange. The feeling and emotion involved are precisely the sense of an acquisition, a flowing into oneself from the nonhuman world of value, and that nonhuman natural world is the source of value simply because it is not human and is possibly the sinless creation of Deity.

Thus Byron's historicism is important precisely because it made possible a transcendence of history into nature. To acquire new friendships in the form of a little group, an ad hoc, as it were, social institution of small scale—a frequent, almost common pattern of Romantic behavior throughout the century from the very beginning of Romanticism and into the twentieth century—is a way of maintaining that new sense of value. To befriend others—a few others—and to be befriended is the confirmation of the capacity both to ascribe value and, just as important, to experience the ascription of value; for both, especially the second, support the self-ascription of value which the self-categorization with innocence and the raw, morally uncompromised power of nature has made possible.

Byron wrote *Manfred* in the summer and autumn of 1816, finishing it in Venice, where he arrived in November. But dissatisfied with Act III he rewrote it, finishing it to his satisfaction in May 1817. He sent the revision at once to Murray, who published the completed work on 16 June 1817. It was the most ambitious work he had yet undertaken, and the most serious, as the wholesale revision of Act III indicates. In the history of developing Romanticism, as well as Byron's version of it, it is peculiarly significant, for it provides further evidence of the links among the creation of a valid personality, self-transcendence, and historicism. The historical factor emerges not merely in the setting of the opening scene in a Gothic hall in what is clearly a medieval castle in the Alps, and in the inclusion among the characters of the Abbot of St. Maurice in the valley of the Rhône, some sixteen miles from the point at which that river flows into the eastern end of Lake Geneva. Historicism emerges even more strongly and more significantly in that the dramatic poem is an inquiry into the past of Byron's personality.

Goethe had proposed that the personality should be treated and created as if it were a work of art. Byron, as we have seen, goes further and is more subtle, since he perceives the construction of a work of art as one aspect of and subsumed by the construction of a personality. Since that construction is, as he has already exhibited in Canto III of *Childe Harold,* a process, it must necessarily have a past. Essentially what Byron does in *Manfred* is what Freudian psychoanalysis later proposed to do. Personality is to the individual as culture is to the society, or, more precisely, personality is the individual's unique modification of culture, of, as Hegel called it, *Geist.* (This formulation of culture is more Jungian than Freudian, for Freud sees biology as the source of personality.) Just as the exploration of a culture's history makes it possible to transcend that culture's present, so the exploration of the individual's history makes it possible to transcend the stage of personality construction at which he has currently arrived. Freud's psychoanalysis is the application of Romantic historicism to the individual. Indeed Freud, fully in the Romantic tradition, came to understand that all individuals are to a certain extent neurotic because a culture, any culture, is necessarily neurotic, since the instructions it generates and the demands it imposes are, since it is a construct, necessarily inadequate to the demands reality makes upon it.

What Byron did in *Manfred* is exceedingly clever and subtle, for it reveals another way of using the past. On the one hand, he explored his own past, but on the other hand he created an alternate past, one in which he dies. After his sufferings are explored and the source of those sufferings (principally his love for Astarte, his sister, for whose death he had been responsible), after he has learned from nature the possibility of a different existence, "the language of another world" (Act III, Scene iv), Manfred accepts completely his own responsibility for himself and above all his responsibility for creating his sense of value, or, in this alternative scenario of Byron's self-understanding, of self-rejection, self-devaluation. His death is the direct consequence of the "Mind's knowledge of its own desert," and the most subtle and most complete form of suicide that Byron could imagine. If self-creation is the process in which the individual must engage if he is to survive, self-destruction is merely the reverse or negation of that process, or an alternate consequence of it.

This self-realization of his own responsibility for his failure is what enables the dying Manfred to repel the demons who have come for his soul. And he mysteriously says not only that he was "my own destroyer" but also "will be my own hereafter." Hell is thus revealed as myth.

"Myth" is the correct word, for *Manfred* is of crucial importance in the development of Romanticism because of Byron's direct facing of the problem of mythology. What he does with the demons, the spirits, Arimanes, Nemesis, the Witch of the Alps, and so on is to create a new mythology. The traditional mythology of Western culture, not only the mythology of ancient Greece and Rome but even the mythology of Christianity, had pretty well lost its literary and cultural viability in the eighteenth century under the impact of Enlightenment rationalism. Not only had classical mythology become mere allegory, so that any abstract word could become a god, but even Christian mythology had become hardly more than allegorical. God, for example, had become for advanced thinkers little more than the ultimate power of nature, and Christ little more than an allegory of moral perfection. The revitalization of the old allegory, whether classical or Christian, into genuine mythology was a widespread effort of the first few generations of Romanticism. The most telling indication of this was the attempt to separate allegory and mythology, or, in the form it often took, allegory and symbol. This involved ascribing a new meaning to "symbol," which traditionally had meant no more than an allegorical sign. There is little point in attempting to explore the widespread struggles of the Romantics with the word "symbol," for none were in fact very successful. Rather, by exploring what they were trying to do by revitalizing mythology it is possible to come to some understanding of what these efforts were aimed at.

The primary reason for the Romantics' effort to revitalize traditional mythology or, as in *Manfred,* to create a new mythology (even though Byron took some names from Zoroastrianism) was their obscure recognition that mythology has a function in human life and culture which is neither identical with nor can be subsumed by allegory. Allegory merely gives for literary or other illustrative purposes a proper name to an explanatory abstraction, to some fragment, as it were, of ideology. But mythology does something more than that. Consider for example Poseidon, who is a god both of sea and of horses. These seem to have little in common until we recognize first that Poseidon has a human form. Thus he has something to do with the human relation to and interaction with both horses and the sea. Interaction with both involves movement by other than the means human physiology provides. Man has learned to sail and has learned to tame and control horses, both for the purpose of moving more rapidly than his own physical equipment makes possible and also of going where his own physical equipment cannot carry him. Poseidon, then, is a god of a certain category of learned behavior or culture. Or take a different kind of god, the avatar type, of which Christian saints are a notable and widespread instance. St. Cecilia, the patron saint of music and musicians, quite obviously symbolizes the learned behavior which we call music making. The Christian God, for whom there is no name, subsumes or governs all learned behavior, all modes of interaction among men and between men and nature. Such a deity is culture itself, while lesser deities are categorizations of culturally learned behavior.

A supreme deity, such as Zeus or the Christian-Jewish deity, since it is culture itself, symbolizes (or more accurately categorizes) the authority of culture, the fact that culture is a control over behavior naturally or physiologically generated. Mythology is concerned with categorizing and explaining how various cultural modes select, guide, and control much naturally generated behavior; but mythology also subsumes how that control is exercised by punishing through the infliction of pain or even death the failure to obey the authoritative guides of culture. That is why a dualistic mythology, such as Zoroastrianism, is less satisfactory than a monastic system, such as Christianity, for the latter subsumes punishment under the authority of the supreme deity, thus showing that punishment is part of cultural control, not its opposite. What the narratives of mythology do is to investigate the interactions of cultural modes and at the same time control those interactions. Culture is control over behavior, and mythology, consisting of gods and narratives, maintains that control by categorizing modes of control and continuously supplying the redundancies which channel behavior in a given society or cultural system—and also change them.

From this analysis of mythology it is clear what the interaction between Manfred and the demons is. Demons and devils categorize the ultimate sanctions by which culture is maintained and behavior is stabilized: deprivation, imprisonment, torture, and execution. When Manfred denies the authority of the demons and asserts that even the hereafter of his death will be his own responsibility, Byron is asserting that the sanctions of culture which affirm the negative value of the individual are for him no longer valid. A more complete rejection of and alienation from one's culture would be impossible to express. Thus the alternative past and its consequences which Byron created in Manfred come to the same conclusion as the consequences which he created and the position he arrived at—the necessity for cultural transcendence. How to achieve that transcendence was soon to become his problem.

Byron's creation of a new mythology was not to end with *Manfred*. As we shall see in the next chapter, he turned to it again, with most interesting results. At the moment it is sufficient to point out the convergence and congruence of his cultural experimentation with mythology with Hegel's comprehension of culture as *Geist* and with Scott's sophisticated cultural awareness, presented in the mode of cultural differentiation, in the Waverley Novels. This coherence can be summed up by the notion that once the Romantic individual has arrived at the point that his unique culture, that is, his personality, is created and constructed, then it is but a step to the realization that behavior not directly generated by and dictated by nature is the creation and construction of the human race. It was to be only a few decades before cultural anthropology emerged as a scientific discipline. It was one of the consequences of Romanticism.

Byron wrote Canto IV of *Childe Harold* from June to December 1817, though most of it was written in June and July. It was published on 28 April 1818. The material for this canto he gathered on a tour in April and May 1817 from Venice through Arqua (the home of Petrarch), Ferrara, Florence, and Rome. The poem follows this route and ends on the hills above Rome, from which the poet addresses the ocean. In pattern and in meaning Canto IV is a repetition, on a larger scale, of Canto III, but undoubtedly with Byron's clearer understanding of what he is doing. His purpose is "To meditate amongst decay, and stand / A ruin amidst ruins." The analogy between the past of Italy and his own past is thoroughly explored, and the Canto ends, as did Canto III, with the identification of the poet and nature made possible less by the presence of nature than, as before, by the absence of man. The subject is again the failure of the human enterprise, the attempt to create freedom, which Napoleon destroyed. The most significant difference between Canto III and Canto IV is so increased a particularity that the poem is almost a kind of guidebook to some of the most important and moving sites of Italy. This particularity was increased by a surprising device, elaborate notes. Nor were these notes the work of Byron. His companion from the time he left England was John Cam Hobhouse, Byron's friend at Cambridge and his companion for the first part of his trip to Greece, described in the first two cantos of *Childe Harold*. Byron had written the less elaborate notes for the preceding cantos, and he clearly wished to show his intellectual seriousness by providing notes of scholarly respectability, the sort of thing the rather pedantic Hobhouse was only too happy to undertake. In fact, the notes proved far too extensive to be published with the poem. Hobhouse, who had returned to England with the manuscript of Canto IV, made a selection of them to be published with that canto and the next year published his full notes as *Historical Illustrations of the Fourth Canto of Childe Harold*. The book included what both Byron and Hobhouse wanted but felt unqualified to do themselves, a survey of the current state of literature in Italy written by Ugo Foscolo, then an exile in England. (See *The Birth of Romanticism*, Chapter III.) And there was one further difference between the new canto and the preceding ones—a far greater poetic power, the result of the self-comprehension and self-creation he had achieved in *Manfred*.

Now in the fall of 1817 there took place a most surprising turn in Byron's poetic creativity. It was even astonishing, unpredicted and unpredictable, a complete contrast with everything he had written so far. He turned to the comic. Evidently in the summer of 1817 he received from England a new publication, *Prospectus and Specimen of an Intended National Work Intended by William and Robert Whistlecraft Intending to Comprise the Most Interesting Particulars Relating to King Arthur and his Round Table*. The author was John Hookham Frere (1769–1846), who had contributed verses to a once famous work appearing in separate numbers in 1797 and 1798, *The Anti-Jacobin.* In addition to ordinary news it published frequently brilliant and almost always amusing satirical verse attacking the English supporters of the French Revolution. In the work always subsequently known as "Whistlecraft" Frere employed the stanza known as *ottava rima,* an eight-line stanza rhyming abababcc. It was a widely used Italian verse form, the dominating stanza for narrative verse, beginning with Boccaccio in the fourteenth century and culminating with Ariosto's marvelous *Orlando Furioso* in the sixteenth. For Ariosto showed better than any of his predecessors that *ottava rima* could be used for both serious, even tragic, purposes and also for brilliant comic effect. Frere, something of a master of comic verse, showed in *Whistlecraft* its possibilities for a lighthearted mode of satire, less solemn than the traditional heroic couplet of Pope. Its appeal to Byron and its suitability for what was to become, after the experiment of *Beppo,* his greatest work, *Don Juan,* needs some analysis.

First it is desirable to examine why the revival of an old metrical device and the importation of such a device from another culture should be so appealing to Byron. By the time he wrote *Beppo* he had become dissatisfied with everything he had written, and equally dissatisfied with the work of Coleridge, Wordsworth, Scott. All of them, including himself, he thought, were on the wrong track in the aim of writing enduringly valuable poetry. This was the first reason for his turning to a verse style unused in the poetry of the time. That is, in typical Romantic fashion he sought for a means of transcending the position he had arrived at, of going beyond the self he had so far constructed, and of going beyond the boundaries of his poetic culture. In order to break up his dependency on two highly approved English verse forms, octosyllabic couplets for his tales and the Spenserian stanza for *Childe Harold,* he sought renewal in the past and in the culture of a foreign language, yet a poetic culture on which so much of English poetic culture had depended. In the largest sense this was part of his historicism, the transcendence of the present by exploring the achievements of alternate possibilities of history. In turning to the stanza form of Boiardo, Pulci, Berni, Ariosto, Tasso, all Italian poets of the fifteenth and sixteenth centuries, he was doing what other Romantic artists did. In these same years, as we shall soon see, Beethoven turned to the Baroque tradition of music and revived the fugue, but he used it in a totally novel context, that of the piano sonata, and eventually of the string quartet. He took a form associated with religious situations and employed it in a purely secular context. In the same way Ingres and the German Nazarenes (see *The Birth of*

Romanticism) sought stylistic renewal and cultural transcendence by turning to Raphael and to his Italian predecessors, thus leaving the tradition of painting which had been founded by the Bolognese reformers of the early seventeenth century. In the same way in the next decade Delacroix was to seek renewal by turning to Rubens and thus escaping from the moribund but still dominating neoclassicism of the Enlightenment. In the same way the architects of these decades sought renewal both in the Gothic revival and in the Classic revival. But in all these instances it would be a mistake to consider these strategies as mere revivalism. On the contrary the revived style always experienced a profound change in the hands of Romantic artists. Indeed, one of the surprising effects of revivalism for renewal combined with historicisim and the steadily improving techniques of historical research was to be, particularly among the architects, the creation of works of art in a style more coherent and stylistically perfect than the architectural works of the style that was being revived. Thus it has been said that the two greatest technicians of *ottava rime* were Ariosto and Byron, for the reason that both responded with extraordinary accuracy and invention to the possibilities of that verse form.

Any kind of assonance in verse, whether alliteration, repetition of vowels, or, above all, rhyme is like the major key in music. It is a sign of aggressive competence directed first of all towards language itself and second by implication towards the subject of the verse. Light verse in English, for example, is almost invariably rhymed, for the point of such poetry is the insouciance of the speaker of the poem, his indifference to any hindrance to his activity, based upon a competence that defeats any attempt to contain his aggressiveness. Thus Shakespearian tragedy and Milton's *Paradise Lost* are not rhymed, but the subject of both is precisely the struggle with the hindrances to human aggressiveness that the experiences of life impose upon the individual, with the individual's failure and, in Milton, with man's failure in his surrender to sin. In Spenser's *The Faerie Queene* and in Byron's *Childe Harold*, the most successful use of the Spenserian stanza except for Spenser's himself, the rhyme is a sign of the ultimate triumph over hindrances.

That fundamental aggressiveness of the poet towards language— it is what makes him a poet—is in English verse manifest in the almost universal movement of any line from unstressed syllables to stressed syllables, towards what is called, illuminatingly enough, the masculine line end on a stressed syllable. What Byron discovered in *Whistlecraft* were the possibilities of ending a line on an unstressed syllable, that is, a line with a feminine ending. The negation of the masculine ending, the feminine ending is a sign not of maintained aggression but of a sudden relaxation or reduction of aggression, an effect which can have the significance of submission.

And submission is exactly the theme of Byron's work in these years, as we have seen. It is also to be found in the last of his octo-syllabic tales, *Mazeppa*, written in 1818 and published 28 June 1819. This is the story of how a Polish nobleman was lashed by a brutal ruler naked to a horse, which then was driven off to its place of origin, the Ukraine. To be sure, the hero is rescued by a lovely girl and be-comes in time a Ukrainian prince, but most of the poem is a superb evocation of helpless submission to a wild and uncontrollable natural force. In *Marino Faliero* Byron again takes the theme of tyranny and a futile rebellion against it (written in 1820, published 21 April 1821). Marino Faliero, the Doge of Venice, is profoundly wounded in his self-esteem because an insult to him and his wife has been frivolously punished by the real rulers of Venice, the patriciate. Tempted by a man of the people who has been insulted just as gratuitously by a Venetian nobleman, he joins a conspiracy to exterminate the patricians of Ven-ice and establish a free commonwealth under his rule. The conspiracy, however, is betrayed by one of the conspirators out of submissive compassion for his noble master, and Faliero is beheaded on the steps of the Doge's Palace. In this play Byron tellingly links willing sub-mission to the preservation of tyrannous political power.

Moreover, the theme of submission in this play is linked to the theme of the victim of social power. The story of *Beppo* again takes up the theme of submission and victim, though comically (written 1817–1818 and published 28 February 1818). Byron was fascinated and amused by the Italian practice of *cavaliere servente*, the publicly ac-cepted and acknowledged lover of a fashionable lady, a kind of second or alternative husband, a practice emerging, of course, from the cus-tom of the arranged marriage, the union for purely practical purposes, ordinarily monetary, and from the conviction that love should have a place in life. Byron himself, to his amusement and with a certain amount of chagrin, became a *cavaliere servente* of the Contessa Teresa Guiccioli, a noblewoman of Rimini. (She was so moral that she suc-ceeded for a time in persuading Byron to give up the composition of *Don Juan*.) Beppo is a Venetian merchant captured by the Turks and thought to have died in captivity. Suddenly he appears one evening at a ball, dressed as a Turk. But instead of revenging himself on his wife, who has taken a lover, he soon makes arrangements with both of them, and all three live happily thereafter, with the lover now an official *cavaliere servente*. Here, then, is comic submission to the customs of a culture. Beppo is comic victim, and the poem is filled with feminine rhymes.

That theme of comic victim was now to become the theme of *Don Juan*. Byron wrote the first two cantos in the fall and early winter of 1818–1819 (published 15 July 1819) and Cantos III to V from the fall of 1819 to the fall of 1820 (published 8 August 1821). He wrote *Marino Faliero* between IV and V. The traditional Don Juan, the heartless libertine, came into literary being in the Spanish drama of the early seventeenth century and continued his life in various Spanish and French plays of the seventeenth and eighteenth centuries. His most recent appearance before Byron took him up was in Mozart's *Don Giovanni* (1787). He was a quasi-mythical creature, almost a god, who subsumed all male activities of pure sexual aggression, an aggression, moreover, which was always successful, and not always punished. In his figure of Don Juan, Byron negates or reverses this tradition. His Don Juan is always a victim, usually a victim of female sexual or other aggression. And like the conspirator in *Marino Faliero* who betrays the conspiracy for freedom, Byron's Don Juan willingly submits to being the eternal victim. He is the victim of his mother's educational ideas, just as his father was his mother's victim. He is seduced as an adolescent, rather than being the seducer. Exiled by his mother, he is shipwrecked, sees his dog and then his tutor eaten and, sole survivor of the wreck, is cast up on an island in the Aegean. There he is again seduced by the daughter of a Greek pirate. Believing her father dead, Haideé and Juan live an idyllic life until her father returns. Lambro promptly seizes Juan and sends him to be sold as a slave, and poor Haideé dies of a broken heart. In Constantinople Juan is mysteriously purchased, led by hidden ways to the Sultan's seraglio, dressed as a woman, and taken before his new owner, the Sultan's wife; the canto ends with the Sultan's complimenting his wife on the charm of her new maiden. And the poem ends for the time being, not to be taken up again until June 1822.

In the political works of these years—for politics may be judged the essence of *Parisina, The Siege of Corinth, The Prisoner of Chillon, Mazeppa, Marino Faliero,* and even, though more subtly and profoundly, Cantos III and IV of *Childe Harold*—Byron reveals the Enlightenment component of his thinking, his ideology of liberation from political tyranny and social oppression. In *Beppo,* in *Marino Faliero,* and above all in *Don Juan* emerges his Romanticism, the awareness of the problematic nature of the relation between victim and oppressor, between seducer and the seduced, of the problematic nature of freedom. From the relatively tame female creatures of Byron there were to be developed in the course of the nineteenth century almost fearsome instances of the dominating woman. In 1847, for example, Prosper Mérimée was to create one of the most notable instances of this type, Carmen, who was to become one of the most powerful as well as popular characters in the history of opera. What Byron is interested in is the relation, the interaction, the fascination that is to be experienced in studying domination and submission. There are today in major cities women who make a living by acting as "dominatrix" for men, often highly successful executives and managers. Perhaps the explanation given by these women, often intelligent, is illuminating to what Byron was studying. These men, they say, so successful in aggressive roles, are exhausted by those roles. They need escape from constant aggressiveness. They need vacations, if only for an hour or two. And this is understandable, for if learning one's culture means learning how to submit to culture, how to accept culture as controls over one's behavior, to accept even the justice of the application to oneself of the ultimate sanction of culture—execution. What Byron is doing in *Don Juan* is subjecting the Enlightenment notion of liberty to the analysis of placing that notion into the context and situations of nonpolitical behavior, even of erotic behavior, for such behavior— he appears to be asserting—is the foundation of political behavior.

With the aid of this analysis it is now possible to understand a little better the astonishing shift in Byron's writing that came with *Beppo* and was brought to a kind of apotheosis in *Don Juan*. Since Canto IV of *Childe Harold* was a more elaborate and poetically more competent version of Canto III, Byron was faced with the problem of all Romantics who arrive at a particular plateau. The self, or the personality, being a process rather than an entity, any apparent plateau must be self-deceptive and must therefore be transcended. The discovery of the intimate relation between aggression and submission, of the ambiguity inherent in the demand for freedom, led to a further alienation from the culture. A glance once again at the rhyme scheme of Byron's *ottava rima* is instructive, for his use of feminine rhymes involved, almost always, a double rhyme, a sign, or indicator, of a higher level of aggression, even though that aggression is softened, though not compromised, by what might well be called a symbolization of a general aggressive competence. But it is, as it were, an overdetermined competence. What it suggests is insouciance, a careless indifference to the demands of culture and society. Thus the comic mode emerges, in *Don Juan*, as a protective mode. From behind the barriers of that protection the author is able to glance satirically or sympathetically at anything in human behavior without being committed to any position. Don

Juan as victim thus becomes a joke. The aggression is withdrawn from the hero of the poem so that the speaker of the poem may be freely aggressive against cultural and social forces which are the source of the hero's victimization.

The question of how that satirical and sympathetic aggression is accomplished now comes to the fore. To understand Byron's effort fully and its place in the development of Romanticism we need to look at the structure of these works, beginning with *Beppo,* in every sense an experimental work. In that poem the narrative or plot takes up only a fraction of the length of the poem. The rest of the poem is about—well, about anything Byron happens to feel like writing about. The source of this device is to be found in the various cantos of *Childe Harold.* Each canto is a journey, but a journey without a goal. It is, then, a wandering. And wandering is one of the central and crucial symbolizations of Romanticism. Why this should be so can be understood if it is recognized that culture controls and *limits* behavior, and that an individual's interest is a strategy for cooperating with culture, a strategy that limits the range of the individual's behavior and protects him against the brain's capacity to produce randomness. On the other hand, study of what we call creativity, the production of cultural innovation, shows that for artist and scientist escape from cultural limitations is a necessary strategy for such innovation, and that significant innovation depends upon a randomization of response, which continues until some response is hit upon which promises significant innovation. At that point, such a response is stabilized as an interest. What the Romantics discovered was precisely the possibilities of randomization of behavior, and in the literature of Romanticism that discovery takes the form of, initially, wandering. Thomas Carlyle in the 1830s was to analyze the emergence of Romanticism in his *Sartor Resartus,* as we shall see later. Here it is enough to point out that he called the wandering stage the Center of Indifference. His hero wanders all over Europe, just like Byron's hero, and "indifference" is a good term for Byron's speaker.

What Byron discovered in *Beppo* and brought to perfection in *Don Juan* was a realization that a symbolization of randomness by means of the metaphor of physical wandering could be transcended by a more sophisticated poetic device. To be sure, Byron sent Don Juan on a course of wandering (he was to go from Constantinople to Russia and thence to England), but the randomization of interests was Byron's or that of the speaker of the poem. Juan's adventures merely provided an excuse for the speaker to discuss anything that crossed his fancy, anything that by sheer chance, it would seem, occurred to

him. The comic mode thus provided in the poem a defense from behind which anything in contemporary culture could be examined
without commitment. The essence of *Don Juan* is a commitment to
noncommitment. The device of randomization even more importantly defends Byron from getting stuck in any ideological position.
It is an instance of the Romantic antimetaphysical metaphysic.

Nevertheless a certain theme may be discerned as running through
all of these digressions. That is the theme of realism, of a particularity
designed to look at culture with the fewest possible preconceptions,
to see the world as nakedly as possible. An example of this is the whole
episode of Juan's shipwreck and the sufferings of those in his boat,
including their cannibalism and the physiological disaster of being too
enthusiastic in eating Juan's tutor. To achieve this realism Byron does
not depend upon his imagination or guesses at what probably might
have happened. On the contrary he pursues a strategy emerging particularly in *Childe Harold* Canto IV and in the poems inspired by his
reading of historical works. And it is evident from his letters that such
reading was becoming one of his principal interests. That strategy was
to become in time, surprisingly enough, one of the crucial strategies
of emerging Romantic culture, the strategy of scholarly research. The
shipwreck episode was based upon Byron's careful reading of published accounts of shipwrecks: cannibalism, suffering, rescue, death—
accounts written by the survivors. This endeavor to achieve realism,
an examination of the world as free as possible from cultural com-
mitments and illusions and hypocrisies, is to be found also in the great
amount of reading and research he put into the writing of *Marino
Faliero* and is an indication that the composition of that Historical
Tragedy, as he called it, was not an inconsistent interruption of his
writing of *Don Juan* but a continuation of precisely the strategies he
was using in that poem. Thus throughout the composition of the complete *Don Juan,* which was to be picked up again in 1822 and continued until ten months before his death in April 1824, he supported his
poem by research and careful analysis of his own experiences. What
these various devices made possible was a new kind of satire, Romantic satire. The satire of earlier cultural epochs had always been
aimed at the failure of individuals to live up to their moral pretensions,
moral ideals which were the ideals and controls of the culture. The
satire of *Don Juan* establishes the mode of Romantic satire, for what
it satirizes, what through satire it denigrates, were the very moral ideals themselves of the culture and the society. The target of the Romantic satirist is not the failure of the individual human, but the
failure of the human mind, the ultimate inadequacy of that *Geist* (as

Hegel called it) which humanity has created. The aim of previous satire is moral redemption; what Romantic satire reveals is that moral redemption is an illusion, if it is taken to assure a stable and final ascription of value to the individual.

LUDWIG VAN BEETHOVEN (1770–1817)

Perhaps it was no more than an accident that Beethoven set to music ten poems by Scott and three by Byron, but at least it was a very appropriate accident, for in these first years after Waterloo Beethoven found it difficult to compose and so spent a great deal of time and energy writing settings for folk songs. To be sure, he chose neither the melodies nor the words. Both were sent to him by George Thomson of Edinburgh, an enthusiast for the folk melodies of the British Isles. Years before, he had persuaded Haydn to do these settings, and Haydn had sent him hundreds. But Haydn ceased sending arrangements to Thomson in 1805, and Thomson started a correspondence with Beethoven. The composer accepted the commission and from 1810 to 1813 set Welsh and Irish songs for voice, piano, violin, and cello, just as Haydn had. He continued to make these arrangements until 1818, principally of Scottish melodies. In time he even had the idea of setting folk songs from many European countries and in fact did twenty-three settings—Danish, German, Tyrolean, Polish, Portuguese, Russian, Swedish, Spanish, and Hungarian. But in the event, these were not published until 1941. Beethoven evidently lost interest in the project, not surprisingly, for by 1818 his period of finding it difficult to compose had come to an end. He was in the middle of his mightiest piano sonata and had already begun to work on two of his greatest compositions, the *Missa Solemnis* and the *Diabelli Variations*.

It is usually said that Beethoven worked for Thomson only for the sake of the money, that it was a pure bread-and-butter project. That may have been so at the beginning, but there are indications that the compositions of these arrangements meant more to him than that. They were his principal musical occupation (in all he set 155 of them) in the latter part of 1815, much of 1816, and even more in 1817, which was otherwise the driest year of all. The first indication that they were of some importance to him is that after Thomson had published three volumes in 1814, 1816, and 1817, Beethoven gave the final volume, published in 1818, an opus number—108—and had it published in Germany. With very rare exceptions he gave opus numbers only to works he considered to be of serious importance. A second indication is that the first important composition after *Meerestille und glückliche Fahrt*, written in the summer of 1815 (see *The Birth of Romanticism*), was the wonderful song cycle *An die ferne Geliebte*, Opus 98, written in April 1816. And the one significant composition of 1817 was a song of extraordinary beauty and originality,"Resignation," written in December. Finally, the most significant indication of the importance of these settings to Beethoven was the care which he devoted to them. And that care was justified, for many of the melodies—all that I have heard in the recording by Dietrich Fischer-Dieskau—are themselves of enchanting beauty, of inexpressible loveliness. When one considers the staggering achievements of Beethoven in the last eleven years of his life, it is impossible to believe that his folk-song arrangements were of little importance to him. On the contrary, it is by no means unreasonable to conclude that writing these settings was critical, was indeed responsible for the astounding rejuvenescence of these final years, years in which he exploded (it is not too strong a word) the piano sonata, the string quartet, the variation set, the symphony, the choral mass, and the song cycle.

The interest in folk art in general, and particularly in the poetry and the music of the peasant world—the folk—had begun in the eighteenth century. It was an aspect of Enlightenment primitivism, the conviction that man close to nature was sinless or at least was purer and more true to natural conditions than the sophisticated individual of corrupt and degenerate urban and courtly high-level culture. It was part of the effort of the Enlightenment to discover the real or fundamental nature of the human race. The ultimate purpose of that effort would be to found a better, a redeemed society, on a natural and pure basis. That notion has developed in the past two hundred fifty years into all kinds of back-to-nature movements, not a few of which have been downright fraudulent, or the benefits of which have been vastly exaggerated. The consumption of vitamins far beyond the supposed daily requirements is a consequence of that Enlightenment ideology of Nature. Such "naturism"—as we may call that ideology—can take two forms. One is the actual effort to live in what are conceived to be natural terms. The other is the turning to nature for a kind of renewal, or a revitalization. This second mode is the way the Romantic tradition has used an Enlightenment idea.

There are sound reasons why that mode should be successful. One of the major scholarly and scientific undertakings of the nineteenth and twentieth centuries has been the discovery, the collection, and the preservation of the art from the cultures we call primitive and from the traditions of the folk, that is, the peasants. The result has been the recognition that the Enlightenment notion of such art as purer or simpler or as more intellectually or aesthetically primitive than the sophisticated art of high civilizations was an error. On the contrary, such art as we encounter it today is the consequence of centuries of subtle and sophisticated aesthetic tradition. An instructive example of how the Romantic artist used folk art is to be found in the career of the twentieth-century English composer Ralph Vaughan Williams. At the outset of his career he turned to folk music not in order to find a foundation for a new music but as a way through an alternate artistic world into a unique and personal style. But he was only one of many composers who have used the same strategy. In the same way and at almost the same time Picasso found through primitive African art a path to a cultural transcendence of extraordinary innovation.

From this perspective it is apparent that it is a serious error to see Beethoven's energy devoted to folk-song arrangements in the immediate post-Waterloo months and years as a mere bread-and-butter activity. On the contrary, there is good reason to believe that he was the first Romantic artist to experience primitive or folk art as an alternate possibility, one that revealed the possibility of going beyond what he had already accomplished, of moving into, as a Romantic artist sooner or later must, a new style, a new vision. The beauty and the mode of sophistication of folk songs questioned the tradition which he was finding inadequate, and therefore enabled him to understand more profoundly the very nature of music itself. The result for Beethoven was the third major work he composed in the final stage of his extraordinary career, the Piano Sonata Opus 106, known as "The Hammerklavier," of which he said that at last he knew how to write music.

Beethoven found the six songs of *An die ferne Geliebte* (*To the distant beloved*), Opus 98, in a collection of poems published in 1815. They were by a young man named Alois Jeitteles (1794–1858) who belonged to a club Beethoven occasionally visited. Perhaps Beethoven met him. More important is the youth of the poet, who later became a doctor in Bohemia. He was probably about twenty when he wrote the poems, and his youth meant that he had grown up in the literary and emotional atmosphere of the German Romantics, an atmosphere reflected in the freshness and charm of the poems. The mood, of course, is yearning, and certainly yearning for a beloved was not a theme unique to Romanticism. Nevertheless in Romanticism yearning has a new quality. It is not a mere yearning for a beloved that is responsible for the intensity of Romantic yearning, but rather that the beloved is a symbol of lost or unattainable value, of, in short, value itself, like the Blue Flower of Novalis. (See *The Birth of Romanticism.*) And again, though examples of the song cycle can be found even in the seventeenth and eighteenth centuries, it was to become a peculiarly Romantic genre, the first important example of which is this work of Beethoven's. It has, however, always been unusual in that the music is continuous from beginning to end. Beethoven also recognized the cyclical character of the work by repeating the music of the last couple of lines of the last poem from the last pair of lines from the first poem, just as Jeitelles had, but with a difference. The first poem ends with a question about the union of the lovers; the last poem ends with a period, an affirmation that the reunion will take place. And Beethoven recognizes this difference. At the end of the first song, what appears to be a concluding chord is transformed by modulation into the opening of the second song. At the end of the last song, the last two lines are repeated, then the last stanza is repeated with various repetitions of the last lines. And there is an instrumental postlude which ends with a remarkable departure from the opening phrase.

The opening phrase ascends to a high note and then falls back almost with, as it were, a sigh. The postlude repeats that pattern but then ends with a rising line that does not fall back but pushes through the barrier of the opening phrase and ends on a high cadence. It is a perfect musical presentation of the overcoming of a hindrance. And then in Beethoven's next major works, something very surprising happens. In both the Piano Sonata Opus 101 and the Piano Sonata Opus 106, the opening phrase of the first theme of the first movement is exactly this "yearning" phrase of the song cycle. And in fact the entire first movement of Opus 101 is atypical. Beethoven heads it with "Somewhat lively and with deepest feeling." It is not the sonata-allegro form but more like a prelude than anything else. Actually, the entire movement is an exploration of the possibilities of this yearning theme; and it ends, like the song cycle, with a sweep upward beyond the point of falling back in yearning and onto a high A, the highest note in the movement. It had been reached only once before, and then only hesitantly and on a syncopated off beat. Even so, the movement ends with a falling away in volume, so that the positive conclusion has a tentative quality.

The second movement is at first glance a striking contrast, "Lively, like a march." The opening theme leaps up from the bass in a dotted movement, one that emphasizes, as do all fast dotted phrases, an intensification of energy release or aggression. It bounds up across several octaves but then repeats the pattern of falling back from an achieved position, the pattern of yearning. This rapid and energetic exploration of the same theme as that of the first movement is interrupted by a trio in counterpoint, the basic theme of which is three notes that rise a tone and then descend to the point of departure. It is a kind of condensation or essence of the motive Beethoven has been exploring in this sonata. The third and slow movement is again a prelude, but of even more preludic character than the first movement. It is entirely an exploration of the possibilities of a turn which falls back on itself and below itself in order, as it were, to gather strength to make a great leap to a higher level. It is a summoning of energy, steadily more successful and at the same time an intensification of yearning, culminating in a cadenza that moves with ease and freedom up and up the keyboard to the greatest surprise of all, a repetition of the opening phrases of the first movement. Here, then, is a further development of the cyclical idea, and its first appearance in piano music. The puzzle this repetition presents is rapidly resolved. The final phrase of the theme is repeated, each time higher in the scale, in his last sonatas to an extraordinary extent, the trill. Here, the trill is maintained in a steady crescendo, accompanied by powerful chords that leap downward a full octave and culminate in the opening theme of the final movement—which turns out to be a sonata-allegro fugue.

It has been said that Beethoven did not write good fugues, but he had a different attitude on the subject. "To make a fugue requires no particular skill, in my study days I made dozens of them. But the fancy wishes also to assert its privileges, and today a new and really poetical element must be introduced into the old traditional form." Aside from the extreme originality of introducing a fugue into a piano sonata and making it the longest and most demanding and most exciting and aggressive movement of that sonata, there is the extraordinary theme of the fugue. The opening phrase, which is repeated innumerable times in the movement and forms, as it were, its propellant force, is a loud leap downward of a major third. From a later work, the opening of the last movement of the Quartet Opus 135, almost the last work Beethoven wrote, we can get an idea of what he was after. That movement is labeled *Der schwer gefasste Entschluss* (The difficult decision, or resolution). The allegro is accompanied by three words, the last two of which are *muss sein* (must be) and are written under a loud downward leap of a fourth. The repetition of the opening theme of Opus 101, the theme of wavering, is now answered by a phrase that means a highly aggressive acceptance of control, the result of which, as the rest of the fugue theme shows, is a release and outpouring of energy.

What could be more emblematic of the acceptance of cultural control than the decision to write a fugue? But, as Beethoven himself said, it was a fugue with a difference. It was more a free fuguing than a strict fugue. But as Beethoven said, he was not interested in strict fugues. He was interested in the transformation of a traditional and severe form into something new. So the control is both accepted and put to use by transcending it. The ending is most appropriate. It is a loud upward leap of seven powerful chords, ending with a loud high chord on A, in reply to the first movement, which ended on the same A but softly. The significance of Opus 101 can be summed up most tersely. It is an instruction to yearn for something beyond what one has achieved, and then to achieve what lies beyond by transforming and transcending one's cultural tradition. It was the perfectly appropriate prelude to Beethoven's astounding achievements of the next decade.

Yet he was still not at the point where he could proceed to extensive and uninterrupted composition of important works. Evidently Opus 101 was finished in November 1816. For more than a year he did little besides folk-song arrangements and sets for piano, violin, or flute, of easy variations on folk themes for Thomson (Opus 105 and Opus 107), an arrangement for string quintet of Opus I, No. III of 1794 (Opus 104), and a fugue for string quintet not published until after his death as Opus 137. It has aroused, it would seem, little interest. But then in December 1817 came the beautiful song "Resignation" (the title is in English), a song such as no one had written before. It is an amazing text for Beethoven to have selected, one he liked so much that atypically he thanked the author, Paul Graf von Haugwitz, for having written it, just as he had thanked Jeitelles for the poems of *An die ferne Geliebte*. In it the speaker tells his light to extinguish itself—what it had once summoned comes no more—the winds are cold. It is the kind of poem that would appeal to one who felt that he had no more to say, yet Beethoven wrote it at the beginning of his greatest period. He could write it because he had experienced resignation so thoroughly he could write about it with full understanding. No longer victimized by resignation he was able to escape from it. For he was about to start or had just started work on his most grandiosely conceived piano sonata, Opus 106, known subsequently as "The Hammerklavier" through a misunderstanding of the title page of the German edition, a mere German version of "pianoforte." Beethoven worked on the sonata until late autumn 1818, and when he finished he immediately set to work on the *Missa Solemnis*.

The opening phrase of Opus 106 is a kind of synthesis of the yearning curve and the downward leap of Opus 101. It begins by leaping up first from a low B-flat to a chord in the center of the keyboard and then to high loud and fast chords in the treble. That opening leap is in various degrees one of the principal motives of the movement, repeated sometimes as a mere third, as sixths, as octaves, and occasionally more than an octave. Here at the beginning the two leaps cover more than three octaves. The phrase curves not at the beginning of the measure, on the beat, but on the off beat of the secondary beat of the measure. Thus the downward leap of a third, taken from the theme of the fugue of Opus 101, begins a measure. This is now repeated from the same bass note but to a third higher than in the first appearances of the phrase. Thus Beethoven establishes what is to be the basic drama of the first movement. The yearning motive is converted into a rapid acceptance of control, but that control is continuously challenged by the aggressive leaps of the opening phrase. The exposition is concluded by a much slower melody that is a return over four measures of a yearning motive, but it is overcome by increasing the tension by means of a long trill over seven measures, leading to rapid chords based on the curve of the immediately controlled effort to raise the level of aggression of the opening phrase. The overall effect of the entire movement is that of an exploration of the implication of the opening theme, a highly energetic thrust of aggression brought under immediate control, but a control that only leads to repeated efforts to overcome that control, an effort that dies away at the end of the movement—except for a final assertive loud and high chord, a final defiance, an indication that the drama is not over.

The second movement, a scherzo, has been called a parody of the first movement. It combines the leap of a third with a curved return to the starting point, but softly. But where the curve in the first movement was a second, this curve is a third. So the mood is less one of parody than of a restrained but optimistic and lighthearted effort to balance the leap of aggression with the imposition of control. The trio of this scherzo is a strangely wavering near repetition of the slow theme at the end of the exposition of the first movement. It is, as it were, a loss of resolve. But that resolve is renewed by a presto section built again on the same curve, but filled with urgency, one that ends with a prestissimo run over almost the full range of the keyboard from bottom to top, followed by something very like a shake of the fist. This is followed by a repetition of the opening scherzo, but with a different ending, a dying away of the curved motive which is suddenly followed by strident octave chords leaping up over three octaves. But then the movement subsides in a repetition of the opening phrases, ending strangely on an off beat.

One may reasonably say that the gay but subdued resolve of the movement has been overcome, but has ended ambiguously and irresolutely. That ambiguity and irresolution is now explained, as it were, by a slow movement, the longest instrumental movement that anyone, it appears, had yet written. Beethoven heads in *Appassionato et con molto sentimento*. After a rising curve, but very softly, the opening melody is presented. It is the reverse of the phrases of the first two movements. It moves downward by two steps to a fifth below the starting note and then moves upward, though hesitatingly and still in the minor, to a fifth above the starting note. It is, then, the pattern of falling back to gain the energy to go forward. And this is behaviorally most accurate, for the acceptance of control, even of control conceived of as hindrance rather than guidance, can enable the individual to recover enough strength to push forward and outward against hindrance. And this is the drama of the entire movement, moving toward an utterly new note of Romantic music, one hitherto not found in music, the ecstatic. And ecstasy can be understood as the sustained experience of unhindered and uncompromised pure sense of value. Once it is achieved in this movement it is re-experienced in episode after episode, and the movement ends in a musical glow of satisfaction, repletion, completion. The great length of the movement, which is in form, as has been pointed out, an enormous aria, is Beethoven's way of saying that such fulfillment must be individually striven for and earned. It is not given, but must be sought and created.

Yet that repletion, that fulfillment that has brought about something very like sleep is not the final answer Beethoven wishes to give. On the contrary the strength gained must be unleashed. And so the final movement begins with something like a summons to awake, a slow repetition of a single note over five octaves, resulting in a release of energy. The movement is from largo to allegro, scale passages rushing up and down the keyboard and culminating in major chords hammered out. Then it retreats to a new summons in a series of trills; and at last there emerges the theme of the enormous fugue (a Beethoven fugue, *Fuga tre voci con alcune licenze*), which concludes the work. The tempo heading tells us the character of the movement and what it is all about—*Allegro risoluto*. The theme opens with a long trill; there are two downward rushes with pauses before and after each one, and then follows a long passage of great rapidity which fights its way with ups and downs back almost to the starting point. It is again the falling-back-to-recover pattern, but here the recovery is not easy and does not take one beyond the starting point. That advance must be earned, the summoning of energy announced by the opening trill must be justified and earned. And that pattern is explored in episode after episode. The end is triumphant. Three trills in both hands proceed upward step by step from A to F-sharp. Two chords lead to high B-flat (the home key of the sonata), repeated an octave lower to establish an equilibrium of aggression, a resting upon success.

As a cultural instruction, Opus 106 is a summons or demand upon the listener first of all for a capacity of sustained attention. At first hearing, for example, the final fugue is bewildering in its complexity and its many episodes, but the series of episodes and their recurrence in recapitulation in the slow movement is hardly less exigent. Beethoven is demanding an attention span no composer had ever demanded, and this increase of the demand upon the listener was to be carried even farther by later Romantic composers, above all by Richard Wagner, who was undoubtedly inspired by Beethoven in his judgment of what can be demanded. Like so much Romantic art Opus 106 is an assault on the listener, the purpose of which is to subject the listener to exactly what the composer had subjected himself, a determination to force him beyond what he thought his limits to be. And in fact in the case of this sonata, it was a long time before it could be played at all. The fugue was judged by some to be absolutely unplayable, and that until fairly recently. Now any well-trained conservatory student can play it and meet all of its technical demands. The point is not so much that piano technique has improved, though that is certainly a factor, as that what the performer can ask of himself and his technique has expanded beyond the limits of Beethoven's time and for most performers long thereafter. What in fact is happening here is the emergence of the Romantic virtuoso, one of the most important cultural innovations of the decades after Waterloo. The significance of the virtuoso is that self-transcendence, originally presented as a possibility, as, therefore, an ideology, is transformed into a behavioral actuality.

Furthermore, as hinted above, such a work as Opus 106 presents the possibility to the listener, if he can achieve it, of becoming a virtuoso listener. By traditional standards of listening, Beethoven was soon to demand, with the utmost musical aggressiveness, virtuoso listeners of such extremity that it is best asserted that he was demanding heroic listeners. For the Romantic hero is not one who fulfills to the highest power the values of his culture but rather one who perceives the necessary inadequacy of those values and determinedly sets out to go beyond the controlling limitations of his culture. He is always, then, something of a vandal, just as shocked musicologists have accused Beethoven of vandalizing the fugue. In the early years of the next decade Carl Maria von Weber was to apply in *Euryanthe* that principle by composing an opera in acts that allowed no interruptions, that had no final cadences, no opportunities for the audience to relax by applauding.

A further virtuosic or heroic demand upon the listener made by both Sonatas 101 and 106 was, as we have seen, the cyclic or recurrent appearance of certain phrases, as well as the inexhaustible analysis of the musical possibilities of those phrases. The listener is thus required, if he is to respond adequately at all, to perceive relationships where before he had been pleased and entertained. The traditional cultural demand upon the artist before Romanticism was to please and to instruct, or more restrictedly to instruct by pleasing, that is, to perform upon the artist's audience an act of seduction. To the Romantic artist, however, to seduce the audience is merely to make it more pliable and responsible to existent cultural demands, to deprive it of its freedom, to use a Romantic term in its special Romantic sense. To force freedom upon the individual responder to the work of art now becomes the moral responsibility of the Romantic artist. Freedom was not a consequence of political arrangements nor the task of the artist, though that kind of political freedom was of course also to be desired. The task of the artist was to create in the individual personality the conditions for transcending the limitations of his culture and that version of his culture known as the personality. This is what lies behind the Romantic act of aggression upon the listener or reader of which Beethoven in these sonatas offered early examples.

Moreover, on finishing Sonata Opus 106 Beethoven immediately began to work on two more works of even vaster extent and imposing even greater demands upon the listener, the *Missa Solemnis* and the *Diabelli Variations*. He took until the middle of 1823 to finish the first of these and until the spring of the same year to finish the second. Three times, however, he interrupted work on these two gigantic works to write three piano sonatas. The first was Opus 109, finished in late summer 1820. It was as original and innovative as the preceding sonatas, though not so long as Opus 106. The first movement begins with an easy rippling and attractive theme. The tempos is "vivace," but after eight bars of exposition it is without warning interrupted by an "adagio espressivo," which has a striking ancestry in the baroque fantasia. The vivace then resumes its almost pastoral character. Once again it is interrupted by the adagio. The vivace resumes and instead of concluding is suddenly transformed by a second movement, a prestissimo. It has an upward thrusting theme, and the movement as a whole has been called, with some justice, brutal. So far, what Beethoven has explored is not the drama of opposing and contrasting emotions but the harsh and unrelated juxtaposition of emotions as opposite to and different from one another as can be imagined, a series which ends with the end of the second movement in an extraordinary surge of violent aggressiveness. If in Sonata Opus 106 he made new intellectual demands upon the listener—and himself—so in this so- nata he makes new emotional demands, ranging from gentle happi- ness to aggressive thrusting power.

The third movement is headed with another instruction, "Gesang- voll, mit innigster Empfindung" (Song-like and with deepest feeling). It is indeed a song in two parts, each of which is repeated; and then begins a series of variations. The balance in the movement up and down of the theme is now put through a series of transformations. The theme becomes an elaborate aria; then it becomes something like a dance; there follows an exercise in relentless energy release; this is succeeded by a slow variation, but one that maintains the steadiness of energy release and is gradually converted into an outburst of pure splendid sonority. By a sudden discontinuity this is followed by an intellectual fugal examination of the essence of the theme. Suddenly a quiet andante variation appears, like the opening, and this is now subjected to the most extraordinary transformation Beethoven had yet achieved, and it is revealed what the whole sonata and especially the last movement had been moving towards, an exploration of the ecstatic beyond that of any preceding work. Page after page of trills accompany figurations which explore with endless invention the pos- sibilities of key modulation. The effect can only be described as rap- turous, perhaps to Beethoven rapturous in the ancient sense, of being carried away or rapt by the divine. At the end that rapture fades away and we are brought back to what is now the ordinary by a simple repetition of the theme. If Opus 101 and 106 were. as we have seen, investigations into the possibilities of musical integration, explora- tions of structure, so Opus 109 is an investigation into the rewards of disintegration, of discovering ecstatic rapture through a deliberate dis- tortion of the senses, as a great French poet, Arthur Rimbaud, was to say many decades later. It is as if Beethoven were asking himself, and his listeners, "What in music is inconceivable, and what is incon- ceivable in the manner in which we experience existence?"

GIOACCHINO ROSSINI (1792–1868)

In the year of Waterloo, Gioacchino Rossini began the great series of operas written for the San Carlo theater in Naples, operas that established Romantic music in Italy. Until recently, Rossini like Beethoven was not thought of as a Romantic composer, but that misapprehension was the consequence of the fact that of his thirty-nine operas only *The Barber of Seville* continued to be performed. Certainly it is a masterpiece, a work that has survived endless bad performances and violations of what Rossini wrote; yet in the history of nineteenth-century opera it is less important than the operas Rossini composed for Naples from 1815 to 1822. In the years after Waterloo Rossini indeed became the darling of the Italian Romantics; after Foscolo (see *The Birth of Romanticism*) he was the first major Italian artist. He became known as the Italian Beethoven.

Rossini was born in Pesaro, a city on the northern shore of the Adriatic, south of Venice. His parents were musicians, his father a horn player and his mother a singer in minor provincial theaters. In 1787, when he was only five, Rossini began to be involved in the political turmoil of Italy that followed the descent of the French under Napoleon. In that year they captured Pesaro, which was in the Papal States, and the citizens of Pesaro soon voted to be a part of the Cisalpine Republic, set up by the French and of course under French hegemony. In 1805 Napoleon turned what had by then become the Italian Republic into the Kingdom of Italy. Rossini and his parents had already moved to Bologna in 1804, and there the boy's musical education began in all seriousness. Handsome and with a beautiful voice, he sang in opera and studied at the famous Liceo Musicale from 1806 to 1810. And in that year he received his first commission, through the good offices of friends of his parents. He wrote *La Cambiale di Matrimonio*, a one-act farce, for the Teatro San Moisè in Venice. It was a success. His career had begun. By 1815, when he became the resident composer of operas at Naples, he was the dominant opera composer in Italy. In less than six years he had composed six short comic operas, two full-length comic operas, and four serious operas. His musical character revealed itself at once; even in *Demetrio and Polibio*, composed (though not entirely by him) in 1808 and 1809, there was an extraordinary charm and freshness of a new kind.

It is not enough to say that this novelty was a matter of sheer genius. We must also consider what released that genius, the political and cultural situation of Italy when Rossini was growing up and when he made his first successes. By 1809 France had control over all of Italy except the island of Sicily. Before he moved to Naples Rossini composed for Venice, Bologna, Ferrara, and Milan, all cities in the Kingdom of Italy, of which Napoleon, the Emperor of France, was also King. In effect, the Kingdom of Italy was part of France, and for most Italians the French hegemony was an era of liberation. Everywhere in Europe that the French penetrated and occupied they brought the Enlightenment, and in Italy the arrival of the French meant a liberation from the oppression of Spain and of Austria. To be sure, the vast majority of the population were peasants, even more so in the old Kingdom of Naples, whose Bourbon monarchy had fled to Sicily, so that the principal excitement of political social and cultural liberation was experienced in the cities. But in Italy to this day each city of any size maintains its memory of the period when it was once a free and independent city-state in the distant Middle Ages. Thus each city has a vivid cultural life and a local pride. The failure of this tradition is *campanilismo,* the indifference of each city to the affairs and the welfare of other cities, even one only twenty-five or thirty miles away. To this day it cannot be said that Italy is unified as France and England are, or even Spain and Germany, let alone Russia and the United States. So we must think of each city that commissioned an opera from Rossini—as well as of the many cities that did not— as a separate burning center of Enlightenment excitement. The new oppression forced upon Italy by the Congress of Vienna in 1815—the extension of Austrian power, the restoration of the Papal States to include once again Bologna and Ferrara, and the return of the Bourbons to the Kingdom of Naples—was experienced, therefore, with great bitterness. It was only a few years before the Carbonari began their struggle for a free and independent Italy.

In this atmosphere of political and cultural fermentation, of an impassioned experience of a new freedom and an equally impassioned demand and hope for greater freedom, a freedom marked by the liberation the French had brought but free from French domination, Rossini grew up and experienced his first successes. As the great Italian leader of the demand for a free and independent Italy, Giuseppe Mazzini, was to say in the 1830s, the essence of Rossini's music is self-assertion. As Mazzini put it, what Rossini meant was "I step forward," a phrase which is an almost exact translation of "aggression." In that phrase is synthesized the two cultures that entered into the emerging and innovative culture of the first half of the nineteenth century at a cultural level below the most advanced Romanticism. The one culture was that of the Enlightenment, the culture of political freedom, of nationalism, of social and economic advance and even leveling, if only a hoped-for leveling upward.

On the other hand was the culture of Romanticism, the culture that proposed that the individual must create his own culture and his own value out of his unique experiences with the political and cultural institutions of his society. The attempted fusion of the two came from the Romantic's insight or vision that the Enlightenment ideal of political liberty was the necessary political and social condition for the cultural freedom of the Romantic. Cultural transcendence, it was believed, could be achieved successfully only in the rationalized Enlightenment state and the rationalized Enlightenment economy. At least that was the most common perception. But there were also those Romantics, as in time we shall see, who saw the potentiality of the rationalization of the state for creating a more consistent and oppressive tyranny over the individual than even the pre-Revolutionary regime had achieved, a potentiality to be fully realized, again and again, in the twentieth century. From these conditions emerged that ambiguity and equivocation or semantic uncertainty and instability of the words "freedom" and "liberty" which obtain still. Thus Mazzini saw in Rossini's "self-assertion" both the assertion of the free individual in a condition of political liberty and the assertion of the cultural freedom of the individual who aims at and achieves cultural transcendence. And to be sure, both of these modes or impulses are to be found in the music of Rossini.

A first example of this self-assertion is to be found in the overtures to many of Rossini's operas, overtures that continued a concert life long after the operas themselves had ceased to be performed. Most instructive is the overture to *Aureliano in Palmira* (La Scala, Milano, 26 December 1813). That work was not successful, and Rossini used the overture again for *Elisabetta regina d'Inghilterra* (San Carlo, Napoli, 4 October 1815). When he wrote *Il barbiere de Siviglia* (Argentina, Roma, 20 February 1816), he evidently composed an overture based on Spanish themes which has unaccountably disappeared. For the subsequent performances and all modern performances, the already used overture to *Aureliano* appeared again. In the same way for *Tancredi* (Le Fenice, Venezia, 6 February 1813), a serious opera, he used the overture to the comic *La pietra del paragone* (La Scala, Milano, 26 September 1812). On at least two occasions, then, Rossini used the same overture for both a comic and a serious work. Once we become aware of this, we cease to look for any connection between Rossini's overtures and the character of the operas. The overture for one of his serious operas may begin with a certain solemn appropriateness and then burst into a lighthearted passage suitable for a comic opera. Thus various of the overtures have become popular concert pieces, particularly since they were revived by Toscanini in the 1930s, simply because they have no dramatic significance at all. What, then, do they assert? And the answer is that they assert Rossini. They were of a new brilliance in European music, intoxicating in their rapidity, their splendidly orchestrated crescendi, their enchanting melodies. Mazzini's remark about the music of Rossini applies most aptly to these delicious overtures. Above all, they proposed to the audience an unrestrained release of pure energy.

This indifference to the conventions of eighteenth-century opera resulted in his abandoning the musical conventions differentiating serious opera and comic opera. On the contrary, he used those conventions indiscriminately in both serious and comic operas. *Tancredi,* his first great success, was a serious work based on a tragedy by Voltaire, but much of the music is of the kind that belonged to the tradition of *opera buffa* rather than *opera seria.* That abandoning of what were by then stale traditions, traditions with which the audiences of the time were weary, was what led to Rossini's great popularity, along with the fire of his music and the sheer beauty of so much of it. Nothing could have been more consonant with and more appropriate to the political, social, and cultural mood of Italy in the years of French domination.

These were the years the Italians discovered freedom and Rossini stated that freedom in his indifference to convention and his transcendence of outworn musical platitudes. Even today critics assert that they experience in these early works before the departure for Naples a freshness of invention not to be found in his later works. The music of Rossini before 1815 was the ebullience of an ebullient period in Italian life. It is not surprising that after 1815, when the Enlightenment was succeeded by an imported Romanticism in Italian culture, what was the manifestation of one cultural period could equally well be interpreted as the manifestation of a new and profoundly different period. The brief period of French domination meant that the culturally advanced Italians of the years after 1815 saw the return in even more tyrannous form of the old pre-French oppression as the more oppressive because it imposed social and cultural controls no longer appropriate to a society that had experienced, though for less than twenty years, the breath of the modern, the breath of freedom. And since political expression was held down, all the Italian desire for modernity and freedom went into music, which could utter the message of freedom in pure sound independent of words. In the coming years, the words of Italian opera could be censored, but not the vitality, the independence, the innovation, the freedom of the music. Rossini's greatness was to show Italy how to experience the character and essence of freedom in an oppressive society, even in Bourbon Naples itself. Rossini so far had learned to respond not to the dramatic situation, responses controlled by convention, but rather to himself, to his genius, to his power to create value musically.

The man who brought Rossini to Naples and was indirectly responsible for a new direction in Rossini's music was Domenico Barbaja (1778–1841), who made a fortune at La Scala in Milano by combining gambling tables with producing operas and from 1809 continued that useful financial synthesis in Naples. He made Rossini musical director for the two principal Neapolitan opera theaters, San Carlo and Fondo, and contracted with him to compose two operas a year. Rossini arrived in Naples in May 1815, shortly after the city and its kingdom had been returned to Bourbon rule. His first opera was well calculated to please the Neapolitan monarch and his wife, Maria Carolina, sister of Marie Antoinette. It was ostensibly about Elizabeth of England and her legendary love for Leicester, but it has so vague and trifling a relationship to historical fact that it could perfectly well have been about a Roman Emperor, Marcus Aurelius, for example, or Titus, or some purely legendary and even imaginary Persian king, in the manner of so many eighteenth-century instances of the *opera seria*. The libretto was based by the poet Giovanni Schmidt on a play by Carlo Federici, in turn, interestingly enough, based on an English novel by Sophia Lee (1783–1785). It is a reminder that the true Romantic historical opera, like the Romantic historical novel, was almost always based upon as much historical fact as current research had so far made available. Scott's *Kenilworth* (1821) is just such a work, an attempt to come as close as possible to the truth of the Elizabeth-Leicester relationship. In Rossini's opera Elizabeth forgives all who offended against her, and in proper Enlightenment monarch fashion. As the chorus sings "Viva Elisa!" the queen sings

> *Fuggi amore da questo seno*
> *non turbar piu il viver mio.*
> *Altri affetti no vogl'io*
> *che la gloria e la pietà.*
> [Flee, love, from this breast,
> No more disturb my life.
> No other passions do I wish
> than glory and compassion.]

Nor was the music a great departure, though often very beautiful and partly borrowed from earlier operas no longer performed (such as *Aureliano*). The principal change was that he dropped recitatives accompanied only by the harpsichord in favor of the French style of recitatives accompanied by the orchestra.

After two more operas for a pair of Roman theaters, a typical late eighteenth-century rescue opera (*Torvaldo e Dorliska*, Teatro Valle, 28 December 1815) and *The Barber of Seville*, an eighteenth-century *opera buffa* full of borrowings from previous works and based on an eighteenth-century play by Beaumarchais (Argentina, 20 February 1816), and another *opera buffa* for Naples (*La gazetta*, Fiorentini, 26 September 1816), Rossini wrote a completely new kind of opera, at least in its third act, *Otello*, derived both remotely and closely from Shakespeare's play. (Fondo, 4 December 1816. Barbaja was rebuilding San Carlo after a fire in April 1816.) The author of the libretto was the Marchese Francesco Berio di Salsa, a man who was, it may be, more important to Rossini's cultural life than anyone else he ever had anything to do with. To be sure, we know little about Rossini's life before his years in Paris much later in the century, but that later life is instructive. We know that in Paris for many years he maintained a brilliant salon, filled not only with musicians but with writers and intellectuals. And we know that when Wagner visited him in March 1860, Rossini said to Wagner that he understood what the German composer was trying to do, to create true music drama that transcended the operatic tradition, because he himself had wanted to do the same thing. But because he had to support a large family, his impecunious mother and father and various other relatives, he could not afford to experiment. He *had* to be popular (it was many years after 1815 before he was wealthy), and so had to write according to the conventions of the traditional opera composed in numbers, with sharp distinctions among recitatives, various kinds of aria, and duets and other concerted numbers. That is, he too was impelled towards that realistic tendency in Romanticism which undermined traditional cultural forms. Now the fact is that in the third act of *Otello* he did indeed move strikingly in the direction of music drama. And it seems more than probable that the impulse to follow his own inclinations or perhaps the first revelation to him of the possibilities of music drama came from his acquaintance with the Marchese Berio di Salsa.

We know something of great significance about Berio from the account published in 1821 of Lady Sydney Morgan's visit to Naples in 1820. There she became acquainted with Berio and came to admire him greatly. He held, she wrote, the finest and most truly cultivated and intellectual salon in Italy, a place where real and serious conversation took place, and there the music was provided by a frequenter of Berio's salon, Rossini himself and his mistress Isabella Colbran, whom he married in 1822. Colbran was probably the greatest singer of the time, and the *opere serie* of Rossini's years in Naples were almost always composed for her voice and acting powers. Berio himself was immensely cultivated and familiar with all the important modern literatures of Europe—English, French, and German, that is, with the emerging Romantic culture. It is true that he has been roundly condemned for his "travesty" of Shakespeare's play, but that is unjust. He reduced it, perhaps with the help of Shakespeare's source, *Hecatomithi* (1565?), by the Italian author Cinthio (1504–1573). All of the action takes place in Venice rather than Venice and Cyprus, and for the famous handkerchief Berio substituted a letter. And indeed the intrigue is not different from that of endless eighteenth-century plays. The third act, however, is an entirely different matter, depending most closely on Shakespeare. And in this act we enter a new world of opera; we encounter something very close to the true music drama, the Romantic effort to bring reality into the opera house, an effort that may be conceived of as having arrived at its fulfillment, or close to it, in the operas of Alban Berg of the 1920s and 1930s, *Wozzeck* and *Lulu*.

The audience, at first relatively cool in their response to *Otello*, was overwhelmingly aroused and made enthusiastic by the third act. One of the most effective and realistic touches was the offstage voice of a gondolier singing a passage from Dante, a passage appropriate in the highest degree to the dramatic situation, Desdemona's fear that she had lost Otello's love. The traditionalists, of course, were horrified by the murder of Desdemona on stage, particularly since for a long time it had been a matter of doctrine that serious operas should end happily, or at least with reconciliations like *Elisabetta*. The flow of music in Act III was almost unbroken, and the sense of composition in numbers separated by recitative almost disappeared. Again, the storm— Rossini was so famous for his operatic storms that even *The Barber of Seville* had one—was dramatically integrated into the action. Those in the audience of modern taste, that is, the early Italian Romantics, recognized the revolution that Rossini had brought about in Act III of *Otello*; and it is true that when we listen to a recording of the work we find ourselves hurled and elevated by Act III into a new world of opera. The achievement of Rossini in this act was so culturally transcending that it is just to say that here nineteenth-century opera, that is, Romantic opera, made its first appearance. As so often in the tradition of Romanticism, the theater was renewed by turning to Shakespeare, a source for regeneration to be found in the next decade even in distant Russia with Pushkin's *Boris Godunov*.

In the remaining operas that Rossini wrote for Naples, he extended and developed what he had learned from *Otello*, nor was Berio absent from this development. He composed the libretto for *Riccardo e Zoraide*, based on Forteguerri's poem *Ricciardetto*, a possible source for Byron's *Beppo* and *Don Juan* (San Carlo, 3 December 1818). His other operas for Naples were *Armida*, from Tasso's *Gerusalemme Liberata* (San

Carlo, 5 March 1818), *Ermione*, from Racine's *Andromaque* (San Carlo, 27 March 1819), and *Zelmira*, after an eighteenth-century French play (San Carlo, 16 February 1822). Three other Naples operas, however, were modern and Romantic. *Mosè in Egitto (San Carlo*, 5 March 1818), though based on an eighteenth-century Italian play, opened with an extraordinarily innovative scene in darkness, the plague of darkness summoned by Moses. Here, for the first time in Rossini's work, the chorus begins to play a dramatic role, as it was to do throughout the nineteenth century. It was the operatic equivalent of the entry of the people on the stage of history which was one of Scott's great themes. It is the more appropriate that Rossini made an opera of Scott's *The Lady of the Lake*. It opens with a beautiful hunting chorus followed by the appearance of the Lady in her boat, sailing from her island and singing a marvelously beautiful aria. *La donna del lago* brings both realism and historicism into Italian opera (San Carlo, 24 September 1819). Finally, *Maometto II* proved too modern for the Neapolitan audiences (San Carlo, 3 December 1820). Indeed, it was less advanced when he rewrote it for Paris in 1826.

Steadily throughout these Neapolitan years Rossini expanded enormously the music resources of Italian opera. There is an increased number of ensembles. By reducing the role of the solo aria, the dramatic effect of interaction is correspondingly intensified. The recitatives become more dramatic and less differentiated from the arias, and the orchestra plays a steadily increasing role, not merely accompanying the soloists, but like the chorus playing an actual dramatic part. Not only were the historical tragedies of Bellini and Donizetti founded on these Neapolitan works but also the grand historical operas of Meyerbeer and Wagner. It is an extraordinary fact that in spite of the political repression of the Bourbons in Naples, a repression that experienced a rebellion of the Carbonari in 1820, the intellectual and cultural atmosphere of that city, as epitomized and concentrated in the figure of the Marchese Berio di Salsa, was responsible (everything points to this) for the tremendous cultural leap achieved by Rossini in his conception and execution of opera during the five or six years after Waterloo. His Enlightenment libertarianism transformed into Romantic individuality evinced itself in the only way it can be properly evinced, in creative innovation, in cultural emergence. As recordings of these operas have become available our understanding of Rossini has been transformed and his greatness as a Romantic composer is beginning to be recognized. Neither the greatness nor the Romanticism can any longer be doubted.

JOSEPH MALLORD WILLIAM TURNER
(1775–1851)

By 1815 Turner had created a wholly new kind of landscape, most fruitfully understood as semiotic constructs of emotional states or conditions. Yet he was not satisfied that he had equaled the man he thought of as the greatest landscape painter of the past, Claude Lorraine. Before again transforming his art in the years 1817 to 1820 he first set out to prove that he had equaled Claude Lorraine and indeed had surpassed him in Claude's own style of landscape painting. In the first years after Waterloo he exhibited a series of paintings which satisfied him that he had succeeded.

Completed 1815: *Lake Avernus: Aeneas and the Cumaean Sibyl* (not exhibited; a commissioned version of a painting of 1798)

Exhibited 1815: *Dido Building Carthage**
Crossing the Brook*

Exhibited 1817: *The Temple of Jupiter Panelennius restored*
View of the Temple of Jupiter Panellenius, in the Island of Aegina

Exhibited 1817: *The Decline of the Carthaginian Empire**

With these paintings out of the way he was ready to go on to something new.

In 1818 he exhibited three pictures of a highly innovative character. The first is *Raby Castle, the Seat of the Earl of Darlington*. It was like nothing he had painted before. Although earlier pictures had been half or more than half sky, there was always some vigorous emergence from the land or the sea into the area of the sky. But in this picture sky and land are almost identical in area. Yet, on the other hand, the distinction between the two disappears in mist. The scene is an enormous landscape in west Durham. The castle itself, though a large building, occupies a small area of the painting, and its towers are far below the horizon line. It is in a shallow valley, and beyond is an extensive plain from which moors rise most subtly toward the hazily suggested crests of the Pennines. The color of the foreground and the hills is a dull almost brownish green, which gives way to delicate violets as the landscape rises toward the distant mountains. But above is a sky such as Turner himself had never yet painted. It is a marvelous complexity of gray and white layers of clouds; in several

---

*Discussed in *The Birth of Romanticism*.

spots the clouds part enough to reveal glimpses of blue sky beyond. The brightest spot in the painting is near the top and just off center to the left, a suggestion that the sun is concealed here behind clouds, a suggestion emphasized by the darkest clouds, almost storm clouds, directly below the spot, a juxtapositional device often used by Turner. Never before in an oil had Turner used such subdued coloring. In the previous Claudian paintings and in the ecstatic landscapes of a few years before 1815, the color was of a miraculous splendor and beauty. Every resource of color available to him at this time was employed. But here there is a sudden refusal of that coloristic excitement and resource. The overall effect is silvery. Turner is moving toward the minimalism of his last paintings, works he never exhibited and which were unappreciated until the twentieth century. In this painting he becomes a virtuoso of restraint.

The second painting exhibited at the Royal Academy in 1818 was a similar departure, for unlike the subdued *Raby Castle* it is, though pale, of an extremely high key. It is *Dort, or Dordrecht, the Dort Packet-Boat from Rotterdam Becalmed*. The dominating colors of the sky, which occupies two-thirds of the painting, are pale violet shading into a pale blue. But such terms are horribly approximate, for the unimaginable differentiation of hues can, in words, be only pointed to. As with all of Turner's greatest paintings, the more one looks at *Dort* the more inexhaustible it seems. The color is made all the more demanding upon the viewer by the brown packet boats (there are in fact several) and their brown reflections in the brownish-greenish water, which also reflects the violet of the sky. Never before had he painted so realistic a sky, one so distant from the conventions of painting. It reminds one irresistibly of Wordsworth's "It is a beauteous evening, calm and free, / the holy time is quiet as a Nun / Breathless with adoration." It is an evocation of muted rapture.

The third painting exhibited in 1818 was the result of his visit of a few weeks to the continent, Belgium, and the Rhine valley, in August 1817. He accompanied *The Field of Waterloo* with a quotation from Byron's *Childe Harold* (III, 28), a fact indicative of his intellectual life and his awareness of current literature. The picture itself aroused some resentment among the critics and the public because, instead of celebrating the glory of Waterloo, it showed a night scene with a heap of dead illuminated by a brilliant moon shining through storm clouds and on the right the burning farm of Hougomont. It is expressive of that side of Turner's personal culture which first appeared fully in *Hannibal Crossing the Alps* (see *The Birth of Romanticism*) and was reiterated in passages he appended to his paintings that purported to come from a long poem, *The Fallacies of Hope,* although in fact there was no long poem but only short passages. The painting brought out Turner's despair over the human condition and was indicative of his alienation from the public, his conviction that to paint for the acceptance of the public would be disastrous, and his determination to believe, quite correctly as it turned out, that no one understood his art.

The third memorial of his 1817 tour was the quite different and highly innovative *Entrance of the Meuse: Orange-Merchant on the Bar, Going to Pieces,* exhibited in 1819. A sketchbook dated 1816 to 1818 contains no less than sixty-five studies of skies and clouds. Some of these were purely realistic, but others, and among them the most beautiful, are obviously studies of how clouds can be used for purposes of emotional semiosis or, to use a more common term, expressiveness—for, that is, constructs of signs of emotion. The clouds of *Entrance of the Meuse* are of this sort. They occupy almost three-fourths of the picture's area. In the foreground are great waves. They are littered with oranges and occupied in part by boats, either boats that have escaped from the wreck in the central background or sailboats coming to the rescue. The clouds surge up in a great diagonal. At the upper left, patches of pale blue sky are visible through remnants and rags of storm clouds. The sky, then, and its clouds are designed to illustrate the great forces responsible for the wreck of the merchantman, expressive of the winds that are carving the waves and troughs in the foreground. The sky, however, is extraordinarily, marvelously beautiful, so much so that one is at first distracted from the terror and suffering of the figures visible in the boat at the left, one of whom appears to be praying. The sky is of the most realistic light that Turner had yet achieved. What Turner is after, it appears, is to evoke in the spectator the response to that natural power and beauty, to feel it in himself, and thus to realize that the painting is not only a sign of natural power and splendor but also a symbol of that power and splendor in the human heart and soul.

An absolute contrast to this picture is the first major result of his 1819 trip to Italy, from which he returned in January 1820. It is *Rome, from the Vatican,* exhibited in 1820. We are looking out over the square of St. Peter's from one of the arches in the loggia called Raphael's from his decorations and paintings of scenes from the Bible. Raphael himself is there, with his mistress La Fornarina and various of his pictures. It is a large picture, eleven feet by nearly six. The viewer is, then, enveloped by the painting, which is, in some way, very strange. On the right we look down the loggia to its end. Thus the arch of the loggia we are looking out of springs diagonally towards the viewer and is cut off about halfway up its curve. On the left, however, is the inside wall of the other half of that arch, and it is painted to be parallel to the plane of the painting, instead of at the angle of the corresponding side of the arch at the right. The other wing of the Vatican is also presented from the perspective of the right hand of the painting and not of that of the left. Moreover, one looks down on the great piazza of St. Peter's embraced by the arms of Bernini's colonnade. One sees it only as one would see it from a window of the facade of St. Peter's itself. Of course Bernini's colonnade was not built when Raphael painted the loggia. The full title of the painting is *Rome, from the Vatican. Raffaelle, Accompanied by La Fornarina Preparing his Pictures for the Decoration of the Loggia.* But in fact the loggia is shown as completely decorated and the pictures include well-known paintings by Raphael that have nothing to do with the loggia, a painting by Claude, and what appears to be an excerpt from Michelangelo's Sistine Chapel ceiling, as well as the plan of St. Peter's with Bernini's colonnade. The distorted perspective pushed to the extreme foreground is as if the loggia were broken and its contents thrust out to the viewer. But the eyes are pulled away from this toward the immense distance covered by a glowing blue sky and a haze at the horizon of mountains, a vast sky echoed by the luminous piazza of St. Peter's, into which a tiny religious procession is entering. The portion of the Vatican at the left, the Palace of Sixtus V, cuts brutally into this expanse of sky.

And so the painting contrasts the artistic energies of man with the sublime indifference of nature. The architecture, the piled-up works of art, the innumerable buildings of the city, including the Castle of St. Angelo, are not only in contrast with but are conceived of as an attack upon the natural world. The almost empty space of the sky with just a few traces of cirrus clouds is echoed by the great empty space of the Piazza, which glows with light. The radiant tranquillity of sky and space and distant mountains is in sharp antithesis to the strangely distorted architecture and the busyness of man, emphasized by the tininess of the figures in the religious procession. The painting has been superficially called a tribute to Italian art, and such an interpretation has its immediate attractiveness. But when one begins to observe and respond to the strangeness of the work—and it is one of Turner's strangest paintings—one is much more inclined to see it as a witness to Turner's feeling and conviction that he had transcended the world of art which had dominated European culture until his generation. Just as the viewer is irresistibly drawn to ignore the foreground details and to escape into the tranquil radiance of the sky and the distant mountains, so Turner himself already had accomplished that escape.

One other work of this period needs to be examined, a watercolor painted in November 1818 at the home in north England of his friend Walter Fawkes, Farnley Hall. It is *A First-Rate Taking in Stores*. It is worth attention not only in its own right but because of the account we have of its creation. The scene is that of a major ship of the British Navy attended by lighters with sails bringing stores to it. We see the whole vast side of the ship, and the scale of what we see is given by two other similar ships in the background. In the foreground are the marvelous waves of a port on a windy day, and in the back is a cloud-scape that erupts from the horizon to the zenith. In the library of the National Gallery in London is to be found the following account of its creation.

There is one thing quite certain as to the Turner traditions at Farnley for I have heard it repeatedly stated by all the generation who were children when Turner was so much at Farnley, and that is, that with one exception, no one ever saw him paint when he was there. The exception was this—one morning at breakfast Walter Fawkes said to him, "I want you to make me a drawing of the ordinary dimensions that will give some idea of the size of a man-of-war." The idea hit Turner's fancy, for with a chuckle he said to Walter Fawkes' eldest son, then a boy of about 15, "Come along Hawkey and we will see what we can do for Papa," and the boy sat by his side the whole morning and witnessed the evolution of *The First-Rate Taking in Stores*. His description of the way Turner went to work was very extraordinary; he began by pouring wet paint onto the paper till it was saturated, he tore, he scratched, he scrubbed at it in a kind of frenzy and the whole thing was chaos—but gradually and as if by magic the lovely ship, with all its exquisite minutia, came into being and by luncheon time the drawing was taken down in triumph. (Martin Butlin, *Turner, Watercolors*, London, 1962)

This description seems incredible, yet Turner left thousands of water-colors of such quality that it is doubtful that anyone ever has equaled him as a watercolorist. But above all it shows in full force the behavior of the Romantic virtuoso, the man who transforms the verbal directions of cultural transcendence, as we have seen, into physical behavior. Turner raised the actual act of painting to a new level. Thus it seems reasonable to interpret *Rome, from the Vatican* as Turner's statement of his transcendent painterly technique, of his status as a virtuoso of painting.

JOHN CONSTABLE (1776–1837)

By 1816 Constable had arrived at a full understanding of what he wanted to do in painting. On the one hand he thought of painting as analogous to music and to poetry. He had most fully realized in his sketches the experience of the moment of revelation, of self-under-standing, of the vision of value and the objectification of an emotional state. On the other hand he thought of painting as analogous to sci-ence. It has long been argued as to whether Constable's sketches or his finished paintings are the more attractive and the finer works of art. The sketches of course have a wonderful spontaneity as well as a mastery in catching the general character of a scene, its *chiaroscuro*, as he called it, its definition through light and shadow. Yet there is a richer fullness of realization in the finished paintings, the big paintings painted for exhibition at the Royal Academy, the pictures on which he wishes to found his greatness. From 1808 to 1815 he had explored in endless sketches and a few paintings the Vale of Dedham (*The Birth of Romanticism*), both realizing his feelings about his home country and at the same time developing a realistic style of recording the appear-ance of that country. Now in the years after Waterloo he set out to synthesize in a series of large paintings that would surpass previous landscape painting his conception of painting as music and as science.

The first step was a commission for a painting of *Wivenhoe Park. The Residence of General Rebow,* begun in August 1816 and perhaps not fin-ished until 1817, when it was exhibited at the Royal Academy. Thus his years of exploring the Vale of Dedham were bracketed by this picture and the earlier topographical painting of a country house, *Malvern Hall,* painted in 1809, the first work in his mature style (discussed in *The Birth of Romanticism*). In the same way Turner in the late eighteenth century had made his start by painting portraits of gentlemen's seats. And Constable in his way was as original in his handling of this tra-ditional subject as Turner. In *Wivenhoe Park* the house of General Rebow is barely visible at the top of a low rise from a lake which occupies most of the foreground. But it is pink, and thus it stands out from the green meadow and trees and the sky filled with clouds that are almost storm clouds; and between them are glimpses and patches of a pale blue sky, somewhat darker at the top of the painting. The pink of the house is beautifully echoed in the exquisite reflections in the lake. The painting catches the areas of sun and shadow and is given interest by various pastoral incidents and touches. There are cattle, swans on the lake, two fishermen in a boat casting a net. On the land all is the perfect tran-quillity of a landed gentleman's estate, but the sky is in contrast, full of turbulent clouds and birds seemingly tossed by the wind. The picture captures both the tranquillity and power of the natural world and the human replication of those attributes of nature. It is a small painting, only forty inches by twenty-two inches, its tranquillity emphasized by its horizontality, its length in contrast with its height, yet that tranquillity is countered by the sky. It was a beginning towards what Constable wanted to do.

The next step was on a larger scale, forty inches by fifty inches. He began *Flatford Mill* probably in September 1816 and exhibited it at the Royal Academy in 1817. This was his first step toward the great series of six large paintings of the Dedham valley known as his "six-footers." But it was not quite a successful step. His father, his uncle, and Farington, the diarist and minor artist, had all told him that his paintings lacked "finish," and that was why they had not sold. This painting also was unsold, in spite of its finish; for it is the most "finished" of his paintings, that is, one in which the brushwork is controlled by the ideal of accuracy of mimesis. The result was that though his scientific ideal was adequately realized, the emotive or musical ideal was not. The high finish meant the disappearance of the most important mark of spontaneity, the evidence of a brush striking the canvas. He was not to make this mistake again.

In the Royal Academy exhibition of 1819 he exhibited the first of his six-footers and the first of his paintings to arouse widespread comment and admiration. It was bought, though by his friend John Fisher, and later in the year Constable was at last elected as Associate of the Royal Academy. The landscape tradition, one which on the whole even Turner obeyed, was that some incident of human activity was required; "staffage" is the technical term. The incident in *The White Horse* is anything but traditional. In the eighteenth century the Stour River flowing through the Vale of Dedham had been canalized, made into a canal navigable for shallow barges by a series of locks. The canal barges were drawn by horses, and at various places, because of one impediment or another, the towpath shifted from one bank to the other. At such points the tow horse was put on the barge and taken to the other bank, the barge itself being poled from one bank to the other. Yet the picture is something of a puzzle, for there is no sign of a towpath on the opposite bank. The fact is that unlike the remaining five large paintings of the Dedham Vale, the exact spot of the picture cannot be located. It is in fact a composed picture, a studio picture. Certainly it is exceedingly beautiful, yet it lacks the sense of spontaneity, of a "spot of time" whether of the landscape or of the painter's subjective vision and life. It is too reminiscent of traditional landscapes, even those of the seventeenth century of the Dutch school, the first great landscape school. The synthesis of painting and science had yet to be achieved. Even at the time, it was recognized that the "soul of landscape" that Turner caught was not in this work of Constable's.

But it was certainly there in the next painting, *Stratford Mill on the*

Stour, begun in 1819 and exhibited in 1820. The scene is west of Dedham and just west of Stratford St. Mary at the very edge of the Vale of Dedham. It is hardly changed today, although the old timber quay of the mill at the left has been replaced by concrete and only the ruins of a later mill remain. In the immediate foreground are two boys fishing with an older fisherman. Farther to the left across the river is another fisherman and still farther a man on a horse just to the right of a corner of the mill and part of the mill wheel. To the right a barge with three men is headed downriver towards Dedham. Deep in the background and framed by trees is a white house. To the right are low hills in shadow in front of which are meadows in shadow and sun. Dominating the picture is a great mass of tall trees in the center. The sky is magnificent with the clouds (some of them rain clouds) and the broken sky of East Anglia, so that the painting is filled with sunlight and deep shadows, and the river reflects both the white clouds and the dark trees. The white reflections on the river lead one's eye deep into the background on a line which continues the line of the quay to the lower left. An opposite implied diagonal line leads from the lower right across the painting to the spot of sunlight beyond the trees where the horse is grazing, its rider sitting quietly on its back. The implied structure of the painting is an "x" pushed flat by the weight, as it were, of the great stand of trees. Further, the perception of the painting is pulled apart in three directions, to the line of the river at the right, to the horseman in a deep recession to the left, and in the center through a tunnel of trees to the distant and small white house.

By these devices Constable has caught in painting the variability of the natural world, its refusal to be captured in the conventions of composition. The scientific aspect of the picture is thus revealed in its composition as well as the exquisitely observed and painted endless and endlessly accurate details. The poetry of the painting, the music, has finally been synthesized with the science. The painting has been called tranquil, but that is a superficial response, perhaps controlled by the fishing boys. (In fact for long the picture was known as *The Young Waltonians,* though not by Constable.) A close look reveals the disturbing character of the great central mass of trees, which all lean to the left in answer to, it must be supposed, winds sweeping from the sea up the Dedham valley. Yet quite opposing that movement is the obvious direction of the clouds, which are boiling from the west. The farthest tree at the left, above the mill, is the darkest, and it is capped by an almost black storm cloud. In this painting Constable has carried to a higher and almost exalted level what he had begun in *Wivenhoe Park,* the simultaneous presentation of tranquillity and passion, here perfectly synthesized. It is Constable's first triumphant creation, a release into a picture of the science that undermines our platitudes of perception and the poetry and music that fills a painting with a revelation of value.

CASPAR DAVID FRIEDRICH (1774–1840)

None of the artists and writers of the immediate post-Napoleonic period responded so strangely to the situation of the years after the defeat of Napoleon and after Waterloo as did Friedrich. In the preceding decade he had painted a considerable variety of subjects—landscapes, ruined abbeys in winter, and various scenes in celebration of the Freedom War of Prussia against Napoleon. Now suddenly he devoted himself for three years, 1816 to 1818, almost entirely to paintings of the sea from the shore, usually with one or two people with their backs to the observer and looking out to sea, where ships are sailing towards a distant horizon, ordinarily at sunset or in moonlight. Sometimes, however, the subject was a harbor filled with ships, or a view across a harbor to a distant city, one based on the towers either of his birthplace Greifswald or of Neubrandenburg. One painting shows two men looking across meadows to a distant and idealized Neubrandenburg silhouetted against the light of dawn. In most of the sea pictures there is a foreground of rocks or of a swampy shore, a few times with a large anchor in the immediate foreground. In these foregrounds Friedrich often stretches out a line of drying fishermen's nets. The virtual termination of these subjects was almost identical in time with his marriage in 1818.

Almost the last of this series was *Auf dem Segler* (*On the Sailboat*), which shows a man and a woman sitting on the prow of what is best described as a yacht and looking across the sea to a distant horizon of buildings which suggest those of Dresden, Greifswald, and Stralsund. Stralsund is the port from which one took a boat to the island of Rügen, which Friedrich and his bride visited in 1818. So this painting may have been inspired by their return. The figure of the man is said not to be Friedrich; though, as we shall see, that may be doubted, and his wife was most probably the model for the woman. Thus the picture may or may not be a souvenir of their trip to Rügen. If the city is the object of the voyage, as it seems to be, are we to think of it as the goal of a return from a journey, as the goal or object of an outward-bound voyage, or as a place not yet experienced?

This obsession with a single theme has been variously interpreted. One school sees all of these paintings as emblems of the movement toward and longing for death. The anchor stands for Christian hope;

the rocks, so frequent, either for faith or for the difficulties of existence; the nets for the complexities of life, the snares of existence. In those pictures which present an empty sea with boats sailing towards the horizon, the boats are said to be the soul or at the least the desire of men for what the Germans call *jenseits*, the other world. In those paintings which show the spires of a distant city instead of an empty horizon, that city symbolizes, it is said, paradise. In certain harbor scenes filled with large ships the masts and spars are interpreted as the Christian cross, and the ships as emblems of one's assurances of an afterlife.

Now all this may indeed be the case. But other interpretations are worth considering, for the reason that if Friedrich was developing a new system of Christian iconography, he was encountering the difficulty of all such attempts in the nineteenth century, and there were not a few. Since meaning is not immanent there is no necessary connection between a verbalization and its symbolization in visual semiosis. This becomes clearer if one considers what is happening when the word "symbol" is used. Since the meaning of any sign is the response to that sign, and since that meaning is not immanent in the sign, a meaning is neither correct nor incorrect but only appropriate in the judgment of some individual, though this does not mean that untold thousands of individuals may not agree. We use the word "symbol," then, when we are proposing that two or more responses to a given sign are appropriate. For this reason "private" symbolization is possible. That is, in the judgment of the maker of the sign, in this case Friedrich, the sign may be an appropriate response to some verbalization ("idea" or "concept") but no one else may grasp its appropriateness. The link between verbalization and visualization, then, has not yet been conventionalized and incorporated into culture and cultural instructions. In these paintings the only well-established symbol is that of the anchor, which in Christian iconography is an emblem of hope. ("Emblem" is the appropriate term when a visualization of a verbalization is well established or is being established by accompanying verbal instructions.) The only clue that a Christian interpretation is appropriate is, then, the anchor. Actually, however, that anchor appears in only two or perhaps three of these twenty-four paintings. The redundancy of the anchor is not sufficient to control the interpretation of all the paintings. Indeed, it is so rare that one is quite justified in thinking that Friedrich abandoned it as not a sufficient guide to the meaning or meanings he was endeavoring to express.

In cases of this sort one turns to other possibilities and, as almost always happens, these other possibilities can be seen to subsume the more limited interpretational possibility, in this case the purely Christian. Thus Christianity itself can be revealed as but one mode of symbolizing a universal or at least very common response to and interpretation of experience and the world. Now it has been suggested that these paintings are not Christian at all but are rather Friedrich's responses, obsessive responses, to the reimposition of political oppression in the years after Waterloo, his response to what was called the Holy Alliance, instigated by Alexander I of Russia, of Austria, Prussia, and Russia, the alliance dedicated to the re-establishment, so far as possible, of the old regime. From this point of view the distant horizon or the distant city represents not paradise but that freedom which was fought for in the Freedom War but which the Holy Alliance wished to suppress. It is worth remembering that it was precisely in these years that a Napoleonic kind of bureaucratized censorship was imposed throughout Europe. There is certainly evidence that Friedrich responded to the new oppression with great bitterness. For example, one of his most famous pictures is *Zwei Männer in Betrachtung des Mondes* (*Two Men Contemplating the Moon*), 1819. One interpretation sees the dead oak tree and the stony path as emblems of the difficulties of life and of death, and interprets the sickle moon as Christ, the promise of resurrection. To a visitor Friedrich interpreted the painting "ironically": "They are making demagogic intrigues." So perhaps Friedrich was setting out a political position.

Yet the source of this political interpretation is in itself dubious and somewhat suspect, emanating from the widespread European tendency in the post-World War II decades to interpret everything by subsuming it under a Marxist ideology. In a sense this is fair enough, for, as we have seen, socialism is an Enlightenment secularization of Christianity, and Marx's ideal classless society no more than a secularization of the Christian Paradise. These paintings can serve one ideology as well as another if the two are merely versions of each other. However, a third possibility has also been proposed. One of the most common themes of German Romanticism is *Sehnsucht*, yearning. To the question, Yearning for what? we have already encountered the answer; yearning for a condition of existence that transcends the present one, more specifically yearning for a culture that transcends the failures of the culture then available.

Of these three possibilities of interpretation, this third one is probably the most appropriate. If Friedrich were merely concerned with a new Christian iconography, there would be little reason for his doing it over and over. That repetition, that redundancy, argues a profounder or at least a different concern. The best evidence for this is that he was asked to create designs for the fitting up of the Marienkirche in Stralsund, and his designs use traditional Christian iconography. Nor is the second, political, interpretation incoherent with the third, the most purely Romantic of the three. For the fact is that whatever private symbolization Friedrich may have given to these paintings, he succeeded in creating a series of beautiful and moving visions of the desire to journey beyond the present possibilities of existence and experience to a possibility undefined, as in the seascapes with empty horizons, or to an exalted vision of possibility, as in those paintings with evocations of distant cities, identified by their spires. Moreover, in 1818 and 1819 and 1820, the paintings become more particularized and give a stronger impression of a specific place on the seashore.

Certainly after his marriage in 1818 and his trip with his bride to his hometown and to the island of Rügen he began to paint different subjects. They are on a large scale and include several of his greatest masterpieces, a rank that only one or two at best of the immediately preceding years can claim. The first two are probably of 1818. *Frau vor untergehenden Sonne (Woman before the Setting Sun)* shows a woman standing at the end of a road. She is facing away from us and, unlike other figures of this sort in Friedrich's paintings, she is large in relation to the size of the painting, two-thirds of the height of the picture. On either side of the road are rocks, and before is an extensive and very beautiful rolling landscape rising up to a low mountain behind which the sun is setting. It sends forth great rays of radiating pink light against a wonderfully variegated yellow, pink, and orange sky. A Christian interpretation makes the end of the road the end of life itself and the distant landscape God and immortality. A more general interpretation sees the road as the cultural possibilities of life as we know it, and the picture is a realization of that and the need to create new possibilities, symbolized by the woman's outspread and welcoming arms before the visionary landscape.

The next picture is *Der Wanderer über dem Nebelmeer (The Wanderer above the Sea of Clouds)*, probably 1818. It shows a man in a frock coat who has climbed to a rock outcropping evidently at the top of a mountain from which he looks out over a great landscape of clouds through which penetrate other outcroppings of rock. Beyond is a vast upland landscape from which rises a great mountain. As in the preceding painting the figure is large though not so large in relation to the size of the painting, itself much larger. It has been proposed that this is a memorial painting for someone who had recently died, possibly a Herr von Brincken, a name which offers the possibility of three different individuals. And of course the painting is easily given a Christian interpretation: a man has reached the aim or end of life, has triumphed over the cloudy errors of existence, and is now ready for triumphant contemplation and perhaps union with the divine. And perhaps that was Friedrich's intention, or he may have simply wished to symbolize the possibility of triumphant self-assertion over the difficulties and limitations of life as it is. For both this and the preceding painting, unique as they are in his work, appear to present such a powerful self-assertion, whether in a Christian frame of reference or not.

In 1819 Friedrich painted what may have been his greatest masterpiece, unfortunately destroyed in Berlin in the bombing of the Flakturm in 1945. It is the great *Klosterfriedhof im Schnee* (*Cloister Graveyard in the Snow*). The first striking fact about this painting is that Friedrich here returns to material and themes of his earliest years of oil painting, 1807–1811, and does so on a grand scale. The picture is one of the largest he had yet painted, 4 feet by 5 feet 8 inches, and one of the largest he ever was to paint. Of a ruined church in the center all that remains is the entrance portal and beyond a towering apse with three lancet windows, based on the apse of the Marienkirche in Stralsund but much higher. In the foreground are two oaks framing the church. All around the church and beyond the oaks are the crosses of gravemarkers. On either side forming a kind of semicircle around the ruins are more dead oaks. A procession of monks is moving diagonally from behind a low rise of ground at the left to the church portal, through which they are carrying a coffin. Far in the distance in the position of the high altar glows a cross with a priest or monk before it, presumably ready to perform the mass of the dead. All of these are themes he had used before. The two great oaks, for example, are simply the reverse of the two oaks in a painting of 1807 in which they flank a dolmen or *Hünengrab*. These same oaks appear in a number of paintings and symbolize the old pre-Christian religion, as they do here. The ruins likewise stand for the dying medieval Christianity, with all of its splendor and pomp, as do the monks moving through the graveyard and bearing the coffin of one of themselves. Yet the pure white and shining cross, almost invisible, suggests the survival of the essence of the Christian religion. That would be consistent with Friedrich's efforts, if such they were, to create a new Christian iconography, efforts which, as we have seen, go far to reveal Christianity as one possible mode of a universal. The real significance of the painting in Friedrich's development is that in what is perhaps his most beautiful painting he was able to turn back to his original sources of artistic vitality and thus renew his powers after the gloomy and discouraging paintings of the preceding years. Whatever interpretation Friedrich might have given to it, it is a witness of his revitalization, of the Romantic capacity to renew oneself after a period of despair and discouragement, of the capacity to transcend an obsession that threatened Friedrich's life as an artist.

That painting was begun in 1817 and finished in 1818. In 1818, probably, he painted a far different picture, also one of his most famous and beautiful, *Kreidefelsen auf Rügen* (*Chalk Cliffs on Rügen*). The point of view of the putative observer is intensely original. We seem to be looking down from something like a bird's-eye view onto the edge of the famous chalk cliffs of the island of Rügen, at this point splintered and shattered into fantastic pinnacles. They make a great V-shape, almost as wide and almost as deep as the painting. Because of the extremely raked point of view, the sea beyond rises up to a distant horizon and fills two-thirds of the V. On the lower edges of the V and on the very edge of the cliff are three figures: a woman in red is pointing down to the abyss below; a man on hands and knees has crawled to the edge of the cliff and is peering down; a second man with folded arms is leaning against a rock at the right and gazing out to sea. At the top of the painting tree branches create an arch from right and left obscuring the sky above the horizon line, towards which two tiny boats are sailing.

Even the commentator most committed to the interpretation of Friedrich's paintings as Christian allegories is baffled by this one. The most striking difference of this from the works of the preceding years is the brilliance of the color. It appears to be an overcoming of the melancholy of the first years of the Holy Alliance. Since there are strong hints that the kneeling man is Friedrich himself and that the woman is his wife, the general tone of the picture suggests a renewed self-confidence and ability to achieve a strong self-assertion. Unlike the figures in the preceding paintings, two of these figures are not looking out to sea. The figure at the right who is and who is wearing the kind of hat some of these sea-gazing figures wore may well signify the past. In the immediate present the woman is pointing to the dangerous abyss of the chalk cliffs, and the man, with great caution, is examining them. His position even suggests that he is studying them. So Friedrich's attention has been turned from *jenseits*, whether that is interpreted as a life after death, as a promise of resurrection, as a desire for a better future free from political oppression, or as a mere longing for an undefined object. It is *diesseits*, this world, that is now being examined, and its dangers.

This possibility is supported by a picture already mentioned, painted at about the same time, *Auf dem Segler.* To be sure there is a visionary city in the distance, but the man and the woman are sailing toward it. For the first time in this series of paintings looking out to sea the perceivers are actually in motion toward a desired object. To be sure the man in the boat wears the same hat as the man lost in contemplation in the *Chalk Cliffs*, but that suggests a link between the two men in that work: the man in the medieval hat is being superseded by the man on the ground studying the realities of his world. If the city is Stralsund, then the figures are Friedrich and his new wife returning from their trip to Rügen to the solid land of Stralsund and Germany and their earthly home; and therefore to a renewal of Friedrich's relation to this world.

In 1819 Friedrich painted another transformation of the sea-gazing pictures. It is the famous *Zwei Männer in Betrachtung des Mondes (Two Men Contemplating the Moon)*, referred to above. Perhaps he really meant and was not being ironic when he said that the two men were plotting *demagogische Umtriebe*. That strange word "demagogic" can perhaps be explained by the assassination in 1819 of the German dramatist and Russian agent and spy August von Kotzebue. The assassin was the student Karl Ludwig Sand, who was a member of the liberal student organization, the *Burschenschaft*, which had grown out of the Freedom War against Napoleon and was bitterly opposed to the oppression of the post-Waterloo years, the oppression by the Holy Alliance guided by the Austrian minister Metternich. The immediate result of the assassination of Kotzebue was the promulgation of the Karlsbad Decrees, drawn up by Metternich and designed to suppress liberal and national movements, since Metternich and his like were activated solely by a fear of the French Revolution. The decrees in effect created a police state throughout the German-speaking world and immediately were responsible for suppressing the *Burschenschaft* as a "demagogic movement." In the picture the man in the cloak has been identified as Friedrich, though he is wearing the same floppy medieval hat as figures not identified as Friedrich. It seems, rather, more appropriate to recognize any man in these pictures with that hat as one aspect of Friedrich, that factor or role of his personality that was primarily engaged in a visionary longing for a better existence, either in this world or after death. In that sense these men are really plotting subversive intrigues. Though they are on a stony path flanked by a dead tree, they are raised above the horizon and are looking *down* on the moon. It is either a moon obscured by current oppression, or it is a new moon beginning to escape from the shadow of that oppression. In either case the men, one of whom is leaning in a friendly fashion upon the shoulder of the man in the cloak, are looking out from the stony and dead waste in which they find themselves towards light, towards value. Because of their elevation above the moon there is something confident, something consoling and reassuring about their stance. The curve that they make with the curved dead tree on the right creates an embrace. The moon is not lost in space but is contained, much as the chalk cliffs and the trees in the earlier painting contain the sea. The composition converts the moon into a possible goal, something to be successfully reached by means of their "demagogic intrigues."

It is fitting, therefore, that in the last painting of these years from 1816 to 1820 Friedrich should have turned once again to a theme of earlier years, but once again transformed, magnificently. It is *Riesengebirgslandschaft mit aufsteigendem Nebel* (*A Landscape in the Sudety Mountains with Rising Mist*). In most of the earlier mountain landscapes the mountains are seen from a distance, usually with an intervening plain or valley. But here we are already in the heart of the mountains. The foreground is an edge of a lower mountain with two dead trees, and beyond in range after range the mountains pile up to a great flattened cone of a distant peak. It is the first of a series of such mountain scenes Friedrich was to paint in the ensuing years. If these paintings are to be given a Christian interpretation, one thinks irresistibly of Psalm 121: "I will lift up mine eyes unto the hills, from which cometh my help." The rest of the psalm turns the hills either into the abode of God or into a symbol of God, depending on whichever interpretation one prefers.

The significant change from Friedrich's previous pictures of mountains is that this peak is not inaccessible. Though to reach it would be difficult, it would not be impossible. The series of ranges are like steps to the summit. It is a painting that does not instruct the viewer to stay where he is, as did the earlier paintings of distant mountains, but rather encourages him to raise the level of his aggressive activity. Just as in the preceding painting the light of the moon is embraced, so here the lofty symbol of value can be reached. The creation of this painting is further evidence of Friedrich's renewal of confidence in spite of the oppressive political and social situation, his determination to continuously renew and transform his art, his ability to transcend his discovered limitations, that ability which is the true mark of the Romantic.

ERNST THEODOR AMADEUS HOFFMANN
(1776–1822)

Waterloo led to the furtherance in Prussia of what had already been begun, the rejuvenation of the Prussian government after the Napoleonic devastations, and to the possibility that Hoffmann would once again get permanent employment in Prussian officialdom. But his first position, as assistant in the *Kammergericht* or Court of Appeals, was without remuneration. He was at the bottom level of a system in which in previous years in Poland he had already proved his competence. He was only an adviser, but at least it was a first step towards employment. So he returned to Berlin in September 1814. On 7 January 1815, he began to receive a full salary, though it was still hardly enough to keep him going. Consequently in the summer of that year he served for a time as a forwarding clerk in a ministry. But at last on 1 May 1816, he received a permanent appointment at the *Kammergericht*. Now he could write in peace of mind, at least financially.

On his arrival in Berlin he was already famous in literary circles because of the *Fantasiestücke*, published in 1814 and 1815. His first task in Berlin was to complete *Die Elixiere des Teufels* (the second part came out in 1816) and to begin writing a new series of stories as well as to push forward the production of his opera *Undine*. That was at last performed on 3 August 1816, and within a year had been given fourteen times, a considerable success at the time. Unfortunately the theater in which it was presented was destroyed by fire on 19 July 1817. Scenery, costumes, and some scores of the opera were lost, and the expense was too great to recreate the opera in the larger Opera House. Also, Hoffmann felt that the work was too intimate for the larger theater. Yet he could take satisfaction that he had created the first truly Romantic opera in Germany. The other satisfaction of these Berlin years was his intimacy with the most interesting Romantic writers in Berlin. Thus until his miserable death in 1822 he not only carried out his judicial duties with the highest professional distinction but also was able to write eight volumes of stories: *Nachstücke* (*Night Pieces*), two volumes in 1816 and 1817; Die *Serapionsbrüder* (*The Separion Brothers*), four volumes in 1819, 1820, and 1821; and *Die letzte Erzählungen* (*The Last Tales*), two posthumous volumes in 1825. He also wrote three long *Märchen* or fairy stories, *Klein Zaches*, 1819, *Prinzessin Brambilla*, 1820, and *Meister Floh*, 1822. There was also the unfinished novel *Kater Murr*, the two completed volumes of which appeared in 1820 and 1821, and a lengthy and brilliant essay on the theater, *Seltsame Leiden eines Theater-Direktors* (*Strange Sufferings of a Theater Director*), 1819. Some of these works, as we shall see, had an impact on literature which is not merely felt but actively continues today.

In the *Fantasiestücke* Hoffmann had established his essential themes and intellectual and imaginative interests. What lay before him in 1815 was the full and profound development of those themes. Yet these various themes can be subsumed under a single theme—the imagination. And indeed Hoffmann became the first great Romantic virtuoso of the imagination, for he exemplifies in some stories how the imagination constructs the world, in others how it distorts the world, in others how the imagination releases destructive forces, and in still others how the imagination redeems itself from its own errors and limitations. For the imagination in Hoffmann's scheme of man and reality is almost identical with the mind itself. He develops Kant's proposal that we know the world in terms of human interests, and the imagination, its ultimate sources mysterious and unknowable, constructs those interests, disintegrates them, analyzes them, reconstructs them, and transcends them. Human beings are both the masters of the imagination and the victims of it, sometimes of our own imagination, sometimes victims of the imagination of another.

The early Romantic decades are haunted by Shakespeare's

> The lunatic, the lover and the poet
> Are of imagination all compact.

For it appeared to these men that it was impossible to draw a distinction between Shakespeare's three human types and anybody else. The human *mind*, then, is of imagination all compact. To explore, to study, to analyze, to understand the imagination became Hoffmann's great theme, pulling into a single task his exploration of the nature of mythology and the possibilities of new mythologies, of the incoherent and multiple character of the personality, of history as the deposit and effect of the imagination, of music as the purest mode of the imagination (for it cannot be reduced to abstractions of words and propositions and preserves the purity of the imagination as well as its ultimate beauty), of the imagination as the human organ or capacity which is continuously engaged in the creation and discovery of value and which most illuminatingly reveals the consequence of the disappearance of or loss of value—but above all the imagination as the source of meaningfulness as distinct from specific meanings. And this again brings us to the importance of music in Hoffmann, because this, to him, is precisely what music does. Thus Hoffmann's conception of the function and effect of music is one of the first and most important steps by which in the course of the next hundred years music was to become the model art, the ideal art, the one art that reveals most purely and directly the true inner character of every kind of art, for it reveals most directly the essence of human behavior.

The title of *Nachtstücke* (*Night Pieces*) is an indicator of the first efforts to analyze the impact of the imagination upon the individual life, the dark and mysterious side of life, the night of the spirit, even its destructiveness. The opening story of Volume I, *Der Sandmann* (*The Sandmann*), is a complex of confusions which apparently have a rational explanation, but that rational explanation is itself undercut by an inexplicable mystery, one that reveals the destructive factor in human life and interaction and imagination. Nathanael as a child confused an ugly figment of a stupid nurse's imagination, a Sandman who steals the eyes of children who refuse to go to sleep, with a hateful figure in his father's life, Coppelius. Doctor Coppelius assists Nathanael's father in alchemical experiments which eventually kill the father and eventuate in Coppelius' disappearance. Coppelius also hates children and quite purposely spoiled the pleasure of the children of the family. Years later an apparently chance error causes Nathanael to confuse Coppelius with Coppola, an optician, from whom Nathanael buys a spyglass. With that he sees in the house across the street the figure of Olimpia, the daughter of Spallanzani. The latter gives a splendid party to introduce Olimpia into society, but only Nathanael dances with her. Everyone else keeps away from her and sneers at her with half-concealed laughter. But Nathanael falls in love with her, only to discover that she is an automaton for whom Coppola has made the eyes. This discovery drives him mad. When he recovers he is again with his beloved Klara and her brother Lothair. Before they leave their native town Klara and Nathanael climb the tower of the city hall. At the top Nathanael takes the spyglass from his pocket, but instead of looking at the landscape looks at Klara. He immediately perceives her as an automaton and attempts to throw her from the tower. She is rescued by her brother, but Nathanael throws himself from the tower and is killed. While he is hesitating to jump the terrible old lawyer Coppelius suddenly makes a reappearance and predicts that he will leap to his death.

Nathanael's initial confusion between the nurse's tale and the sinister lawyer evidently lays the foundation, or, to use a perhaps more instructive metaphor, creates the template for further confusions, which result in his inability to distinguish an automaton—so popular in the eighteenth and early nineteenth centuries—from a real girl. Again the association between this confusion and the spyglass throws him into a paroxysm of madness in which he confuses Klara with Olimpia. The result is his suicide, the disintegration of a personality as a consequence of a childhood confusion. But at the very end in a typical Hoffmann-esque manner this rationalist explanation is undermined by the reap-pearance of the sinister Coppelius, the man responsible for Nathanael's father's death. Was he then indeed the Sandman of Nathanael's mother's use of Coppelius to get the children to go to bed and also the Sandman of the nurse's horrifying story? This puzzle is Hoffmann's way of pointing out that rational explanation of imaginative disorders (and orders as well) are limited, that beyond them lies an impenetrable mystery, the fundamental incomprehensibility of human existence. Finally, it is similarly significant that Klara should be the near victim of Nathanael's final madness, for she was the first one to offer him a rationalizing explanation of his imaginative disturbances.

In "The Jesuit Church in G———," the third story in Volume I of *Nachstücke*, Hoffmann sets out to explore the problem of the creative imagination, that is, the difficulties of the artistic imagination in attempting to manifest its genius. Berthold is a painter of great promise who is unable to realize his talent either in landscape or in history painting until he has a sudden quasi-visionary encounter with an ideal woman. The result is the release of his powers in a series of religious pictures in which the woman is the central figure. But when he rescues her from her burning palace at the time of the riots in Naples resulting from the Napoleonic invasion of Italy and escapes with her back to Germany, that is, when his visionary ideal is actually in his possession, he is at once unable to paint anything but the most lifeless picture. He treats his wife and child so badly that the authorities are about to interfere. Suddenly all three disappear. Later he turns up in G——— and paints architectural frames for chapels in the Jesuit church. That church contains his barely unfinished masterpiece with his wife and child, painted after he had separated from them, and it must be covered with a cloth to make it possible for him to work. Illness had prevented its completion. Hoffmann, who has presented himself to the reader as the author of *Fantasiestücke*, learns Berthold's story from others and asks him if he has killed his wife and child. He denies it vehemently, threatens Hoffmann with his life, and shortly after disappears, possibly a suicide by drowning.

Just as Berthold was unable to paint successful landscapes, in spite of the perfection of his mimetic technique, in the presence of nature, so he was unable to paint successful figures in the presence of an ideal model. The point that Hoffmann is making is the inadequacy of the mimetic theory of art. Artistic value has its true source within, in the activity of the imagination. The story is one of the many Romantic indications of the shift from a mimetic to an expressive theory of art. At the same time the story itself is an instance of Romantic realism, exhibited in the precise description of the town and of the Jesuit church and especially of the life of German artists in Rome in the late eighteenth century. Realism is further intensified by the disturbances in Naples at the time of the Napoleonic invasion of Italy.

That same realism set firmly in an historical setting dominates two stories in Volume II of *Nachstücke*, stories which repay examination in the effort to understand Hoffmann and his importance to the development of Romanticism. The first is *Das Majorat* (*The Deed of Entail*). It takes place on the shores of the eastern Baltic in the second half of the eighteenth century and before the partition of Poland. The plot is in fact one of immense Hoffmannesque complexity, constructed around the desire, ultimately a desire coming to nothing, to found a great landed family. It begins as a ghost story but is developed into a tale of legal complexities such that only someone like Hoffmann, a professional member of the legal establishment, could have devised. And this legal realism carries the story far beyond the Gothic romance ghost and moves it toward what another story in this volume also moves closer to—the mystery story. *Das Gelübde* (*The Vow*) is so direct an imitation of Kleist's *Die Marquise von O——* (*The Birth of Romanticism*) that it is clear that the difference is what Hoffmann is interested in—the effects of the disordered and destructive imagination. In Hoffmann's story the woman is not raped while she is unconscious; rather, in the throes of an hysterical confusion triggered by the resemblance between her betrothed and his cousin, she seduces the cousin (hopelessly and fruitlessly in love with her) into an imagined marriage and an immediate consummation of it. She believes herself, then, to be pregnant by the man she loves, whom she believes she has married. And like Kleist's story this is firmly set in an historical situation, the efforts of Poland to regain its freedom and in the Napoleonic wars. Thus Hoffmann carried further his aim of setting the activity of the imagination firmly in the events of the ordinary, the familiar, the "real" world.

In the four volumes of *Die Serapionsbrüder* Hoffmann published twenty-eight stories. The first two volumes appeared in 1819, the third in 1820 and the fourth in 1821. Eighteen had already appeared in various journals and annuals, some as early as 1814. The title refers to the presentation of the stories by four members of the Serapion club. Three of them, and perhaps the fourth as well, are aspects of Hoffmann himself. Thus he analytically disintegrates his own personality into various interests and functions, a notion coherent with his previously presented conviction of the non-unitary, almost accidental, structure of one's personality, although "assemblage" would perhaps be a better term for Hoffmann's conception of the personality than "structure."

Not all of the stories are of equal interest or importance. Some of them merely present in different form ideas already presented. The first story of significance in Volume I is *Rat Krespel* (*Councillor Krespel*). (Like a number of the stories this has no title assigned by Hoffmann but is known by a title given it by subsequent editors.) The theme is his further exploration of the psychic essence of the artist. Antonia, the daughter of Krespel, an eccentric love of music and seeker of the secret of great violins, has inherited from her mother a glorious voice and an ever greater artistic gift in using it. But the character and quality of the voice is the result of a mysterious illness of such a nature that if she sings she will die. At length she is tempted by her love to sing for her beloved—and she dies. This is an early and perhaps the first appearance of what Edmund Wilson was to call the "wound-and-bow" thesis of artistic creativity: Art is a compensation for some deep psychic wound which eventually destroys the artist or at least his creativity. The thesis is a further instance of the perception of the Romantic artist as so alienated from his culture that the exercise of his art destroys him. The legend of Byron, for example, and those of Shelley and Keats as well, were to become exemplars of this notion, which fundamentally is an expression of Romantic alienation combined with the Romantic notion of artist as both prophet and priest. Thus only the artist is capable of redeeming society, or at least introducing value into the social order, but that order is so wrong that the very effort of the artist recoils upon himself and destroys him. In the course of the last couple of centuries this notion of the artist often takes the form of perceiving the artist's later works as evidence of his deterioration, both as a human being and as an artist. Even his physical degeneration becomes part of the theme. Indeed, the idea has become so pervasive that if an artist's style changes radically, his work is rejected. Likewise, if it does not change, as it should according to the Romantic ideal of continuous self-transcendence, that fact is itself taken as evidence of his deterioration and failure.

The next story of importance also appears in Volume I of *The Serapion Brothers*. It is *Die Bergwerke zu Falun* (*The Mines of Falun*) in Sweden. In it Hoffmann develops further and experiments more profoundly with a new mythology in order to account for the relation of man to his environment and that relation as conditioned by and perhaps determined by the imagination. A sailor weary of the sea is persuaded by a powerful old miner, who, it turns out, has been dead for several hundred years, to leave the sea and become a miner. In the depths of the mine he has extraordinary visions of the veins of metal deep in earth which bear gems as if they were flowers. He sees the spirits of the earth and on his wedding day plunges into the mine and is possessed by a vision of the goddess of the riches of the earth. That vision kills him; a collapse in the mine buries him; and his body is not recovered until years later, when his betrothed, now an old woman, recognizes his perfectly preserved form before it crumbles into dust. Here Hoffmann is exploring how the imagination can be the source of insight into the nature of reality and also can be the source of a dangerous and ultimately destructive obsession.

In the summer of 1818 Hoffmann wrote *Klein Zaches gennant Zinnober* (*Little Zaches, surnamed Zinnober*) and published it in January 1819. It is a fairy story of some length, the kind the Germans call a *Märchen*. It is of wondrous complexity, partly because Hoffmann is also concerned with satirizing every matter which annoyed and amused him—the pretensions of the tiny principalities of Germany; the elaborate titles and costumes and honorary orders found in such places; soulless and unimaginative science; and above all the Enlightenment itself. At the deepest level the work is not merely a justification of the imagination but an exploration of its most important and perhaps fundamental task. In a tiny principality where everyone lives an Arcadian life and the reigning prince finds it quite unnecessary to rule, the fairies also have found an idyllic abode. But when the old prince dies and his son and heir Paphnutius succeeds, the new prince determines to rule and in gratitude to his valet for a trifling service makes him his Prime Minister whose task it will be to bring the Enlightenment to his country. Everything must now be done according to rational principles, strict rule to impose reason becomes central, and the fairies—since they embody Hoffmann's myth of the imagination—must emigrate. A few, however, are left and are given mundane tasks. One of them finds beside the road a weary and despairing old peasant woman and her misshapen son, three feet high and unbelievably hideous and as stupid as ugly. In pity the fairy plants three red hairs in his scalp. The effect is that everyone now sees the little monster as a beautiful and intelligent and gifted child. The prince, lost in admiration, makes him his prime minister, for everything that anyone does splendidly, whether writing poetry or singing, is immediately ascribed to Klein Zaches, even though the actual creator of such beauty is present. A young student in love with the girl Klein Zaches is scheduled to marry learns his secret, catches him, pulls out the magic hairs, and Klein Zaches drowns in a great silver pot.

Hoffmann said himself that the story was not to be taken seriously; certainly it was his most brilliant example yet of the virtuosic imagination. Yet he cannot be permitted to have his way here, for the point of the tale, no matter how wreathed in imaginative complexities, emerges with clarity. The fairies, of course, are myths of the imagination, and when all but a few are forced to leave, a remaining fairy finds it too easy to create an illusion. Overcome by pure reason, the population has no defense against magic, against illusion, against the imagination used for deception rather than understanding. As Hoffmann shows in the figure of the scientist, the reason without the aid of the imagination can engage itself only in trivialities of research. The reason is truly and significantly creative only when it is governed and inspired by the imagination, a point that sophisticated scientists and philosophers of science of the late twentieth century would certainly agree with. Deprived of the free use of the imagination, the mind has no defenses against the destructive use of the imagination in the capacity of the mind to accept illusion, to be unable to distinguish between illusion and reality. Thus the fundamental task of the imagination is to defend the mind against the misuse of the imagination. Therefore reality cannot be apprehended in itself by pure reason but only by the imagination in the service of essential human interests. This is why when the fairies were free and at home in the principality it was an Arcadian world.

Another tiny principality is the setting for *Lebens-Ansichten des Kater Murrs nebst fragmentarischer Biographie des Kapellmeisters Johannes Kreisler in zufälligen Makulatarblättern.* (*The Life and Opinions of Kater Murr, with the Fragmentary Biography of Kapellmeister Johannes Kreisler on Random Sheets of Scrap Paper*), 1820 and 1821. The joke is explained in the "Editor's Preface": "When Kater Murr wrote his life and opinions, he unceremoniously ripped up a printed book which he found at his master's and simply used the leaves, partly as an underpad, partly as blotting paper. These papers remained in the manuscript and, by mistake, were printed as if they belonged to it." (Translated by Leonard J. Kent and Elizabeth C. Knight.) Thus the tale alternates between the biography of a cat and a narrative about Kreisler, the eccentric musician who was one of the main figures in *Fantasiestücke*. The principality itself, of which Kreisler is the *Kapellmeister,* the court officer in charge of all music and music making in the court, is nonexistent, having been absorbed in a larger principality by Napoleon when he ended the Holy Roman Empire and created a new and more consolidated political structure out of which, after Napoleon's defeat, emerged the German Confederation. But the prince cannot accept the fact that he is no longer a ruler and maintains a phantom court, a pretended court, one which hardly deserves the title of "imaginary." The whole story in this part of the book is designed to give Hoffmann a chance to explore the fantastic figure of the musician Kreisler, at times loving and tender, at times apparently cruel, at times joyous, at times bitter and satirical. What Hoffmann is proposing is that music, as the purest mode of the imagination, has the effect of revealing the truth of the personality, the fact that personality is not coherent, the fact that it is a package or assemblage, the fact that in ordinary circumstances this rich complexity of personality is concealed behind a self-imposed social mask of consistency.

This point is brought out by the characterization of Murr the Cat, who learns to read and to write and fancies himself a genius, though he is in fact the dullest of pedants. All kinds of things happen to him and he gets into a great variety of scrapes, but he always and to himself successfully rationalizes his misadventures—his inability, for example, to keep the affection of the cat he loves and marries—by summoning a coherent and internally consistent conception of himself. Unlike Kreisler, who is often a victim of melancholy and depression, one who is capable of experiencing to the full the instability of one's own sense of one's own value, Murr is the Perfect Philistine—especially in sneering at Philistines—who, totally self-complacent, never questions his own value. Thus Hoffmann reveals self-complacency, the stabilization of self-value, as the very source of rationalization, of reason uncorrected by the imagination's power to see oneself from a differing perspective, from, so to speak, as others see one. So the two parts of *Kater Murr* as complements to each other comprise one of Hoffmann's subtlest and most thoroughgoing instances of psychological analysis.

That very ability to be a *doppelgänger,* as Hoffmann called it, to be both the self and another simultaneously, to accept and exploit the reality that the individual is a social dyad, not a monad, becomes the theme, the great liberating theme, of Hoffmann's next and final major work, the most fantastic and imaginative and virtuosic of all, *Prinzessin Brambilla,* published in 1820. This *Märchen* takes place in Rome in the eighteenth century and during a carnival. It was at least in part inspired by a set of engravings by Jacques Callot, who, Hoffmann claimed, had been the source for his *Fantasiestücke in Callots Manier.* These were carnival figures and figures from the old *commedia dell'arte;* eight of them became illustrations to Hoffmann's story. True to the spirit of carnival the story is rich in masks, costumes, *doppelgänger* figures, transformations, deceptions, illusions, theatrical pageants, and so on; and it cannot possibly be summed up, except in exceedingly reductive form. Briefly, Giglio Fava, a pretentious and pompous actor in eighteenth-century tragedies, equally pompous and pretentious, and his beloved, a seamstress called Giacenta, are transformed by incomprehensible carnival events into brilliant actors in the new style of the comedies of Gozzi.

Carlo Gozzi (1720–1806) was an eccentric Venetian aristocrat who wearied of the plays of Goldoni and Chiara and set about to revive the dying *commedia dell'arte* in a series of Fantastic plays. (In the twentieth century three of these have been used for operas by Busoni and Puccini [*Turandot*], Prokofiev [*The Love of Three Oranges*], and Henze [*King Stag*].) These were to become more popular in German translation than in Italy. For Friedrich Schlegel, for example, Gozzi stood by the side of Shakespeare. This last opinion explains why Hoffmann chose to use the emergence of the style of Gozzi for his myth of cultural transcendence. Thus in a duel with his double, Giglio Fava is defeated; his empty costume is discovered to be stuffed with pompous tragedies. After this the true, innermost, essential Fava reappears as a newborn actor in fantastic comedies with a serious meaning, just as this story is. Within *Brambilla* is another *Märchen*, a story of an unhappy king and queen who see themselves in a lake created by a benevolent magician. The king had lost his sense of harmony with nature, but in seeing himself mirrored upside down in the lake and as part of nature his good temper is restored. It is, of course, the seeing oneself free from the masks of convention and roles of society that makes a self-transcendence possible. And the essence of this, as the whole tale makes clear, is humor. The story thus links perception of oneself as other to transcending oneself, particularly since the former self was a product of the conventions of society and culture. But Hoffmann is not so naive as to imagine that to transcend oneself as mask is to arrive at a "true" or unmasked self. On the contrary, what needs to be done is the creation of new conventions, just as Giglio and Giacenta become comedians, or role-players, actors of the conventions of a new kind of drama. This new drama is in the manner of Gozzi, for it is the imagination, released. In building his story on actors and acting, Hoffmann is asserting that although we are all actors, role-players, only those who with the aid of humor recognize themselves as actors can be free masters of their culture and not enslaved victims of it.

Hoffmann was to write further stories, as well as a second part of *Kater Murr* before his death in 1822, but *Prinzessin Brambilla* was his culminating achievement. To be sure, of great importance for the future was *Das Fräulein von Scuderi* (*Mademoiselle de Scuderi*), published in 1820 in Volume III of the Serapion series; for it is the prototypical murder mystery. Ultimately a series of murders is discovered to have been committed by a famous jeweler in order to retrieve his own creations; because of a childhood experience he is obsessed with them. The tale is an exploration of how the artistic imagination can become destructive; and in the contrast between the two sides of Condillac's personality, the gentle and creative and the murderous and destructive, it is one of several of Hoffmann's innovations of the Jekyll-Hyde theme. Yet in the *Märchen*, beginning with *The Golden Pot* (see *The Birth of Romanticism*) are to be found Hoffmann's greatest achievement and his greatest contribution to the development of Romanticism—the releasing of the imagination, or better, the unleashing of the imagination.

What Hoffmann revealed to generation after generation of European and American writers was not only that the literary imagination can be freed of the bonds of convention, but also how it can be released, how it is linked to the deepest and most obscure motivations and forces of the personality, forces often embodied in the soul during infancy or childhood, and how art and humor and the perception of oneself as other—how, in short, self-alienation and sociocultural alienation, when their connection is grasped, can free the imagination to its proper task, the transcendence and transformation of one's culture. And in so doing Hoffmann revealed as it had not been hitherto revealed the significance and importance and immense value of the Romantic virtuoso, a mode of creativity of which he himself was one of the most remarkable examplars Romanticism had yet produced.

SAMUEL TAYLOR COLERIDGE (1772–1834)

It is appropriate to turn from Hoffmann, the supreme imaginative writer of the early decades of Romanticism, to Coleridge, the preeminent English theorist of the imagination. And it is the more appropriate in that both of them depended upon and derived from Schelling. (See *The Birth of Romanticism*). Indeed Coleridge added very little to Schelling's concept of the imagination and not very much to the notions of the imagination developed in England and Germany in the late eighteenth century. Nevertheless some brief account of Coleridge on the imagination deserves a place here, if only because of the impact his discussion of the imagination has had and continues to have upon English-speaking culture.

Coleridge dictated his *Biographia Literaria* to his friend John Morgan in the summer of 1815. His recovery from opium addiction, though impressive under the circumstances of how little was then known about addiction, was only partial. As early as 1809 and 1810 he had composed twenty-seven numbers of his periodical *The Friend*, but that book is marked by the same difficulty that is to be found in *Biographia Literaria*. It was a difficulty that had dominated his life for years. In both works he spends a great deal of time talking about what he is going to do, and then fails to do it. Thus in *Biographia Literaria* he spends several chapters, much of them plagiarized from Schelling, to lead up to his great chapter on the imagination—and then breaks it off shortly after it has begun. So his discussion of the imagination and the fancy takes only a few paragraphs, and in itself that account is exceedingly mysterious.

Yet modern scholarship has attained a fairly clear notion of what Coleridge was trying to say. His first point concerns what he calls the "primary imagination." The very act of perception, then, is an imaginative act. The senses do not give us the world as it is but rather apprehend it and comprehend it, grasp it and put and hold together those graspings. The categories of perception are not derived from the world but are imposed upon the world. Coleridge's notion of the "fancy" as opposed to the imagination, though not fully coherent with the rest of his thinking upon the subject, implies that the source of the categories with which we organize the categories of perception is the memory. That is, to put it in more modern terms, the categories are learned from the culture. The fancy merely combines in novel ways those categories. The secondary imagination he conceives not as a higher form of the fancy, as was traditional among many writers on the subject, but as a faculty of a different order. (To be sure, this whole scheme is vitiated if one abandons a facultative psychology in favor of a functional psychology, an abandonment that has long since obtained.) The secondary imagination analyzes, restructures, reorganizes the categories which the fancy can only combine mechanically, and it does so in a way that can only be conceived of as—dangerous word—organic. Thus it is enabled to innovate at high categorical levels—high in the sense of regressive from the senses. What Coleridge is trying to get at here is the notion of significant cultural innovation. His examples of the distinction between the fancy and the imagination are by no means convincing, and it is doubtful that they have ever convinced anyone who considered them with any care. Rather, whether one judges some rhetorical device in a poem, for example, as either the product of the fancy or of the imagination appears to be a matter of taste. But that is of no importance. For it is the inspirational tone and effect of Coleridge's account that is significant.

His account of the secondary imagination provided a rhetorical possibility which the Romantic tradition needed—the possibility of emergent innovation or radical creativity. The reason is thus relegated to an admittedly lofty task of dealing with the material the creative or secondary imagination has produced, but in itself it is lifeless, without creative potentiality or power. Moreover, Coleridge ascribes to the creative imagination an extraordinary validity, asserting that it is the equivalency in the human mind of the creativity of the divine and indeed, he strongly suggests, is the manifestation of the divine in the human. This notion was to become of crucial importance to the subsequent Romantic tradition in the English-speaking world, which in the course of the nineteenth century became a very large world indeed as the British empire expanded. What the notion meant to that tradition is that the imagination is *the* source of value.

The significance of that lay in Coleridge's further assertions in various places that the purest and most creative mode of the imagination's activity is to be found in poetry, by which he meant all of the "fine arts." This idea provided the theoretical foundation for what the Romantics already believed in, the poet as prophet and priest. Thus the task of art is revealed as, if not redemptive (establishing an individual's value with the solidity and permanence of entry into heaven), then at least redemptionistic. The way was prepared for the secular to absorb the function of religion, of the sacred. The poet or artist, as Coleridge implies so strongly in "Kubla Khan," has truly "drunk the milk of paradise."

Furthermore Coleridge discerns a further function for the imagination, one little noted or appreciated at the time or since, but one which showed which way the epistemology of the Romantic tradition was developing. In *The Friend*, which Coleridge reworked and issued again in three volumes in 1818, he asserts that the best system of government is that of expediency, in spite of the fact that elsewhere he has attacked expediency. He says that he will clarify and justify this apparent inconsistency, but of course he does not. However, we can do it for him. The discussion of the imagination in both the original and revised *Friend* and in *Biographia Literaria* takes place in an atmosphere and context of continuous attack upon the Enlightenment. What Coleridge seems to have been one of the first to grasp is that in the total cultural history of the nineteenth century the spread of Enlightenment ideas was far greater quantitatively than the spread of Romantic ideas. Coleridge saw the consequence of the defeat of Napoleon and the effort to come to terms with the severe economic and political difficulties following that defeat as the increasing influence and popularity of the kind of rationalism which he felt, quite rightly, had led to the Napoleonic tyranny. Thus he saw the consequence of an absolute rationalism to be the destruction of freedom. And in this perception he was of course quite correct, agreeing with Hegel, though he did not know it. Hence he described his own epistemological position as one of an idealistic or rationalistic empiricism.

He saw intellectual and cultural vitality in the tension between senses and reason, and he saw the imagination as the mediator—the creative mediator—between the two, a mediator which was alive and organic simply because its mediation could never become final. Coleridge seems surely to have been the first to bring together in creative dissonance idealism and empiricism, a notion which in the twentieth century could still be presented as novel. In this context his defense of political expediency makes sense.

The kind of expediency he objected to was that of the eighteenth century, the purely egocentric expediency, the unprincipled expediency of those who unanalytically accept the notions of the reason and thus have no defense against the transformation of the reason into a *caput mortuum*, as Coleridge called it, a dead absolute. The expediency of which he approved was an expediency which adapts the principles of the reason to the actual demands of living situations. He can praise such expediency because clearly it is the equivalent in political activity of the imagination; or rather it *is* the political imagination, living and organic. Expediency in this sense is the analytic imagination at living work.

What we witness in this defense of what we justly may call Romantic expediency, a life-giving expediency, is the birth of what many decades later and in the United States of America was to be called pragmatism. And this is not surprising, once it is realized that the necessary consequence of the Kantian position, though it was a long time coming, was precisely pragmatism. It is greatly to Coleridge's credit that he arrived at this epistemological position so early, though it must be admitted that he did little with it, sidetracked as he was by a regressive religiosity. Obviously his very terminology, "expediency," embarrassed him and interfered with the full development of his idea.

THE NAZARENES

In *The Birth of Romanticism* it was proposed that the idea of the Nazarenes, the group of German artists who had gone to Rome determined to revitalize art, was that a truly effective and successful cultural revitalization lay in the revitalization of Christianity, and that could be accomplished by art. Thus even in a situation of sincere and devout religious conviction [one having been born a Catholic and another having converted in 1812] the redemptive force was truly Romantic, for it was to be discovered and released in art and in the creation of art, not in religion itself. By 1815, then, as previously discussed, they had become sufficiently successful for the Prussian Consul General in Rome, Jacob Salomon Bartholdy (1779–1824), the uncle of Mendelssohn, to commission them to fresco a room in his Palazzo Zuccari near the top of the Spanish Steps. Bartholdy's proposal was the decoration of a room used for social occasions. That they chose to decorate such a room with the legend of Joseph and his brothers reveals the Nazarenes' interests. The artists involved were Peter Cornelius (1783–1867), Johann Friedrich Overbeck (1789–1869), Wilhelm von Schadow (1788–1862), who had joined the Nazarenes in 1813, and Philipp Veit (1793–1877), who had become a member in 1815.

The frescoes in the Palazzo Zuccari aroused the intensest interest. After the end of the Napoleonic wars in 1815 hundreds of artists descended upon Rome from all over Europe, and every one of them, it seems, felt it necessary to visit the Legend of Joseph and his Brothers. In spite of the opposition of the expiring school of David, engravings of the frescoes were even published in Paris. That the Nazarenes had achieved something of an artistic revolution and a salutary one was widely though of course not universally acknowledged. Almost immediately—early 1817 or even at the end of 1816—they received another commission, the decoration of the walls of the Casino Massimo with scenes from Dante, Tasso, and Ariosto. (The proposal to decorate a fourth room with scenes from Petrarch was never carried out.) The casino was a little building in the garden of the now destroyed Palazzo Massimo near the Lateran. Like the room in Bartholdy's palace it was a building designed for social purposes; and the Marchese Carlo Massimo and his guests must have been overwhelmed by what the Nazarenes achieved, for the rooms are small but the frescoes, which have survived some damage and repainting, are brilliant in color and more serious in subject than decorative.

Cornelius executed only a few designs for the Dante room before he left for Munich, called by the Crown Prince of Bavaria to decorate the new Glyptothek, the museum of Greek and Roman antiquities, the first building to be built in Europe as an art museum. Philipp Veit took Cornelius' place, but after executing the ceiling decided the task was too much for him. The Marchese called upon Joseph Anton Koch (1762–1839) to do the walls of the Dante room. Koch was a neoclassic painter whose specialty had been heroic landscapes, but rather surprisingly he was able to adapt his style to that of the Nazarenes. As he turned to a medieval subject he tended to depend upon the style of Dürer, who had, of course, been one of the sources for the Nazarenes. His figures, however, were larger than theirs and overscaled and oppressive for the size of the room. Overbeck took the assignment of the Tasso room, but by 1822 he had finished only the ceiling. In that year he began the wall frescoes, but abandoned them in 1827 when the Marchese died. The room was finished by a young Czech artist Joseph Führich (1800–1876). The only room to be decorated by a single artist was the Ariosto room, the central room and the largest. Julius Schnorr von Carolsfeld (1794–1871) came to Rome and joined the Nazarene group in 1817. He worked on the Ariosto room from 1821 to 1827.

It is a sad and a revealing story. A great enterprise designed to carry out and exemplify both the artistic principles of the Nazarenes and their social principles, a restoration of a perhaps nostalgically fancied community of artists, reveals instead the disintegration of the group. But it reveals more than that. It shows that the Nazarenes had made a fun-

damental error in departing from the main and developing, though to
be sure not yet absolutely clear, path of Romanticism. More than the
Zuccari frescoes the Massimo frescoes depend upon Raphael, Pintu-
ricchio, even Signorelli. Rome was, perhaps, too much for them. They
were too much at the mercy, as it were, of the High Renaissance. Because of the difficulties of the papacy until well past the middle of the
fifteenth century, Rome is not rich in early Renaissance paintings. The
finest examples were the relatively late frescoes by Botticelli, Pinturic-
chio, and others in the Sistine Chapel executed from 1481 to 1483. And
even in these frescoes, wonderful as they are, especially now that they
have been cleaned and adequately lit, one can see the effect of Rome
and the weighty ideological demands of the Church upon artistic genius. One can even discern it in the incomparable frescoes in the Vatican of Raphael and Michelangelo, and the effect is nearly constant
throughout the city in the churches and the palaces.

It is possible, after some time in exploring the art of Rome, to become
not so much weary as oppressed, to become aware that these undoubtedly glorious works of art and architecture were the result of forcing
the genius of the artists, all of whom were imported to Rome, beyond
the natural and reasonable limits of their taste and talents. Whether it
is true or not that Michelangelo was forced into painting the Sistine
Chapel and to do something he did not want to do—and it must be
admitted that the current cleaning of the ceiling is revealing that it was
painted with greater bravura and pleasure than for centuries has been
imagined—nevertheless the story is appropriate, a response, perhaps,
to what the visitor to this day can feel. The truth is that though in the
nineteenth century endless hordes of artists descended upon Rome, by
the end of the century it was no longer fashionable, not to become so
again until after the second World War. And the reason is obvious. Almost no important painter, almost no important artistic emergence,
came from Rome or the Roman experience. As we shall see probably
the only important exception is that of Corot. But Corot responded not
at all to the art of Rome but only to its appearance, to the city as landscape. The importance of Rome to him was that he was not in Paris,
that he was isolated and could experience the force of Romantic alienation.

The effect of Rome, then, can be the forcing of one's talents, not the
exploration of them by testing them against the phenomenal world—
not, that is, the way of Romanticism. When they arrived in Rome the
Nazarenes were already deeply involved in an ideological commitment,
the justification of art through its power to bring about a religious revival. That ideological commitment was given enormous force by the

greatness of an ideologically committed art with which they were surrounded. As we have seen often enough already, the thrust of Romanticism is to question, to criticize, to undermine ideology. Ideologically, Romanticism is an anti-ideological ideology. The effect of this is that tendency observable from the very beginning of Romanticism, what is known as "realism," which far from being as traditionally claimed a reaction against Romanticism was intrinsic to Romanticism from the very beginning.

For what unites all forms of realism is precisely the testing of mind against sense, of ideology against actuality, of finding—as Coleridge was already finding—for ideology at best only a pragmatic function. The subsequent careers of the principal Nazarenes, especially Cornelius and Overbeck, was such that further discussion of those careers is unnecessary. It is enough to point out here that technique and style became increasingly stable and inflexible, for their interest and avowed intention was to reverse their original program. That is, instead of art regenerating religion, religious ideology became the primary justification for the existence of the work of art. The turning point was indeed the Massimo frescoes, for in the work of Cornelius, though not carried out, of Overbeck, and of Veit the remarkable, fascinating, and genuinely emergent compositional devices were abandoned in favor of those taken from the Renaissance paintings around them, including the late Raphael frescoes in the Farnesina and even, it appears, the Raphael tapestries. Frequently there are frank and bold borrowings of individual figures and compositional dispositions.

In short, Romantic painting developed and was to develop by eschewing traditional perfection of composition and technique in favor of modifying both by subjecting them to the visual demands of the phenomenally observable and to the physical, or even physiological, demands of putting paint on canvas or wall. The pro-ideological position at which the Nazarenes had arrived put them in the position of obscuring as much as possible the physical activity of the unique and uniquely individual artist by the creation of a technically perfect surface, what was to become known as the "licked" surface. Nor must it be imagined that what was in question was the mere individuality of the artist; rather, the inadequacy of any perceptual construct of the phenomenally visible world was the anti-ideological factor of cultural emergence. Thus it has been claimed that the most important German paintings done at Rome in these years were three oil sketches by Johann Georg von Dillis. Born in 1759, he evidently felt strongly the cultural forces that were already disintegrating artistic traditions. One of these sketches is *View of St. Peter's from the Villa Malta, Rome,* 1818. The Villa

Malta is behind the church of SS. Trinità at the top of the Spanish steps and therefore near the residence of the Nazarenes, the home of the French Academy at the Villa Medici, and the home in those days of Ingres.

The striking aspect of Dillis' painting is first its strict division by the horizon line, a perfectly straight line broken only by the dome of St. Peter's and the cupola at the top of the dome of a nearer church. In the right slightly more than half of the lower part of the picture and occupying little more than a quarter of the total surface but less than a third is a jumble of roofs and walls. Thus the compositional interest and even—it is not too strong a word—excitement of the picture lies in the contrast and complete discontinuity between the richly and almost cubistically arranged complexity of those buildings and the nearly featureless character of the rest of the painting. The power of the work emerges from its revelation of the selective and constructive and interested power of the eye itself, of vision, and in the tension of the picture, for one's perception is pulled between the interesting jumble of buildings, with their almost formally significant interlocking shapes, and on the opposite diagonal the emptiness of the sky and the featureless city plain below it. It is important because it shows a power of compositional originality and cultural emergence which the Nazarenes had originally approached and from which they had now turned away. It is not surprising, then, that a competent art historian and critic has called these three sketches the most important paintings in the history of German art. Their significance lies precisely in the fact that a German artist had seized upon the possibilities of painting which Turner and Constable for some time had been exploring in England. The sketches are important because they show that German painting had the potential for a genuine Romantic painting, and that painting was in time to emerge.

J.-A.-D. INGRES (1780–1867)

The years after the fall of Napoleon and the departure of the French from Rome were difficult for Ingres. His best customers, the French occupying administrators and officers, had left, and his only profitable customers for portraits were tourists, mostly English, who were in Rome only briefly and interested only in pencil portraits. These are, to be sure, among Ingres' most miraculous works. Of his major portraits these years in Rome saw only the completion of that of the Vicomtesse de Senonnes, which had been commissioned and begun in 1814. It is instructive that when we think of Ingres today we are most likely to think of his portraits. Yet these are far less numerous than his subject paintings, and Ingres disliked portraiture and thought of himself in the traditional manner as a painter of "histories," or subject paintings—religious, historical, and imaginative. So in these years he did a number of small paintings of historical subjects, most of them commissioned. In each he endeavored not only to achieve an extreme historical accuracy in the various properties—costumes, furniture, architecture, fabrics, and so on—but even to paint more or less in the style of the painting of the period of the subject. Thus, he denied vehemently that *Paolo and Francesca* (see *The Birth of Romanticism*) was painted in the fashionable Parisian "Troubadour Style" but insisted it was done in a truly medieval fashion, especially, one would guess, in what he conceived to be the style of medieval illuminated manuscripts. To us today he hardly seems to have been successful, but to his eye and to those of his time no doubt it was a reasonably convincing evocation of medieval style. The real point is not his success in that endeavor or lack of it but rather that he attempted it. It was a genuine effort at a profoundly Romantic historicism. The new subjects of these five years were *Henry IV Playing with his Children*, *The Duke of Alba at St. Gudule*, *Philip V and the Marshal of Berwick*, *The Death of Leonardo da Vinci*, and *Roger Freeing Angelica*, in which he clearly attempted a style appropriate to Ariosto's life in the High Renaissance. But these pictures present a puzzle or at least a significant problem, for like those "small histories" painted before 1815 he repeated them, sometimes five or six times, in oil, in drawings, in watercolors, for the rest of his life. His last major painting, *The Turkish Bath* of 1859–1863, was a transformation of the *Bather of Valpinço* of 1808, which he repeated several times with the same figure placed in a Turkish bath. In *The Turkish Bath* she makes her final appearance, seated on the floor but otherwise unchanged and with the same turban. She is surrounded, of course, by a whole crowd of nudes. This obsessive repetition demands more of an explanation than that which has been recently proposed—the pursuit of perfection.

As a first step toward grasping this difficulty it is useful to examine the two major paintings which bracketed these five years, *The Vicomtesse de Senonnes* and *Christ Giving the Keys to St. Peter*. In the portrait he continues the earlier tendencies in his portraits: the emphasis upon the surface of the painting, achieved here by having the subject lean forward and place her right arm in a powerful curve parallel to the picture plane, by placing behind her a large rectangular mirror which is ambiguously painted so that it appears both parallel to the surface of the painting and, judging by its reflection, at an angle, and by the superb arabesque of the tangled lines of the drapery, the cushions, and the subject's dress, and by the outline of her dress against her shoulders and breasts as well as by the perfect egg shape of her face. And of course there is again the sumptuousness of color, deep red and greenish gold, though the shoulders and head are outlines against the almost black mirror, that outline again compounding the effect of the arabesque. One could say that it is one of his greatest portraits, were it not for the fact that all of his major portraits seem equally great and completely convincing, an effect in part achieved, oddly enough, by the flatness and the arabesque. For when one sees one of these portraits, not a reproduction but the original, the effect is always breathtaking, almost shocking. It is not entirely absurd or even inappropriate to compare it to suddenly perceiving in the tangle of lines of a Jackson Pollock—perceiving without error or hallucination—a tiger leaping out at you. In this sense *Vicomtesse de Senonnes* is something of a new step or departure for Ingres: she has an aggressiveness not found in previous portraits but almost never missing in the portraits to follow.

Quite different and quite unconvincing is *Christ Giving the Keys*. It is not merely that it is derived so clearly from Raphael's design for the tapestry of the same subject. It is also apparent that it is derived from a different and rather surprising source, the Nazarenes, who, as pointed out in *The Birth of Romanticism*, were Ingres' neighbors in Rome. The painting was commissioned by a Count Blacas for SS. Trinità dei Monti, the church at the end of Ingres' street and opposite the Palazzo Zuccari. One can admire the splendor of Ingres' technique, but the composition is too arranged, too obviously formalized. The figures are too obviously models, just as the cloak of St. Peter is too carefully arranged. One can almost see Ingres making the golden cloak hang just so, even though an attempt at realism is the effect of the cloak dragging behind St. Peter as he has knelt to receive the keys. The composition is also too obviously contrived. The lower three quarters consist of a dark square of landscape against which the figures stand out. (Judas is barely visible at the left.) The cloak of St. Peter, a key, Christ's pointing finger, and his raised arm pointing directly at the upper left corner imply too obvious a diagonal line. To it there is a counterpoint of a less vigorous implied line from the lower left through the arm of St. Peter and the folds of a disciple's cloak to a head. So there is implied a lopsided x against a square.

The painting is as unconvincing as almost all the religious art of the nineteenth century, including Ingres' other efforts in that genre, *The Vow of Louis XIII* of 1824, *Saint Symphorien* of 1834, and *Jesus among the Doctors* of 1842 to 1862. These works irresistibly remind one of the religious kitsch that has filled Catholic churches all over the world in the last nearly two hundred years, just as in Germany and elsewhere the paintings of the Nazarenes were the source of much of that pictorial vulgarity. And even Ingres' nonreligious historical paintings share something of that unconvincingness, as does most of the historical painting of the nineteenth century executed in the "slick" or "licked" almost academic style of Ingres and the Nazarenes.

Why should this be so? Why is it so difficult for us to admire what was so widely (though by no means universally) admired when these paintings were created? The first clue is to be found in Ingres' compulsive repeating of the paintings which he first painted in Rome, the "small histories." Instead of a pursuit of perfection this obsessiveness argues rather a lack of confidence not in himself—for his incredible technique was perfectly obvious—but in his imagination, that is, ultimately, in the ideology which drove him to these historical subjects, to "histories" in the traditional definition. The changes from version to version were generally minor and fussy, in that they made little compositional dramatic difference. Even though he used such subjects for small paintings, a size traditionally limited to genre and landscape, the necessary superiority of history painting, the hierarchy of subject matter which Romanticism was abandoning, was a conviction he could not surrender. As we have seen again and again in both this volume and in *The Birth of Romanticism*, the emergent drive and power of the Romantic tradition lies in maintaining the tension between imagination or the constructive and synthetic power on the one hand, and reality, the deconstructive and analytic power, on the other. The Nazarenes abandoned that tension originally so powerful in their work, and in *Christ Giving the Keys*, inspired by the Nazarenes and commissioned for what might be called the neighborhood church of both Ingres and the Nazarenes, Ingres also abandoned it, just as the Nazarenes in these very same years were abandoning it.

Ingres detested paintings in which the brush stroke was apparent, as in, for example, the work of Delacroix, whom he loathed. Yet, as we have seen, that evident brush stroke is only superficially an expression of Romantic individuality. Rather at a profounder level it is a symptom of the tension involved in transforming and distorting the visible world by the act of the constructive and synthetic imagination. For Ingres the pragmatism which we have discerned in Coleridge's phrase of political expediency—for the essence of pragmatism is precisely the recognition of that tension I have been discussing—is to be found in the great and unsurpassed series of portraits, beginning with the Rivière family of the period before he left Paris and concluding with the almost inconceivable greatness of the portraits of his final years, such as the portrait of Madame Moitessier seated. The arabesque and the tendency to bring out the two-dimensional flatness of a painting is Ingres' equivalent of the visible brush stroke. It is his awareness that he is painting a picture, not a subject. The superb quality of *Vicomtesse de Senonnes* was not to be matched until 1820, when Ingres left Rome for Florence and in 1824 for Paris. In 1820 he painted the portrait of Lorenzo Bartolini, in 1821 the portraits of Jeanne Gonin and Count Guriev, in 1823 those of the Leblancs, in 1826 the portraits of Madame Marcotte de Sainte-Marie and of Count Amadée David de Pastoret. After 1830 there were only nine or ten, not counting replicas. The rarity of these portraits is evident. And yet, for the reasons given, they are his finest works.

It will not be necessary to return to Ingres. Of him it may be finally said that he was a Romantic painter but that he could not accept his place in the history of art and of culture and did his greatest work in spite of himself. Only in his portraits did he allow that ruthless and dismantling aggressiveness of the Romantic artist to emerge, and then only by presenting that aggressiveness within the form of a fashionable sitter for a portrait. Thus he masked his own aggressiveness against a tradition which he could not wholeheartedly repudiate.

JEAN-LOUIS-ANDRÉ-THÉODORE GÉRICAULT (1791–1824)

Another painter who tried residence in Rome in the years after Waterloo was Géricault, with results very different from those of both the Nazarenes and Ingres. He was born in Rouen to old and established and well-to-do Norman families. His parents moved to Paris in 1795 or 1796, where his father prospered in a tobacco firm and was able to improve the fortune that had come with his wife. His son inherited enough to be independent and in time developed into something of an elegant man-about-town, something almost of a dandy, in spite of the bold originality of his paintings. Although he attended the teaching studios of two fashionable painters, Carle Vernet (1758–1836) and Pierre-Narcisse Guérin (1774–1833), he was more self-taught than instructed. Wealthy and of a highly independent personality he went his own way. The first result was a surprising picture at the Salon of 1812, *The Charging Chasseur.* Although it was obviously influenced by and even derived from the Imperial propaganda paintings of the Baron Gros (1771–1835) and taking much from Rubens, though perhaps by way of Gros, it was of astonishing originality.

First of all it was big, more than nine feet by more than six feet, most untraditionally scaled for what was but a single man on horseback, though some justification was offered by minute scenes of battle and a few suggestions that the rider was leading his troops into battle. The rearing horse is leaping to the right, diagonally towards the depth of the picture, but the rider, twisted in his saddle, is looking back to the left. The horse and rider occupy the full height of the picture from the horse's left rear foot to the rider's plume, the top of which almost touches the top center of the picture. The opposite directionalities of rider and horse create with great force that tension which almost always is to be found in the work of Géricault and, as we shall see, is particularly powerful in his greatest painting, *The Raft of the Medusa* (1819). And the painting is also the beginning of a long series of paintings of and with horses, for the horse becomes so obsessive for Géricault that it is apparent that it must be considered an emblem of energy, fiery independence, and aggressiveness. For *The Charging Chasseur* is more than anything else an aggressive attack upon the still dominating school of David. It was a defiance of neoclassicism. Yet it was still in the heroic mood of the Napoleonic Empire.

Not long after the opening of the 1812 Salon in November news came of the retreat from Moscow, which had in fact begun before the Salon opened, and the next years saw the crumbling of the Empire and in 1814 the Abdication. When Géricault next exhibited, it was at the Salon of 1814, unexpectedly announced in a city occupied by foreign and conquering troops. In unconscious preparation for it he pursued his studies of horses. There is, for example, an extraordinary oil which presents three strips of the rear ends of horses (with one exception), some twenty-four studies of superb quality. They were to Géricault what the Thames Valley studies had been to Turner a few years before and the oil sketches of Stour Valley to Constable. (See *The Birth of Romanticism.*) All his life it is clear that what nature first meant to Géricault was beauty, energy, and power. His tragic conception of nature was still to come. It had been adumbrated, however, in his first major picture—the struggle of man to control a force of nature.

Yet in spite of all these studies—and there are dozens of them aside from those that have been lost—in the picture he painted for the Salon of 1814, again in a great hurry, the horse is strangely distorted. The picture was a counterpart or companion piece to *The Charging Chasseur,* which he re-exhibited so that the two paintings made a pair. The new picture was *The Wounded Cuirassier Leaving the Field of Battle.*

Géricault's father was a Royalist, and Géricault himself seems never to have been in any way committed to Napoleon and the Empire. There is no question that this new painting was an emblem of the defeat of the Empire and the fall of Napoleon. This significance of the work is emphasized by the fact that the cuirassier seems to be slipping or sliding down an inclined plane, attempting to support himself by his sword and, most significantly, by at once restraining the horse and by grasping its bridle near its jaw evidently also attempting to support himself. The theme of the first horseman, there subtly adumbrated, is here more salient—the opposition between the furious will of the horse, rearing against its restraint, eager, one is tempted to say, to go on fighting, and the will of its master to leave the battle. And again he is looking away from the horse, back toward the battle. With regret? With fear? In despair? It is impossible to say. But at any rate an important theme for Géricault's future work is put forth, the indifference of the world of nature, as in this animal, to the wishes of man.

After these paintings Géricault seems not to have known what to do next, what direction to take. The path he took led him first to Rome. Indeed, he hoped to win the Prix de Rome and evidently in his attempt to do so endeavored to master the Davidien neoclassic manner. Or perhaps he was already pursuing a different train of painterly thought. He began by doing sketches in the neoclassic manner, going back as far as Flaxman (see *The Birth of Romanticism*), but his real interest soon began to be apparent. The more sketches he did the more powerful they became. Instead of the neoclassic grace and harmony they were filled with Romantic violence and tension, both in subject matter and composition. In particular he painted at least two large "academies," studies of male nudes, as different from those of David and Ingres as can be imagined. They are presented not as mere posed models but as actively engaged in struggle. One of the most effective shows a male standing in water, his legs thrust apart. He is pulling at a rope, and behind him is a quite fully developed stormy sky. Failing to win the Prix de Rome Géricault went to Rome on his own, arriving in November 1816, after a stay in Florence, primarily to see the Michelangelo sculptures in the Medici Chapel.

His efforts began to make clearer what he was struggling towards. On the one hand he did a number of sketches of classic themes, like those already done in Paris, and on the other he did, like so many painters in Rome, sketches of the picturesque street life of the city. But Géricault's sketches were by no means picturesque. Rather they translated ordinary Italian city dwellers and peasants into a heroic guise, a pictorial heroism modeled on the classic tradition. What he was attempting to do became completely lucid in the series of sketches in various media leading up to what in fact was a large uncompleted and not really started canvas. He abandoned it when he suddenly left Rome in 1817, a year before he had planned to. The great uncreated canvas survives in a series of oil sketches. The final one, splendid enough to be accounted a complete picture, is *The Start of the Barberini Race*, the race of riderless horses down the Corso from the Piazza del Popolo to the Piazza Venezia. The practice was to torture the horses in order to drive them into such a frenzy that at the starting it was almost impossible to restrain them and at the end it was of extreme difficulty to stop them and bring them under control.

In a series of sketches, many of them fully developed, Géricault converted a contemporary scene into a classic scene, one of horses and nudes, with classic architecture in the background. This classicism marks his full emergence as a Romantic artist, for again and again as we look across Europe in the early years of the nineteenth century we see the effort to revive the art of Greece and Rome and to revitalize the classic tradition. Thus it is clear that in Rome Géricault was far more interested in ancient sculpture than in Renaissance paintings. In the next chapter we will see both Keats and Shelley devoting major efforts to that revitalization. Greek Revival architecture was part of the same struggle to create a Romantic Classicism. Examples are the new Glyptothek in Munich, 1816–1834 (by Leo von Klenze), the Royal High School in Edinburgh (by Thomas Hamilton), and innumerable homes and churches in the United States. A more aggressive attack upon Enlightenment neoclassicism can scarcely be imagined. Romantic classicism was an effort to rediscover the very sources of European art and at the same time was a determination to reveal how neoclassicism had perverted those sources, almost parodically. But again as with Keats, so with Géricault. The modern world is presented as noble, as energetic, and as tragic as the ancient world, and as beautiful. The troubled recognition in these very years of the authenticity and greatness of Lord Elgin's Parthenon sculpture and soon of the Aegina sculptures, and the recognition that Roman sculpture was an inferior imitation of Greek sculpture, were part of Romantic classicism. One of the great themes of the Romantic tradition, traditionally so closely identified with medievalism, is the rediscovery of the true character of Greek art and Greek culture. The worship of ancient Greece was to become one of the great and central themes of nineteenth-century Romantic culture.

The triumphant affirmation of this discovery, of Géricault's determination to recreate in modern terms the greatness of that remote past, was a painting that first was to its observers simply a puzzle; but a few, such as Delacroix, recognized that French painting had been newly founded. It was *The Raft of the Medusa*, exhibited in the Salon of 1819. To traditionalists everything about it was so wrong that the work was totally perplexing. Its size was wrong, its subject was wrong. Paintings of such enormous size—it was twenty-four feet by sixteen—were properly devoted, it was affirmed, only to heroic subjects of national glory and, to be sure, of religious splendor. But here was a painting that focused upon the climax of one of the most scandalous affairs of the Restoration, the wreck of the Medusa.

On 1 July 1816, the government frigate *La Médusa* was on its way with soldiers and settlers to Senegal. The incompetence of the politically appointed captain wrecked it. As many as possible crowded into the few lifeboats. A raft was constructed and fitted with a mast, a sail, and a tent for shelter from the sun, and provisioned, it would seem, principally with barrels of wine. The idea was that the boats would tow it to the shore. But in panic or poltroonery or both the officers in the boats cut the lines and cast the raft adrift. On 17 July the men on the raft were finally rescued by a brig which had been sighted but which at first did not see the raft. After several hours it returned and rescued the survivors. Of the one hundred fifty men and one woman placed on the raft, fifteen were still living. They had survived mutiny, terrible suffering, and cannibalism. At first the government attempted to suppress the story, but an official account of it was leaked to the press; and in a year or so two of the survivors wrote a complete account of what had happened. Géricault determined to use an episode of this narrative for a major picture, to mount a powerful attack on the painting establishment.

After experimenting with various episodes of the event, Géricault finally settled on the first sighting of the brig, hardly more than a speck on the horizon. There is no effort to achieve a classic detachment. On the contrary the nearest corner of the raft would, were it not concealed by waves, penetrate the frame of the painting. The figures (there are more than the historical fifteen) are for the most part arranged in a great curve which ascends from death and despair at the left across the raft and across the picture to an implied pyramid at the right where two men are holding up a Negro who is waving a cloth. The brig is barely visible, emphasizing with utmost force the impossibility of the brig's occupants seeing the raft. Almost all the figures are turned away from the viewer, and most have their backs to him. The counterweight to this immense triangle in the right third of the picture, an implied triangle made by piled up bodies, most of them naked, is a triangle to the left which is not like the other one; it is presented almost without implication. It is formed by the tent, but it is not a stable triangle since it is tilted to the left and has no base. A third triangle is formed by the two ropes that hold the mast. It encloses the preceding triangle. It too has no base. Thus the human figures are shown as attempting to escape from a kind of cage, an effect strengthened by three figures, arranged in a lesser implied triangle, who stand in the center of the canvas and next to the tent. They look toward the brig, except one who with arm outstretched and pointing toward the brig appears to encourage the figures in the great curve of bodies.

At the time of the Salon the painting was not thought to be a political comment on the incompetence of the new Bourbon regime, nor is it. The theme that Géricault has been adumbrating and approaching for nearly ten years had now arrived in full force. Critics and observers at the time were baffled by the picture, but Géricault's theme in the context of Romanticism and in the context of his preceding work is virtually inescapable. It is the indifference of the natural world to mankind, an inscrutable and incomprehensible indifference, presented with all the power of ancient art. That is why the men on the raft are naked, for the Greeks had discovered that the naked human body reveals as no other artistic device both the strength and the vulnerability of the human condition. Géricault had found in his own life that the fundamental experience of humankind is suffering, an incomprehensible and pointless suffering. Human incompetence is made understandable and comprehensible and forgivable once we face directly the appalling natural situation in which man finds himself. The survivors of the wreck of the *Medusa* are both emblems and concentrations or intensifications of the human condition.

Géricault's masterpiece breaks with the Enlightenment notion of the possible harmony of man and nature, a harmony that was no more than the secularization of the Judeo-Christian myth of Adam and Eve before the fall. From death the figures in this painting crawl and struggle and climb to a confrontation with—emptiness, indifference. The painting is the triumphant explanation of the charging chasseur, the struggle between man and animal, between mankind and nature that wills his opposition. In the year before that in which Géricault finished and exhibited his manifesto of human failure, a German philosopher, Arthur Schopenhauer, provided an even vaster explanation of what the painter had grasped. But first it is necessary to examine the philosopher whom Schopenhauer thought of as his greatest enemy.

GEORG WILHELM FRIEDRICH HEGEL
(1770–1831)

After the defeat of Napoleon in 1814 and again in 1815 Germany began to reconstruct its university life, which had been disrupted by the invasions of Napoleon and the struggle against him, the Freedom War. So in 1816 Hegel was called from his headmastership in Nürnberg to the University of Heidelberg, and in 1818 to the relatively new University of Berlin, of which Fichte had been the first Rector. That university was deliberately set up on a new model. For the first time the emphasis in university life was given to the advancement of knowledge, to research, an attitude thoroughly compatible with and convergent to Romanticism. In the teaching of philosophy it was traditional in German universities to provide the students with a printed and published outline of the course. Thus Hegel was forced, or at least seduced, into at last doing what he had set out to do fifteen years before, the creation and publication of a philosophical system, a task for which the *Phenomenology* had been the necessary preparation. (See *The Birth of Romanticism.*) So in 1817 he published *Enzyklopädie der philosophischen Wissenschaften im Grundrisse: zum Gebrauch seiner Vorlesungen* (*Encyclopedia of the Philosophical Sciences in Outline Form: for Use in Connection with his Lectures*). The first edition consisted of only 188 pages made up of 477 numbered paragraphs. In 1827 Hegel brought out a second edition. He added a long preface and with further additions doubled the size of the book and added nearly a hundred numbered paragraphs. Although in 1830 a third edition was of about the same length, Hegel had made thousands of changes. After his death a fourth edition appeared from 1840 to 1845, the work of three different editors, who based their massive changes on their and others' notes on Hegel's Berlin lectures.

To understand what Hegel proposes it is first necessary to comprehend what he means by his technical term *Begriff*. This term is often translated as "concept" or "notion," but both terms are inadequate and even misleading. In English these terms usually subsume certain words or sentences. That is, they are words that subsume other words. But Hegel in his term *Begriff* is after something quite different. In the first place it is a metaphor, a very common one, of course, and for other philosophers "concept," "notion," and "understanding" are adequate translations. Hegel, however, is playing upon the metaphorical roots of the term and reviving its metaphorical power. What he is getting at is the fact that when the individual establishes a relation with something not himself (to speak loosely, for here "not himself" can mean, for example, his own physiology) he "grasps it" by using the full resources of "*Geist.*"

Now, as was proposed in *The Birth of Romanticism*, the most satisfactory translation of *Geist* is "culture," in the anthropological sense, that is, in behavioral terminology, learned behavior. Moreover, what Hegel had demonstrated in his *Phenomenology* is that *Geist* or culture was a history. Thus any individual grasp of the world is both the product of history and is itself a moment in history. Furthermore every moment of judgment about the world is capable, minimally at the very least, of modifying *Geist*. Self-consciousness as it emerges in Hegel's philosophy is the most advanced historical self-consciousness simply because it recognizes itself as both a product of the history of *Geist* and a contribution to its history. That contribution arises from the tension between on the one hand the individual and culture, that is, his modification of culture because of his own limits of personality and of his historical situation; and on the other hand between the individual and the world, between, in traditional terminology, subject and object. Thus *Begriff* in Hegel's use refers to a grasp of the world which, as opposed to a mere rational idea or sentence or word, brings to bear upon some segment of the world the full resources of culture and of the individual's modification of culture. The *Encyclopedia* is a systematic exploration of those resources. It is Hegel's famous "system," and in the complete edition of Hegel's works it is given that title.

The work is divided into three major parts: "The Science of Logic," ("science" is used in the premodern sense of organized, structured, coherent discourse), "The Philosophy of Nature," and "The Philosophy of *Geist*." (I shall continue to use that word rather than any translation of it by "spirit," or "mind," or even "culture," because it properly subsumes culture, a society's modification of culture, and the individual's modification.) The first part is a digest or précis of the major *Logic*, published in 1812, 1813, and 1816. As proposed in *The Birth of Romanticism*, Hegel's point about logic is that it struggles to control the categories (which he later recognized as words), which are constantly being modified by their use in grasping the world. That use exposes or at least brings about contradiction, incoherence, inconsistency. The famous Hegelian dialectic, as he once explained to Goethe, is simply the awareness that every category, since it is only partly successful in grasping the world, reveals that which it does not grasp, its negation. And that awareness of negation is the dynamic of thought. Ultimately, what Hegel is getting after in the idea of the dialectic is that the historical process of *Geist* brings into existence negations and contradictions in its categorical instruments. Thus dialectic must always be thought of as process, as historical process, always as part of actual historical situations. All this may be summed up as Hegel's revelation of the necessary instability of all thinking and also that progress in self-consciousness of that instability means progress in the understanding of the world. Therefore he turns next to the philosophy of nature.

So long as Hegel's system is thought of as constitutive, that is, saying what the world really is, it is misapprended. It is rather instrumental, and it is best grasped when one is aware that two of the greatest American pragmatists, George Herbert Mead and John Dewey, started out as full-fledged Hegelians. Pragmatism focuses on what these men saw as the crucial aspect of Hegelianism: How does novelty in our grasp of the world emerge? To use a bit of the terminology used here, what is the *process* by which cultural emergence takes place? Looking at Hegel from this historical point of view, as according to his own analysis he ought to be looked at, Hegelianism implies an instrumentalism or pragmatism, and Hegel's system is an analysis of the resources we have (and do not have) which make novelty or cultural emergence possible, unavoidable, and necessary.

Thus the fact that much of Hegel's philosophy of nature is out of date and even the fact that he made mistakes are irrelevant. For unlike the other philosophers of nature, such as Schelling, Hegel's account is not constitutive, does not say what nature really is or provide a foundation for the further development of the natural sciences. Rather, his aim was to show how the categories of thinking are used in exploring and grasping the natural world. It must always be remembered that Hegel is not an idealist, in the sense that man can grasp the world in its totality and say what it really is, but is indeed an empiricist, in the sense that the categories of thought are, in comparison with the solidity of the real world, but shadows, constantly changing and shifting, as it were, in the blinding light of nature. Thus in the Philosophy of Nature Hegel uses his extraordinarily detailed knowledge of current science in the three realms or spheres of mechanics, physics, and organisms. He is employing the current state of the natural sciences to show how the *Geist* performs in its dealings with nature. For, as we shall see, the logic of the categories is not self-sufficient, self-creative, and independent but in fact is dependent upon a higher sphere, that of Absolute *Geist*. But we are not yet ready to turn to that.

From the philosophy of nature Hegel turns to the philosophy of *Geist*, first as it appears in the individual, for the ultimate source of *Geist*, since Hegel is an empiricist, is nature itself. So he first considers *Geist* as it emerges from nature and proceeds to full self-consciousness, as the free *Geist*. (In this section he gives a kind of précis of the *Phenomenology*.) In modern terminology this consideration of, as he calls it, the Subjective *Geist* is simply psychology. But since that subjectivity is the subjectivity of the individual, the next step is to examine what forms the individual which is not nature. That forming power or controlling power of the Subjective *Geist* is what he calls the Objective *Geist*, consisting of law, morality, and, interestingly and most penetratingly, custom as the highest of these, subsuming the others. Again, in more modern terms, what he is talking about are social institutions.

The institutions Hegel proposes are, however, under the control of the Absolute *Geist*—by which he means those cultural forces, traditions, values, and so on, which are, he believes, independent and at a higher level than institutions and which subsume and control institutions. At the same time, through self-consciousness they emerge from institutions, just as the subjective *Geist*, controlled by institutions, emerges from nature. In the Absolute *Geist* he proposes three levels, each higher than the preceding one: art, revealed religion, and philosophy. (Clearly by "revealed" he means religion which purports to be revealed—that is, religion which claims a supernatural authority and claims not to be developed out of social institutions. Such a claim is, of course, in error.) To use a modern term, though one probably developed from Hegelianism, these three form the realm or sphere of ideologies. They are the highest level of self-consciousness, and of course Hegel thinks of philosophy as the highest level of all, because in philosophy (and it is difficult to argue with him) *Geist* is at its fullest expression of self-consciousness. "Fullest" is appropriate, not "completest," because *Geist* is unstable, is historical, and therefore cannot be complete.

From this level of absolute or institutionally independent spirit are derived the categories with which man endeavors to grasp and control nature under the direction of what he conceives to be his true interests, though these too, being historically emergent, are always necessarily inadequate.

To sum up (and hopefully not too grotesquely), what the individual man does when he grasps the world is to use (if he is sufficiently self-conscious, that is, historically modern) the full resources of logic as subjective, objective, and absolute *Geist*, that is, of individuality, of social institutions, and of ideology. It is also necessary in understanding this system to bear always in mind that the realms of *Geist* are as unstable as the realm of logic, as fluid, as full of the capacity for negation, contradiction, and impermanence, and that man is always both the triumphant and free creation of history and its suffering and tortured martyr.

A particular problem in the understanding of Hegel that emerges from the *Encyclopedia* is the notion of the necessary movement of mankind towards freedom, even, in the distant future, absolute freedom. At times even Hegel was tempted to give this interpretation to his work, though at others he denied it. The notion arose from the fact that the study of "Subjective *Geist*" concludes with *Der freie Geist*, ordinarily thought of in a limited, individual, or personal sense of *Geist*, and thus as a discussion of the very attractive notion of "the free spirit." So it is assumed that freedom increased through the stage of "the Objective *Geist*" to its culmination in philosophy as the conclusion of the apex of "the Absolute *Geist*," the term "absolute" being as attractive and tempting as the term "free." But this is to miss Hegel's point. It is true that when the individual emerges from or is placed under the control of social institutions he both loses and gains in freedom. He has of course lost a great deal of freedom of choice and behavior; he is not, for example, free to kill anyone he wants to, but on the other hand as a member of an institution he has access to forms of behavior and to satisfactions that are inaccessible to him as an isolated asocial individual. Likewise in the sphere of Absolute *Geist* the individual in art, religion, and philosophy has transcended institutions and institutional controls; he has, therefore, a freedom of thought which as an obedient member of an institution is denied to him. On the other hand that freedom of manipulating categories is countered by the fact that those categories are not subjected to critical analysis by what Hegel calls logic. So Kant at the highest level of philosophy in his moment of history simply took the categories from the philosophical tradition without subjecting them to critical analysis; from the Hegelian point of view his philosophical behavior was virtually naive. The sophisticated analysis of categories as carried out in Hegel's logic corrects or transcends this limitation of the Absolute *Geist*, but is itself corrected by dealings with nature. To use the categories as analyzed by Hegel in investigating and mastering the natural world is to subject the freedom of logical analysis to limitations. And these limitations are necessary if the categories of logic are to transcend and leave the realm of shadows and have an effect on the natural world.

Thus in every movement from one sphere of *Geist* to another (and from one level to another within each sphere) there is both gain and loss, what Hegel calls *aufheben*.

Yet even if one is aware of this gain and loss there still appears to be a notion of progress, of man's greater freedom from natural limitations, in the whole history of the operation of *Geist* upon nature. Hegel lived at a time of great advances in science and also of an increasing rate of scientific advance. It looks very much as if the whole system, from the point of view of the progress of science, does indeed involve a progress, does indeed have an optimistic character. Thus the constitutive rather than the instrumental interpretation of Hegel could lead, and did for many or most Hegelians, to a belief in a purpose or teleological realization of the Absolute in this phenomenal or natural world. It may be regarded as the synthetic rather than the analytic response to Hegel. It is an indication of how difficult it was for the analytic attitude to take hold in a culture still, and to this day, overwhelmingly synthetic.

Yet today we can have a very different response to Hegel's philosophy of nature. For we know how the triumphant advance of scientific control of nature has led to irreparable damage to nature—has led, is leading, and will continue to lead to such damage. The scientific negation of science had not, in Hegel's time, yet appeared. The enormous damage the automobile does, from killing tens of thousands of people annually to air pollution and toxic runoff from highways, is but an easy example among endless examples.

What, from the Hegelian point of view, is the source of this scientific negation of science? It lies in the fact that science has used categories not uncritically but selectively and incompletely. It has operated in the spirit of the Absolute, a spirit which Hegel so perceptively condemned in politics, where absolute freedom necessarily leads to, and historically has often enough led to, absolute tyranny. In his own lifetime there was the French Revolutionary Terror, carried out in the name of Absolute Reason. Thus science in the past couple of hundred years has made enormous advances precisely because it has acted with a complete moral irresponsibility, believing that the pursuit of scientific truth is Absolutely justified. The result, as we can see all around us, is a scientific control over nature that negates scientific control over nature, a control over nature that destroys nature.

So Hegelianism is both optimistic and pessimistic. On the one hand man as a whole, like the individual, is moving towards freedom, is progressing towards freedom, but on the other hand that freedom can never be absolute because it is always and necessarily compromised by history, by the limitations of a given historical moment, by an actual situation, by eternal effort to stabilize and hypostatize the categories. So Hegel could affirm that his position is optimistic but at the same time affirm that it is not. That is his way of asserting the necessary and unresolvable tension between subject and object, between man and the world, mind and empirical reality, thought and sensation. And that is what makes the system of Hegel, as expounded in the *Encyclopedia*, one of the greatest of Romantic texts. The greatness of Hegel is that he understood his place, his moment (to use his own term) in the history of human culture as no man had before, and perhaps as no man since. At the time very few could grasp what he had done and mistakenly thought it was an idealistic account of what the world really is, an attempt to derive reality from thought, simply because they had not arrived at Hegel's position of self-consciousness, of historical self-consciousness, of Romantic self-consciousness.

ARTHUR SCHOPENHAUER (1788–1860)

In some ways Schopenhauer was the most Romantic of philosophers. No one stated so clearly and so powerfully, or with such extensive application, the Romantic loss of value. Few Romantics in their lives willfully experienced so complete a social alienation. To be sure he proposed a metaphysic, but it was so reduced, so intellectually threadbare, that as he himself said it consisted of only one idea. In the same way his epistemology was so reductionist that, like his enemy Hegel, he proposed an incipient or primitive pragmatism. And few acted out so thoroughly a Romantic literary pattern we have observed several times, aimless and obsessive wandering.

He was born in Danzig to the wealthy banking and mercantile middle class. In 1793 his father moved his family and his business to Hamburg, in order to escape the Prussian possession of his once free city. After his father's death in 1805, probably by suicide, and particularly after his mother granted him his share of the family fortune in 1809, giving him financial independence, Schopenhauer left the business position in which his father had placed him and studied in the universities of Gotha, Göttingen, Berlin, and Jena. The last granted him a degree for his dissertation, *On the Fourfold Root of Sufficient Reason*, published in 1813 in Rudolfstadt (near Jena), where he had written it. After joining his mother briefly in Weimar and quarreling with her so bitterly that he never saw her again, he went to Dresden, where in the next few years he wrote the work that after many years was to make him famous, *The World as Will and Representation*.

After its publication in 1818 (dated 1819) Schopenhauer fled to Italy, then back to Dresden, then to Berlin, where he vainly lectured in opposition to the increasingly popular Hegel, then to Italy again, to Munich, back to Dresden, then for six miserable years again at Berlin, always longing for reputation and recognition, and always baffled, at last in 1833 settling down in Frankfurt.

Yet in the last decade of his life recognition and fame were finally to come. But that decade of the 1850s followed the failure of the widespread revolutionary efforts of 1848 and 1849. And that failure, to those in the Romantic tradition, marked the end of the hope for an alternative culture and an alternative society, a redeemed society, one in which value would be built into and enshrined in the social structure. It marked the end of the last lingering nostalgic connection with Enlightenment redemptionistic hope. That hope had found its most lasting embodiment in a few pages of Marx, who himself, after 1848, was unable to complete *Das Kapital*, in spite of the steady financial support of Engels, in spite of that comfort and security. Baudelaire, like so many others, turned to a grim realism, almost a pessimism, and Wagner changed the ending of the *Ring* from an optimistic reconciliation of man and gods, of behavior and ideology, to an ending of utter disillusion. In that decade, then, Schopenhauer was at last recognized; for his reductionism, in spite of his lingering metaphysical bias and in spite of his philosophical weakness, was to be the most powerful attack yet proposed on the superstructure of Western culture, a superstructure, so many then felt and have felt since, that had led to a faith in illusory hopes. Indeed, more successfully than any other Romantic he had self-consciously proposed a functional equivalent for original sin.

In *Die Welt als Wille und Vorstellung* he had, he said, but one idea. The two greatest influences on him were Kant, whom he revered though with whom he often disagreed, and Buddhism and Brahmanism. As so often in philosophical treatises the presentation of his one idea in his major work is prolix and often tedious. The curse of philosophers is that they try to convince other philosophers, by elaborate argument and usually in vain. Schopenhauer also asserted that his one idea could not be understood unless the whole book were read not once but twice. But that is an exaggeration. One of the reasons for his eventual popularity is the clarity of his style, brilliant, aphoristic, and pungent. His one idea depends first of all on Kant's proof that we cannot know the world in itself, that is, the world without human interests. For human interests are not derived immediately from the world as we know it, but are imposed upon it and are instruments for manipulating and controlling it. Thus we know the world only in terms of our interests, as a representation, or re-presentation by means of the perception of the senses, to the knowing mind. Like Hegel, Schopenhauer denies the adequacy of Kant's unexamined categories, revealing them as unstable and capable of moving legitimately and convincingly in opposite directions— to both good and evil, for example. A further similarity to Hegel is that instead of the *Begriff* of the *Geist* (or culture) he proposes the aggressiveness of the Will. The reason for this similarity is that Kant had left unresolved the problem of where these interests (or ideas) come from.

Schopenhauer insists that we know ourselves as representation but also that we know ourselves in another aspect, as creatures whose sole effort is to control that which is not ourselves. We know ourselves as pure Will. Thus in this twinned behavior we know ourselves both as subject and as object. As object we are mere representation; as subject we are the objectified will and indeed the highest objectification of the Will. Between the aggressiveness of the subject and the resistance of the world we know only as representation there is, in typical Romantic fashion, an irresolvable tension, at least in almost all human activity. But why is the world as representation so resistant to the individual? Why is it that the world as object is only representation yet is frustrating to the Will?

In that phrase, "the highest objectification of the Will," Schopenhauer proposes his answer to these questions and does so by a dependence upon a tremendous analogical leap. Since as subject man is Will and since man is part of nature, it follows, Schopenhauer proposes, that nature or the world as thing-in-itself is also Will. That is why the world resists and baffles man, for the world, like man, man being a part of the world, is an opposing Will. The world is not, he often insists, an *expression* or *manifestation* of the Will; it *is* the Will, an objectification of the Will, as he says again and again. But that is an unsatisfactory way of putting what he seems to mean, for it implies a separation between the (hypostatized) Will and its objectification. What he appears to mean is that the Will is the object which the subject knows as the world and its representation. Or, truly we can in fact *know* the world only by knowing it as Will and by means of our own Will. Thus if we seek to control the world—and the "world" includes all other human beings— the world seeks to control us, that is, the world as Will in all its individual objectifications. Taking a phrase from Thomas Hobbes, Schopenhauer asserts that life is a war of all against all. This is how he reduces the vast structure of, for example, Kantian epistemology to simply an exercise of the Will. And this, of course, is the source of his incipient or proto-pragmatism. And in that he is once again analogous to his enemy Hegel. This reduction of knowledge to simply the struggle of the human Will to impose itself on all other human or nonhuman objectifications of the Will is his most powerful attack upon the superstructure of Western culture. It is, moreover, a superbly complete manifestation or expression of a total loss of value in reaction against the Enlightenment and its failure in the French Revolution. So Schopenhauer says that the individual life of a human being is either one of suffering or, if an attempt is made to withdraw from the suffering, boredom.

There is a further reductionism in his scheme which almost reaches an antimetaphysical position, though since he never recognizes his book as an expression of the Will characterized by an aggressive attack upon other philosophers, particularly Hegel, Fichte, and Schleiermacher, and thus does not undercut his own position, it remains, although minimally, metaphysical. That further reductionism is to be found in his basing his whole argument upon a simplistic analogy between man and nature. Since man is Will, nature must be Will. We have seen previously in other Romantics the tendency to reduce argument to analogy, the recognition that all arguments are ultimately reducible to analogical argument.

As suggested above, this conception of the war of all against all, this reduction of human activity to suffering or boredom is a functional equivalent of original sin, although Schopenhauer himself says rather that it explains the existence of that theory. Yet as so frequently happens in at least the early decades of the Romantic tradition—and sometimes in much later decades—the functional equivalent of redemption also appears. And as so often in the Romantic tradition—for more than a hundred years, in fact—that redemption is art. The basis of Schopenhauer's argument for the *almost* supreme value of art is that the basis of representation is perception, also conceived, of course, as an act of the Will. To save art from being a manifestation of the Will, since his cultural pattern demands some kind of redemptive activity, he uses an idea of Kant, the disinterestedness of art, and perceives aesthetic activity as pure perception, whether of nature or art, "pure" perception in the sense that the tension between subject and object is resolved, even to the degree that the distinction between subject and object is done away with, disappears. The subject and the object become one. This, of course, may be doubted, and both Kant and Schopenhauer may be rejected on the grounds that it is possible so to interpret any situation that no action is required. The disinterestedness is not in the perceptual act or in the perceptual object, art or nature, but in the situation. Art, which is an important member of the redundancy systems of a culture, those systems that stabilize behavior, is of course not disinterested, nor is the artist, who is invariably under ideological control, even when struggling to reject and escape from ideological control. So it may be reasonably said, in Schopenhauer's own terms, that in aesthetic perception the Will is interested in quieting itself.

The same objection applies to a quieting of the Will—a quieting which is superior even to aesthetic perception, even to art. And his scheme of thinking requires that something must be superior since the experience with the work of art, though it quiets the Will, does so only temporarily and evanescently. This superior mode is, he thinks, asceticism, which must begin with sexual asceticism, since the sexual organs are the most powerful manifestation of the Will in human and animal life. Schopenhauer particularly admires those who quite leave the world, hermits who withdraw to the deep woods and caves where they are free from human importunity and can exercise the asceticism which alone is capable of quieting the Will. Of himself Schopenhauer once said that he preferred observing human action to participating in it. And this and his reductive asceticism can profitably be understood as typical Romantic alienation. But again it must be pointed out that this exercise of supreme and severe control of the interests of the body-as-Will depends upon perception, representation, and the exercise of the Will. What this mode of redemption amounts to is that the war of all against all is reduced to the war of the individual against himself. But it is still war. Thus ultimately Schopenhauer's Romanticism emerges in his inability to construct a convincing mode of redemption.

Schopenhauer as philosopher may be unsatisfactory and even, as many claim and continue to claim, simply, as philosopher, inferior. Nevertheless his appeal is profound. The belief that suffering-and-boredom is the fundamental character of human existence has a wide, even a universal, appeal, and it is an appeal not altogether founded on self-pity. What Schopenhauer is urging corresponds to what everyone has felt at one time or another, but if one belongs to a cultural tradition from which the traditional consolations for and restorations from such a valueless orientation have failed and departed, then to respond to Schopenhauer is more than and other than self-pity. What it comes down to is that Schopenhauer presented the Romantic loss of value and the Romantic explanatory collapse more profoundly and, at least in its rhetoric, more convincingly than anyone else. That his book is philosophically inferior or a failure is quite beside the point, is quite irrelevant. That is why, unlike the tremendous majority of philosophers, he has stepped across the fence that surrounds philosophy and has become a living part of the general culture. His survival in popular and semi-popular modalities is witness to the vitality of the Romantic struggle with the Romantic problem, of the continuing vitality of the Romantic tradition.

CHAPTER TWO

1820–1825
The First Romanticized
Generation

JOHN KEATS (1795–1821)

In the work of Géricault and, though less obviously, of Rossini can be seen emerging a problem which was to become perennial, in one form or another, in the Romantic tradition. To categorize oneself, whether that categorization is self-selected or imposed by others, initially in most cases by the individual's parents, is to be able to draw upon the bank, as it were, of cultural instructions that shape, control, and guide members of that category. Thus the individual locates for himself a kind of ecological niche; to organisms that maintain their existence by means of learned behavior, the institutions of society and the culture which maintains those institutions are the forces of environment as much as climate and biological inheritance and circumstance. One of the most powerful and long-lasting effects of Romanticism was the calling into question the controlling attributes of certain categories of individual, the result of social and cultural alienation and even more of the new ideal of cultural transcendence. One of the richest occurrences of this problem of "identity," as he called it, is to be found in the poetry and the letters of John Keats.

Keats belongs in this second chapter because he presents this new problem so sharply: now that the emergent culture of Romanticism was established, what did it demand of one who categorized himself as a poet? What was he supposed to do? What kind of poetry was he supposed to write? Thus Keats marks with singular effectiveness the impact of the newly emergent Romantic tradition upon those individuals who grew up in that tradition rather than, like the individuals considered in *The Birth of Romanticism* and the first chapter of this volume, those who created that tradition, who first experienced the necessity for romanticism. To Keats Wordsworth was the example to be followed, the guide to a new poetry, particularly the Wordsworth of *The Excursion*, the major work by Wordsworth that Keats could have known. (*The Prelude* was not to be published until 1850 and was known in manuscript only to a few friends of Wordsworth and to members of his family.) After him came Scott, both of the narrative poems and the novels, Byron, and with the publication of *Biographia Literaria*, Coleridge.

In 1818 Keats succumbed to the Scott fashion by taking a long walking tour through the Scottish Highlands. Various minor figures, such as his friend for a few years, Leigh Hunt, also were of some importance to him. He was intensely aware of the fact that he had emerged from a youthful love of older poetry, above all Spenser and Milton, and an endeavor to study medicine, into a world, in his own words, of "great spirits." In the figure of the Solitary in *The Excursion* he could find brilliantly set forth the impact of the French Revolution and its failure, so that he could say that Napoleon did almost irreparable harm to the cause of liberty. The Great Spirits recognized what had happened and were great, to Keats, because they were endeavoring to create a new culture. Thus, with his limited experience, he could admire the enormously ambitious but not first-rate artist, Benjamin Robert Haydon.

For Haydon did Keats an enormous service. He introduced him to the marvelous sculptures which Lord Elgin had recently rescued (or stolen) from the Parthenon. These were not yet canonical. Many thought them inferior Roman imitations or copies of Greek originals. Haydon's one great achievement was to recognize and assert their magnificence, and to Keats they were sublime because they gave him a vision into the Greek world, could inspire him to set about, as did a number of early and later Romantics, revivifying Greek mythology, rescuing it from the incrustation of the now dying Renaissance tradition. Above all they suggested instructions and controls for an aspiring poet. Haydon's enthusiasm and penetration enflamed Keats and gave him what was already becoming a central theme in his thinking and in his poetry: transformation, self-transcendence, and self-transcendence as a mode of cultural transcendence.

And there was another reason why that experience of transformation was of such supreme importance to him. He was a victim of the rigid English class structure, as rigid today as it was in his time. Unlike the poets so important to him he was of neither the professional or the aristocratic classes. His father had worked and married his way up from the working classes into the lower middle-class of small businessmen, that of owner of a livery stable, into which his mother had been born. Unlike Wordsworth, Coleridge, Scott, Byron, and Shelley he did not attend a university but only a reasonably good school which he left when he was sixteen to be apprenticed to a surgeon. So in time he was to be called, sneeringly, a "Cockney" poet, a designation that wounded him. And with reason. For he was a young man of high intelligence, and even when still at the Clarke School in Enfield he set about a self-transformation which was to give his poetry an astonishing air of wide literary experience and learning. Though he took the Apothecaries' Society's Certificate he never practiced as a surgeon. He had already determined to be a poet, to transform his self-categorization, and he could make that decision because of an inheritance from his grandparents, his mother's family, that made it possible to pursue his ambition without having to earn a living. He was one of the first important artists of the nineteenth century to profit from the rapidly growing wealth of England. Nor is it surprising that politically he was a liberal and intensely aware of the efforts after Waterloo to restore the repression of the prerevolutionary societies.

As for his determination to be a poet, when he said that the poet has no identity, is a chameleon-like figure, the remark amounted to saying that the cultural instructions of how to be a poet had failed. Yet there was still enough instruction about being a poet passed to him from the old tradition that he knew that to be a poet he must be learned. And more than that, he must be able to bring his learning to life, to prove it, as he said, upon one's pulses. Thus in a famous phrase he could cry out for a life of sensations rather than of thoughts, and to arrive at his impressive notion of "negative capability," the ability *not* to arrive "irritably" at conclusions, the ability to accept tensions and uncertainty and the unresolved. Remarkably he absorbed thus early the antimetaphysical metaphysic of Romanticism, its irresolvable tension between subject and object. The main thrust of his intellectual and artistic development was to move from an adoration of ravishing and ecstatic beauty to an awareness, via worship that shifted from Milton and Spenser to Shakespeare, of the inexplicable bitterness, cruelty, and suffering of human life, and to that Romantic realism which we have already met so often. It is not accidental that his writing career was confined to the years from 1815 to 1819, to the years which saw emerge the visions of Géricault and Schopenhauer. Yet he properly belongs in this chapter, for the July 1820, publication of his most important volume, *Lamia, Isabella, The Eve of St. Agnes, and Other Poems*, is an appropriate beginning for a new stage in the development of the Romantic tradition.

It was not his first volume. In 1817 he had published *Poems* and, in 1818, his longest work, comprising almost a quarter of his total output, *Endymion*. And it is from that work, so unsatisfactory in many ways, that the essence, to use one of his favorite words, of Keats and his poetry must first be determined. *Endymion* was an extraordinarily daring undertaking. Keats had written very little when he began *Endymion* in the spring of 1817. He was taking a great risk, and in undertaking a long poem he was setting out, in his own words, on an unchartered ocean. Only by carrying out his plan in a poem of more than four thousand lines could he prove to himself that he was justified in attempting to become a poet, and also learn how the tradition of being a poet had to be transformed. The example of Wordsworth, though he was later to turn a little away from his great predecessor, was an example of the loftiest seriousness, of a genuine effort to achieve what was still called the sublime. Moreover, he was determined to give new life to one of the most worn-out and exhausted materials of European culture, classical mythology, particularly that of Greece. In doing so, he was not only culturally convergent with other artists and writers of the time, but he was also attempting something that his great spirits, Wordsworth, Byron, Coleridge, and Scott, had not attempted. In the most astonishing way, by taking old and worn-out material he was creating something new. After all, one may say, in responding so deeply and so adequately to the Elgin marbles he had seen the gods as the Greeks had seen them.

We may postpone the essential accomplishment of *Endymion* for a moment in order to glance at and consider certain major themes of the work. What is *Endymion* about? It is a question critics have puzzled over for a long time. Indeed, it is a question that has been taken entirely too seriously. There is some doubt if Keats knew himself. In spite of his intelligence and his poetic genius, Keats has been taken, if anything, too seriously. It must be remembered always that he was still a very young man when his poetic career ended in 1819, and in spite of his efforts at self-education he was, after all, self-educated, only approximately educated. Yet certain themes and patterns can be discerned.

First Keats resorted to a typical Romantic reductionism to get at the essential story. From the complex story of Endymion, available in several versions, he analyzed out the theme of the love of Diana for Endymion and the final consummation of that love which raises him to the skies, translates him out of human existence. This simplification opens up the figure of Endymion to a rich humanization and revitalization. From longing Endymion moves to consummation, clearly sexual. And thus the poem, like Friedrich Schlegel's *Lucinde*, discussed in *The Birth of Romanticism*, begins the Romantic tradition of redemption through—not love—but sexual consummation. In the nineteenth century that tradition existed covertly, but in the twentieth it entered into daylight, particularly in English-speaking countries with the work of D. H. Lawrence. The Christian pattern of redemption, secularized in the Enlightenment, was to survive as sexual competence—the successful orgasm—as a source of individual value. But in Keats' poem it is not at all that simple. Before that consummation are four thousand lines of highly wrought poetry. Before Endymion can recognize that the Indian maid is Diana herself, he must go through a kind of erotic education, an exploration, in almost Hegelian fashion, of the culture and history of eroticism, both in myth and in actual human lives. Thus Endymion goes through what Keats himself had gone through and was going through, a self-transformation or self-transcendence through learning. Value, Keats is saying though he may not have known it, can be achieved only through mastery of one's culture.

That notion leads to the principal accomplishment of the poem. It is not merely in the frequent passages in which Keats endeavors to achieve the ecstatic, or sustained sense of value, a central Romantic motive, as we have seen. Rather, it lies in Keats' obvious effort to explore the possibilities of poetry, to incorporate into his own sensibility and his own poetic capacity and technique, the possibilities of poetry as they are to be found in the English poetic tradition and the classic as well. What does it *now* mean to be a poet? Keats asked himself, and this was his answer, the answer of the virtuosic artist. As we have already seen, the Romantic virtuoso establishes the sense of self, of identity, of artist, and above all the actuality of cultural transcendence by precisely this sustained virtuoso performance. What is *Endymion* about? It is about the demands Romanticism was making on the artist. It is about the Romantic artist pushing himself beyond the limits that tradition had set for the artist. In the tradition of English poetry, *Endymion* is an astonishing performance. Keats could now make that self-transformation, that self-transcendence, into his central theme because in writing *Endymion* he had experienced on a large scale and over a period of six or seven months of sustained creative labor what he had briefly experienced before the Elgin marbles.

While he was still busy preparing the revised *Endymion* for the press, he wrote an utterly different kind of poem. *Isabella, or the Pot of Basil* is a retelling of a particularly sordid and cruel story from Boccaccio. And for it Keats settled on a style that was a negation of the style of *Endymion*. *Isabella* has often been condemned or dismissed as a failed or minor effort, but such judgments fail to understand what he was doing in this work. As compared to his previous poetic style, the work is almost entirely without Keatsian lushness, or luxuriousness, as he called it. It is an essay in a reductive style, suitable for the realistic subject, "realistic" in the sense that it is devoted to what Keats was increasingly interested in, the bitterness, the ugliness, the horror of human life. Keats finished the poem late in April 1818, went on his walking tour of Scotland in the summer, and in September began his next major undertaking, an epic poem, *Hyperion*. By April 1819, he had abandoned it. While he was still working on it, in January 1819, he wrote a kind of companion to *Isabella*, *The Eve of St. Agnes*, together with the uncompleted and exquisite "The Eve of St. Mark."

Endymion and *Hyperion* are exercises in classic revivalism, both using the mythology of archaic Greece, but the other poems are set in the Middle Ages. Like the German architect Karl Friedrich Schinkel (1781–1841) Keats endeavored to revivify both the classic and the gothic (or *Romantik*) stylistic modes. *The Eve of St. Agnes* is a step past *Isabella*, for in it Keats turns again to the lush, luxurious style he had virtually perfected in *Endymion* and at the same time vividly presents the drunken, brawling celebrants in the castle in which the lovers meet and from which they flee. The poem is also remarkable for being an early instance of the open end: Porphyro and Madeline "flee into the storm" and nothing more is heard of them. Without being a fragment as it would be by the previous standards of closed narrative, the poem has the closure of a fragment.

The Eve of St. Mark is even more convincingly medieval than its companion. It is difficult to believe that Keats had not seen medieval illuminated manuscripts, though where he could have seen them is not easy to know. At any rate, the poem deliberately evokes the color and elegance of medieval art. It is strikingly convergent with the paintings that Ingres was doing in those years in what the French called the troubadour style. And as striking is Keats' evocation of the atmosphere of an old cathedral town. The note of nostalgia is sounded with the most delicate reverberation, supported by a convincing historicism.

Hyperion (published in 1820) was to remain a fragment, and his second attempt, *The Fall of Hyperion* (published in 1857), undertaken in the summer of 1819, was also abandoned. Keats felt that the trouble with the first effort was that its style was an artificial Miltonism, too closely, slavishly, modeled on that of *Paradise Lost*. There were even long narrative passages directly derived from that poem. The new sections added in *The Fall of Hyperion* were in a plainer style, modeled on Dante, or rather Cary's translation of Dante, which Keats read with great eagerness and pleasure. And that new section is also modeled on Chaucer's dream poems. So, just as in *The Eve of St. Agnes* he attempted a synthesis or at least a combination of the ravishingly beautiful and the realistic, so in *The Fall of Hyperion* he attempted a combination of classicism and medievalism.

The trouble with the Miltonic style of the first attempt was that it was not new, it was not culturally emergent, it was not stylistically transcendent; for the theme of the poem is precisely that. The old gods are defeated and superseded by the new. The Titans lose their power to the new and rebellious Olympians. Of the old gods the one who still retains his glory is Hyperion, the god of the sun and of poetry. Though the old forms of divine control over human life are worn out, poetry (and perhaps art in general) still retains its glamour. Thus the real theme of the poem, emerging only towards the end of the fragment, is the triumph of Apollo over Hyperion. But the question Keats is really asking is, How does this triumph take place? In more general terms, What is the psychic strategy by which self-transcendence, cultural transcendence, and transformation do in fact take place? So the key to the answer is how Apollo comes to recognize his task, becomes a god. And it is instructive that this whole section is hardly Miltonic at all. The crux of it needs to be quoted. Apollo has been addressing Mnemosyne, the goddess of memory.

> I can read
> A wondrous lesson in thy silent face:
> Knowledge enormous makes a God of me.
> Names, deeds, gray legends, dire events, rebellions,
> Majesties, sovran voices, agonies,
> Creations and destroyings, all at once
> Pour into the wide hollows of my brain,
> And deify me, as if some blithe wine
> Or bright elixir peerless I had drunk
> And so become immortal. (III, 111–120)

Only in one way is this a new notion for Keats. It is the same idea as that of *Endymion*, for the hero of that poem is also made a god through knowledge, a knowledge that enables him to perceive Diana under the veil or mask of the Indian Maid. What is new in Apollo's transformation is the kind of knowledge, historical knowledge, the knowledge imparted by Mnemosyne, who is indeed less the goddess of memory than the goddess of racial memory, of history itself. Nor is this knowledge by any means atypical of the Romantic tradition. Quite the contrary, for we have already seen how scholarship and learning, particularly historical scholarship and learning, are close to the essence of the Romantic tradition. This historical consciousness and awareness could have come to Keats from several sources; from Wordsworth (*The Excursion* begins with the shock of history that transforms the individual), from Byron, and above all from Scott. On his tour of Scotland, inspired by Scott, Keats wrote a poem to Meg Merrilies, a character in *Guy Mannering* (1815), one of Scott's most striking and famous characters. Thus by his continuous exploration of the problem of psychic transformation Keats has arrived at an historicist realization of cultural transcendence and has embedded the individual, that is, himself, firmly in history. Hence the new long introduction to *The Fall of Hyperion* is devoted to the temple of Moneta, the mother of the muses and the goddess of memory.

Before his illness quite destroyed his power to create, Keats wrote in the summer of 1819 still another narrative poem, *Lamia,* based upon a tale in Burton's *The Anatomy of Melancholy,* in the language of which he particularly delighted. In it a snake-woman, perhaps a demigoddess, persuades Hermes to transform her from snake to woman, for she is in love with a youth of Corinth, the traditional city of eroticism. With her illusion-creating powers, she summons into apparent being an exquisite palace. But at the wedding banquet of Lamia and Lycius, her lover, the philosopher Apollonius, his teacher, carefully *not* invited by Lamia, forces the creature to dispel her illusions. She vanishes, her palace of illusion vanishes, and Lycius dies. The poem is a tour de force, a virtuoso performance, the most accomplished of his narratives. Only a poet of extraordinary talent could have written it. But the point of it? It seems clear enough. Knowledge destroys the illusion of eroticism as the source of value and destroys whoever surrenders to that illusion. And even more significantly it is an adumbration, an early example, of what was to become a central theme and problem of the Romantic tradition, belief as a mode of illusion—and also the theme of the human desire for illusion, for self-deception.

And is not the poem also an attack upon the imagination? In his letters Keats makes fairly frequent use of the word, so that "Keats and the Imagination" is one of the common topics of literary scholarship and criticism. Yet never does he use the term with such precision that one can be sure of what he is talking about. Of course it must be admitted that vagueness is true of virtually all discussions of the imagination. In Keats' case there is little doubt that a letter of November 1817 gives the best clue to the importance of the word to him, for it includes certain phrases which are clearly related to Coleridge's *Biographia Literaria*, published in the preceding June. Unsatisfactory as Keats' remarks about the imagination are, nevertheless an examination of his use of the term goes a way towards revealing why it was so important to the Romantics.

First, however, it is necessary to approach the notion in the simplest and most direct way possible in order to grasp the superstructure that Romanticism imposed upon it. To begin, it is necessary to get rid of the term. Just as "memory" is an inexplicable term, one that cannot be tied down to anything observable, but "remembering" enables us to observe something, so for the hypostatized term "imagination" it is extremely helpful to substitute "imagining" and from this to derive "the imagined." Now clearly in this term the root term "image" is metaphorical. It is fairly obvious that what "imagining" or "the imagined" subsumes are overt or covert semiotic constructs which are emergent in the behavior of the individual in question. From this can be derived the notion that an "imagined" is emergent in the culture of the individual and is unique in that culture, though this is not a necessary attribute of the term, at least in ordinary usage. And again, in ordinary usage, the actual material or subject matter of the imagined construct can be anything from a new way of semiotically constructing the most ordinary, platitudinous, day-to-day material to constructing the most bizarre, fantastic, unrealistic, and innovative material.

Upon these simple meanings it is possible to construct such elaborate theories of the imagination as Coleridge proposed to provide but only hinted at in the most mysterious, pompous, and inflated manner possible. But his hints were enough to enflame the English Romantics and the whole Romantic tradition of criticism and literary theory ever since. Though without actually using the term, the three greatest odes that Keats wrote in 1819 enable us to grasp why the word was important to him and what he was trying to do with it. These three odes are "Ode to a Nightingale," written in May 1819, "Ode on a Grecian Urn," written sometime in 1819, probably in the spring or summer, and "To Autumn," written on 19 September 1819. In the first of these the speaker imagines himself transported to the heart of a copse where a nightingale is singing in the shadows of moonlight. It is an ecstatic experience, but it brings the speaker to a longing for death. That longing transforms the nightingale into a transcendent nightingale, an immortal nightingale, an *unreal* nightingale. The simple word "forlorn" breaks the enchantment, reminds the speaker of his loneliness in a world of pain and suffering, and makes him realize "the fancy [that is, the imagination] cannot cheat so well / As she is fam'd to do, deceiving elf." The song of the nightingale has so inspired the poet that he transforms the world in which he finds himself and himself with it.

Hence to the question Keats was struggling with in his major poems, What is the source of the transforming, the self-transcending, the culturally transcending capacity? or What is that capacity? the answer is the imagination, the imagining capacity itself. More clearly than anyone, the half-educated and the naive and intellectually innocent Keats hit upon the centrality of imagining, of "creativity," in the Romantic tradition. It is the power that redeems one from alienation by constructing alternative modes of existence, and this is the capacity to transcend one's culture, to escape from and go beyond its limitations and its inadequacies. And it is also the capacity to deceive and destroy.

This is borne out in the "Ode on a Grecian Urn." Few passages in English poetry have been so exhaustively quarreled over as the last two famous lines of this poem.

> "Beauty is truth, truth beauty,"—that is all
> Ye know on earth, and all ye need to know.

T. S. Eliot called the lines senseless. Yet a certain sense can be made of them. Both beauty and truth can be reasonably and traditionally thought of as manifestations or emblems or exempla of value. In that sense beauty and truth are indeed interchangeable. In the world of art, the world of the Urn, the world of perfect beauty which never experiences the disappointments and despair that follow upon the consummation of any mode of behavior, in that world of unconsummation, of promise that never experiences the bitterness of fulfillment, in the world, then, that imagination can construct, there is nothing to be gained by making a distinction between beauty and truth. If we enter that world, then indeed we need to know nothing else—whomever the "ye" may refer to, and that has never been decided, nor can be. (Yet it does seem probable that "ye" are the figures on the urn.) But that world is a deception, as "The Ode to a Nightingale" has told us. And no one knew better than Keats that truth and beauty are very different indeed. He had begun his career by devoting himself to ecstatic sustained beauty, and he had learned the truth of a bitter reality, "Here, where men sit and hear each other groan . . . / . . . Where but to think is to be full of sorrow." If the imagination, the transforming capacity, can construct for us only a world of illusory beauty, then it is indeed a cheat. So Keats is struggling with the problem of what to do with this transforming capacity and power, of how to use it.

In "To Autumn" he appears to propose an answer. The power of imagining is to be used not to construct an ecstatic world of unreal beauty, the poetry he had begun with, but rather to exploit knowledge. It is the capacity to transform knowledge into value, knowledge of the real world as it actually is and, as history can tell us, has been. So the exquisite "To Autumn," the most perfect of his poems and perhaps the most perfect poem in the English language—at least one always feels that when one has just read it—synthesizes his marvelous but hitherto scattered power of "snail-horn" (to use his term) observation and sensitivity into a vision of process—from emergence through maturity to departure. Here the capacity for imagining is at its most powerful because it is at its most ordinary task, so constructing the world perception immediately gives us that the world of process emerges from perceived valueless squalor into a vision—or better still and more accurately—an experience of value.

Thus Keats at the end of his career has arrived at the very heart of Romanticism and the Romantic tradition: the capacity to construct the emergent is the power to create value. For years he had kept doggedly at the problem of understanding self-transformation, and before his tuberculosis first made him powerless to write and then killed him, he had arrived at an understanding of what he had set out to understand.

PERCY BYSSHE SHELLEY (1792–1822)

Shelley was so intensely interested in politics, in philosophy, in science, and in human behavior, about which towards the end of his life he planned to write a book, that it is surprising and even perplexing that he became a poet. His interest in politics he caught, it would appear, from his late-eighteenth-century *nouveau riche* family. His grandfather, who had become wealthy by a judicious combination of financial manipulation and marriages, had indeed become Sir Bysshe Shelley. Both his grandfather and his father were politically active Whigs. Thus there was a faint suggestion of liberalism in his political background. But more important was the late-eighteenth-century culture in which young Shelley grew up. As I proposed in *The Birth of Romanticism*, the late Enlightenment was marked by both a neoclassicism and a neo-Gothicism, both justified by a simplistic conception of "nature." The precocious youngster absorbed both and the personality culture that accompanied both, the culture of emotional lability. His early writings were purely late Enlightenment, including a Gothic novel. His first extended work in verse, *Queen Mab*, was an exemplification of radical late Enlightenment ideology, in particular an uncritical acceptance of the principles of the French Revolution. Moreover, this Enlightenment ideology sustained him, though with increasingly idealistic modifications, to the end of his short life. Since the spread of Enlightenment ideas in the nineteenth century was quantitatively far more important than the spread of Romanticism, it is not at all surprising that *Queen Mab* was pirated in the 1820s and became an important influence on the growing English labor movement, though more for the notes than for the poetic text itself.

The emotional instability of Shelley has always been noted, even by his contemporaries, and has been something of a puzzle for which elaborate psychological and physiological explanations have been proposed. Rather, it seems to have been a self-induced personality trait, one easily traced to the cultural ideal of emotional lability—as a personality attribute more "natural" than the approved emotional stability of the dominant pre- or early-Enlightenment culture. An unsentimental examination of the details of his life suggests very strongly that Shelley wanted to be emotionally unstable and worked at it. Certainly that instability is a constant theme in the poems that have been called autobiographical, mistakenly, as we shall see.

Of the various theories for the failure of the French Revolution Shelley adopted the betrayal theory. According to that theory of the failures of Enlightenment-based social efforts, whether capitalistic, communistic, socialistic, rationalistic, or national socialistic (that is, Fascistic), those failures could not have arisen from theoretical inadequacy or ideological incoherence but only from betrayal from within or attack from without. Evidently Shelley came to combine the Napoleonic dictatorship with the Bourbon restoration, the one the only possible response to the attack upon the Revolution by external tyrannies, the other the destruction of what was left of the Revolution by the imposition of the Restoration by those same tyrannies. This is implied in his highly idealized retelling of the Revolution in his longest poem, *The Revolt of Islam*.

The growing protest against English government policy, reaching a momentary climax in the 1819 attack by troops on a peaceful assembly at Manchester, known as Peterloo, and the Spanish and Neapolitan revolutions in 1820 supported Shelley's belief that the destruction of current society and its replacement by a regime of liberty, equality, and fraternity was imminent. And of course he was not too far wrong, since there was an Enlightenment-based alleviation of European repressiveness in the course of the nineteenth century, one which has continued to the present, in spite of fascism and communism. It has been the relative success of moderate Enlightenment ideology as opposed to the relative failure of extremist Enlightenment social modes. Nevertheless Shelley's last work, *The Triumph of Life,* though unfinished, suggests that current modes of social life were far more deeply corrupt and corrupting, more profoundly vicious, than he had originally judged. There will always be the question as to whether or not he was moving in the direction of a Schopenhauer-like pessimism. His drowning has made that question forever unanswerable.

Yet in spite of his Enlightenment ideology Shelley has always been counted as a Romantic. Indeed his simultaneous Romantic and Enlightenment tendencies have been responsible for a frequent confusion between Romanticism and Enlightenment. The source of this confusion is the assumption that a personality is coherent, especially the personality of a great poet, an assumption in itself, as we have seen, anti-Romantic. To account for Shelley's incoherence it is useful to employ for an understanding of cultural history the metaphor of stratification. The attributes of this metaphor propose that different behavior patterns coexisting in a society can have a different historical origin. Thus stopping at stoplights originated more recently than marriage customs, though both exist concurrently and in the same individuals and are quite unrelated. This notion can be extended to ideologies since they are, after all, but verbal behavior patterns. Thus the Jehovah's Witnesses, for example, originated in the second decade of this century but ideologically belong to early seventeenth-century culture. Nor is this surprising; that religious sect developed out of a sixteenth-century religious ideology which persisted into the twentieth century and still persists, particularly in the American South. The metaphor of stratification makes it possible to understand that both Romantic and Enlightenment ideologies continued simultaneous development throughout the nineteenth century and still continue together with medieval, reformation, and pre-Enlightenment rationalistic ideologies. All are different cultural strata.

As suggested above, the spread of Enlightenment ideology was more massive than that of Romantic ideology, primarily because it was a reaction against a lower stratum, the still more massive Reformation ideology. Thus Shelley is an early and highly conspicuous example of what has been a constantly recurring phenomenon in the culture of the last two hundred years, the simultaneous acceptance by a single individual of both Enlightenment and Romantic cultural ideals. As we shall see later in this volume, Marx is a remarkable instance of this cultural phenomenon. But generally speaking, Romantic artists have tended to be, politically, sympathetic to Enlightenment liberalism, simply because such a political attitude provides social space for Romantic experimentalism and cultural deviance and transcendence. Artistically Shelley became a Romantic, and became increasingly Romantic as his poetic career developed. His first Romantic poetic work was written in late 1815, significantly, after Waterloo.

"Alastor, or The Spirit of Solitude" was published as the title poem of a volume with a few other poems in March 1816. There are clear references to Wordsworth in the prologue and epilogue to the poem and echoes from his work. Although in that same volume Shelley published a sonnet attacking Wordsworth for his desertion of the cause of truth and liberty, of his position as that of a "lone star" shining on a "frail bark," a frequent image of Shelley's self-conception, of his position as "a rock-built refuge," he also praised the older poet for the "Ode on Intimations of Immortality" and for being "a poet of Nature." Shelley had an endless admiration for the earlier work of Wordsworth, particularly "Tintern Abbey," to which he often referred; yet for him, as for Keats, Wordsworth's major work was *The Excursion*. And worth mentioning again is the widespread admiration for that poem when it was published and for long thereafter. Only in this century has *The Prelude* usurped its place. As I discussed in *The Birth of Romanticism*, the subject of *The Excursion* is how the solitary, the man hopelessly disappointed by what had happened to the original promise of the French Revolution, is moved at least a step out of his isolation and alienation and despair, his solitariness, his solitude, by a group of friends and well-wishers who persuade him to take a day's walk with them.

Nor was Wordsworth alone in exploring solitude and alienation. By 1815 Byron, who Shelley was to admire all his life and who was to become a close friend, had published his studies of solitariness and alienation, the first two cantos of *Childe Harold*, *The Bride of Abydos*, *Lara*, and *The Corsair*. Shelley himself was bitterly alienated from his home and his father and from his first wife, Harriet, from whom he had separated. There are also indications that his relation to Mary Shelley, with whom he had eloped in July 1814, and could not yet marry, Harriet being still alive and divorce being virtually impossible, had turned out not to be all that his sexual sentimentality had thought it would be. Indeed he was to fall in love with several other women before his death, less an indication, perhaps, of the unsatisfactory marriage with Mary, though that was certainly a factor, than of his cultivated emotional instability. What the Solitary forced Shelley to face was the fact that Wordsworth's finest poetry had been written after his rejection of the Revolution (even though Shelley could not have known the whole story as revealed in *The Prelude*), and that perhaps there was at least a certain insufficiency in his Enlightenment ideals. His conception of himself as the poet of a new society founded on those ideals could not adequately explain the alienation and isolation which he found in Wordsworth and Byron and which he was experiencing himself. "Alastor" is Shelley's first step towards a new self-conception.

The narrative structure of "Alastor" is that of one of the central Romantic symbolizations of solitariness and alienation, aimless wandering terminating in this poem in the protagonist's death. That aimless wandering is repeated in the dreams of sleep, presented as another Romantic theme, the Waste Land. Indeed the landscape of the waking wandering is also a waste land. There are almost no other human beings. The protagonist sets out from the "lone Chorasmian waste," the area between the Aral and the Caspian seas, and in frail bark, the symbolic function of which in Shelley's poetry we have already seen, sails across the Caspian and enters into a highly unrealistic blasted and tortured Caucasus, filled with strange streams and whirlpools and valleys that seem to defy gravity and geography. At length he dies, gazing over a vast and empty landscape from a cliff over which the stream that has brought him plunges in a waterfall dissipated in the winds. His solitude destroys him, but it is not the solitude but the isolation and alienation, the inability to love others, to be in sympathy with members of humanity. Now to Shelley social and individual love were the same, including the most intense manifestation of love, sexual love. It is not that the failure to love is the cause of his hero's solitude but rather that the failure to love *is* solitude, *is* isolation, *is* alienation. The value the poet-hero of the poem granted to the noblest history of man and to the natural world is not sufficient to sustain him, is a mere consolation for isolation. His death is the failure to ascribe value to other human beings, for this is what Shelley has come to mean by "love." And, as we have seen, it *is* the romantic problem.

In Shelley's case a vision of a satisfactory future society could only make more poignant the horror of the one he was living in. In that one there was no source of value, for what the French Revolution so briefly offered had been destroyed by betrayal and by its enemies. Despair and dejection continued to haunt Shelley during the rest of his life. In part it was the despair and dejection endemic in the Romantic tradition, the result of the tenuousness and instability of strategies for maintaining the sense of value; but in part it was the consequence of the tradition of emotional lability, which leaves the individual defenseless against depression. "Alastor" is Shelley's realization of the difficulty of creating and sustaining value from one's unique resources, of sustaining the tenuous and uncertain and unstable character of the romantic self and selfhood. "Alastor" is witness to the fact that Wordsworth and Byron and his own failures had made him aware of the difficulty of the problem he was faced with. So in poem after poem he turns to the analysis of the self-conception he wishes to create and the value he wishes to bring into existence. That is why it is insufficient and inaccurate to call these poems autobiographical. They are struggles to bring a Romantic self, a self-sustained selfhood, into being.

Because of the turmoil of his personal life, the suicide of Harriet and the failed effort to gain legal custody of his children by her, Shelley wrote little until the spring of 1817. Then he set out on his longest effort, originally called *Laon and Cythna; or, The Revolution of the Golden City: A Vision of the Nineteenth Century*, published in the fall of 1817, but suppressed and republished as *The Revolt of Islam* in January 1818. (By an odd coincidence he was working on it during the same summer Keats was working on *his* longest poem, *Endymion*.) The reason for the suppression was the theme of incest. The hero and heroine were brother and sister as well as lovers in the first version. In the revision they are merely brought up together. The explanation for that incest motive is to be found by examining the initial vision of the poem, the allegorical struggle between power and value, between an eagle and a snake. That the eagle should be the emblem of evil power is easily explained by the frequency with which the eagle appears in the heraldry of the ruling families of Europe. And turning the snake, the traditional emblem of evil, into the emblem of the helpless good and valuable is the indication of Shelley's determination to reverse traditional morality, of his conviction of the evil of existing institutions and human relations. The presentation of incest as a good displays the same determination. Moreover, this reversal is an indication of an increasing bifurcation or diremption in Shelley's thinking, between a liberalistic and realistic proposal for parliamentary reform and a conviction that a future society could not be a correction or improvement or redemption of existent society but must be something wholly new and as yet unimagined and unimaginable.

At the end Laon is executed and Cythna willingly joins him in the flames that are killing him. Suddenly there is a transformation and the pair find themselves beyond the veil that parts life from death and in a paradisal world. But it is not the Christian paradise. They embark in the boat of a seraph, the spirit of Cythna's child, who had died of the plague when they died, and voyage to the Temple of the Spirit. That was first encountered in Canto I; there an empty throne is taken by the snake transformed into its original shape, that of the spirit among the many spirits of the great individuals of the human past, those who had created from human experience the ideals of liberty and of love. So Laon and Cythna, first encountered in Canto I and whose story they have told in the intervening cantos, are among those spirits. Shelley is here making his first effort at a transcendental, not transcendent, mythology, a device to categorize the efforts of those men and woman of the past who have created human value. But this is a departure from the Enlightenment position that the natural goodness of man has simply been perverted through the errors, natural errors, of priestcraft and tyranny.

Human value is then not a naturally given quality but a quality that has been created by human beings. And this is what Shelley means by "intellectual beauty," the subject of "Hymn to Intellectual Beauty," written in Switzerland in the summer of 1816, the summer he and Mary spent with Byron as their neighbor:

> The awful shadow of some unseen Power
> Floats though unseen among us,— visiting
> This various world with as inconstant wing
> As summer winds that creep from flower to flower,—
> . . . .
> Like aught that for its grace may be
> Dear and yet dearer for its mystery.

That power is the source of "Love, Hope, and Self-esteem." It has been identified as Necessity, but this interpretation makes little sense, since the "unseen Power" is clearly identified as unknowable, inexplicable; but necessitarianism, particularly of the Enlightenment sort which Shelley earlier had accepted, is not inexplicable nor does it make the world incomprehensible. Quite the contrary. Nor is Necessity unconstant, and in the "Hymn" Shelley emphasizes again and again the power's uncertainty, inconstancy, instability. Clearly the emphases on "self-esteem," so constant a theme in Romanticism, make it most reasonable to identify this power as the human power to create value in a world which in its natural condition, that is, without humanity, is without value. Value in this poem and in *The Revolt of Islam* is the creation of mankind in its most exalted state, the state Shelley aspires to, to be achieved, as he makes clear in *A Defence of Poetry*, written in Pisa in 1821, by the poetic imagination. In that sense poets are the "unacknowledged legislators of the world," for they create the purely human value from which all just laws must be derived and on which they depend. Furthermore, Shelley's recognition of the instability of value, above all the value of the self, or self-esteem, was the impulse that led to the major effort of *Laon and Cythna*, the effort by means of the poetic imagination to stabilize value, at least for the duration of the experience of the poem and of the experience of writing it.

Only a few months after the second publication of *The Revolt of Islam* Shelley set out for Italy, and in the fall of 1818 he began a year of extraordinary achievement, made possible by what he had accomplished in that poem. In September and October 1818, at Este, he composed the first act of *Prometheus Unbound*. In March and April 1818, in Rome, he composed Acts II and III, thinking the work to be finished. From May to August he wrote his extraordinary tragedy, *The Cenci*, and at Florence in the late fall he returned to *Prometheus Unbound* and composed the exultant and celebratory Act IV. And these two works are best considered in that order. Indeed Act IV of the first of these two dramas is virtually an independent poem, and as we shall see, its importance is that it adds almost nothing to the ideas of the first three acts.

Prometheus Unbound is stylistically such a departure from *The Revolt of Islam* and is, quite simply, so beautiful that the first major effort has been to a certain extent neglected, partly because the lyrical drama, as he called it, is so much an ideological exemplification that it can be responded to as poetry without the reader having to pay too much attention to the ideology that governs it. Thus the story is of the utmost simplicity, and although in the Preface Shelley denies that it is didactic poetry, a kind he abhors, and offers, he says, only "beautiful idealisms," the fact is that the action of the work is more than merely susceptible to an allegorical interpretation. Briefly, as the work opens, Prometheus is revealed as bound to a precipice in the Indian Caucasus. He has been bound there by the order of Jupiter, whom he has cursed. But now he recalls his curse. That recall releases the power of Asia, who summons from the depths of the world the inexplicable Demogorgon. Demogorgon overthrows Jupiter. Prometheus is released by Hercules and with Asia retires to a lovely cave in a forest.

There the Spirit of the Earth tells him of the blessed consequences of Jupiter's fall.

Asia is intellectual beauty, the embodiment of value-creating forces in the Temple of the Spirit. Prometheus is the civilizing, the inventive power of mankind, subject to the brutal power of political domination and force. That brutal force cannot be defeated by a counterforce but only by love, by the power to ascribe value to *all* human beings. It is the recognition of the failure of his curse, the counterforce, that enables Prometheus to release the value-creating power, which, as we have seen, is the highest manifestation of humanity. Demogorgon, often identified with Necessity, is more properly identified with historical process, since he is brought to Jupiter's heaven by the Spirit of the Hour. The defeat of Jupiter is inevitable, but on the other hand the historical process that brings about that defeat can be, as it were, triggered only by love, by intellectual beauty, by the value-creating power. If force is destroyed by a counterforce, then that counterforce itself must be destroyed. Is Shelley asserting that the freedom-creating force of the French Revolution destroyed the very freedom it had created? It would seem so, and this assertion would be consistent with his growing interest in reform rather than revolution. Thus he evidently believed that little would be accomplished by the various revolutions around 1820, except that the struggle for liberty would be kept alive and vigorous.

To make his point clearer, Shelley told the story all over again in his tragedy on the legend of the Cenci, a legend which he took to be historically correct. Historical study in the later nineteenth century dispelled much of the glamour that had accumulated about the figure of Beatrice Cenci, who may have been as bad as the father she had murdered, or at least not very much better. But in Shelley's time the saintliness of Beatrice and the absolute villainy of her father were unquestioned, and had been since the sixteenth century when the famous story of the Cenci family took place in Rome.

The legend and Shelley's version of it amount to this. Francesco Cenci treated his children and his second wife with the utmost, with inconceivable brutality, even raping his daughter Beatrice in order to subdue her to his control. His brutality was imitated by several of his sons, who died disgraceful deaths. But Beatrice, her stepmother, Lucrezia, and one of her brothers resolved to kill the father. They did so with the aid of hired assassins and were themselves apprehended and executed, except for the youngest brother. Francesco Cenci is a reappearance of Jupiter, and Beatrice is the reappearance of the opposite of Prometheus and Asia. She is destroyed by the exercise of the force she summons to destroy a persecuting and irredeemably vicious tyrant. Yet—and this is Shelley's important point—she is ennobled by her act. In *Prometheus Unbound* Shelley examined force and rebellion and freedom in the human mind. In *The Cenci* he examined them in the family. And the implication of both works is that identical forces and counterforces and value-creating powers are to be found in society and in the family. *The Cenci,* perhaps inspired by Scott, places these factors of human behavior in a historical situation. Beatrice's act is an act of familial revolution, and Shelley's point is that even though a counterforce is destroyed by its rebellion, a step forward has been made in the movement of mankind toward freedom, brotherhood, and equality, toward the resolution of human misery. It is as if Shelley were saying that the beautiful idealisms of *Prometheus Unbound* are all very well and justifiably inspiring, but the existent historical situation demands that counterforce must be used against tyrannous force. It must fail, but even so a step forward has been made.

Thus the ideology of both plays is a modified and as it were progressivist version of Enlightenment ideology. But at the same time the growing diremption of Shelley's work is powerfully evident. For the purely ideological or allegorical factor in *Prometheus Unbound* is, quantitatively, not dominating. What is dominating is a sustained poetic beauty, a sustained imaginative constructionism. There emerges in the first three acts of the work a poetic virtuosity, and that becomes almost the sole character of Act IV, with a repetition of the moral of the first three acts tacked on the end in the words of Demogorgon. Act IV is astoundingly original. Nothing like it had ever been written in any European language. It is one long ecstatic celebration sustained by an astonishing virtuosity. It is Shelley's manifestation of the power of imagining to create sustained value. He has analyzed himself as Prometheus, and has again analyzed himself as Beatrice Cenci. The intensity of those analyses and the consequent self-understanding has released his poetic power in a display of supreme sustained virtuosity. His greatest lyric poetry and his greatest single narrative were to follow on this consequence.

Moreover, in Act IV he was endeavoring to move beyond the allegorical into the mythological. His ideological position led him to reverse the mythological role of Jupiter from beneficent to evil power. That released his comprehension that mythology can not only be changed; it can be originated. His aim now was to create a genuine mythology of the forces in nature and in humanity that can bring about liberty and joy, or value. He wished to reveal that those forces in man are sustained by forces in nature. Hence the revelry of the Earth and the Moon. And hence also Demogorgon is hailed by the Earth, the Moon, the universe beyond earth and moon, the dead, the elemental powers, the spirits of all living things, beasts and lightning and wind, and man as the power which releases. And thus in his final speech Demogorgon reveals what power he is, the power in nature and man as part of nature that can overcome and destroy political and social force, the force, whatever its source may be, that tyrannically oppresses liberty and joy.

When *Prometheus Unbound* was published in the summer of 1820, Shelley included a number of short poems, three of which, added to the title poem, make it one of the most remarkable volumes in the history of English poetry, as extraordinary as the 1820 volume of Keats. These three lyrics have long since been recognized as among the greatest achievements in English lyric poetry. The first is "Ode to the West Wind," written before the last act of *Prometheus Unbound* and closely related to it. It is, first of all, another exercise in self-definition or at least hoped-for selfhood, and the poem also attempts a new mythology. The west wind destroys, preserves, and in the spring brings the plant world once more to life. It is a power of recreation, then, and is another myth of exactly the same power Demogorgon represents. And Shelley gives it, as with Demogorgon, a specifically political-social power. It is the power, now conceived as cyclic, that destroys forms of human value and then creates new forms. And the poem is a passionate wish that Shelley, as poet, should be the instrument of that power. Like other Romantic mythologies, it is an effort to create the functional equivalent of religion, for as the instrument of that value-creating power the poet himself becomes value-laden.

Shelley's "Ode to the West Wind" was written in Florence. In January 1820, he moved to Pisa and thence to Leghorn. In the spring in the latter city he wrote the other two supreme lyrics of the 1820 volume, "The Cloud" and "To a Skylark." The scientific or naturalistic basis of the first is the creation of clouds from moisture drawn up from the waters of the earth by the sun. The poem is another mythological endeavor, an attempt of the utmost virtuosity and sustained ecstasy to identify by using the first person the force that lies beyond the re-creative powers of man. The theme is once again that of Demogorgon, but stripped of that figure's portentousness and refined to a being of the purest joyousness, the indestructible, though cyclical, natural power to create and re-create human value. And this natural source of ecstatic rapture can be transmuted into a message the world of mankind would gladly listen to if the poet, Shelley, can learn from the skylark. Shelley is again creating a myth of the natural source and fountain and support of the ability of mankind to overcome its failures and create a satisfactory human condition. Above all, all three of these poems display what Shelley had achieved as a poet, the virtuosic mastery of powerful aggressiveness to subject all the attributes and aspects of language to the poet's will.

In that same summer of 1820, in August, Shelley composed what can arguably be deemed his poetic masterpiece, *The Witch of Atlas*. The fact that the stanza he used, *ottava rima*, is the stanza of Byron's *Beppo* and *Don Juan*, poems which Shelley admired prodigiously, suggests that he was determined to achieve in his idiom that insouciance, that playfulness, that easy mastery which Byron had so signally accomplished. Shelley creates a good witch who had come into being before Error and Truth "had hunted from the Earth / All those bright natures which adorned its prime, / And left us nothing to believe in." She is again a creature of myth, of Shelley's new mythology, and she subsumes those powers which he had before presented in the three great lyrics as well as in Prometheus himself. But in this new poem composed, amazingly, in three days, Shelley is more precise. The witch is a myth of the power of transformation. Thus from fire and snow and love she created a Fair Shape, a Living Image, a hermaphrodite. And she made soldiers dream of being blacksmiths and made gaolers set liberals free in the streets of Memphis.

All these deeds (and there are many of them of both a similar and a more varied sort) can be made even more precise by identifying the witch as the transforming power of the imagination, of poetry, and therefore of the power that can transform human life, human societies, human political systems. And so it can perhaps be correctly said that the witch is Shelley's version of what we have already seen as the power to achieve cultural transcendence. Thus far has Shelley's poetic genius moved him away from his Enlightenment ideology and towards a genuine Romanticism, even, it may be, arriving there; for in this poem the central Romantic theme of the creation of value out of purely human resources, the gods being dead, as she says in the first stanza, achieves Shelley's most purely joyous and rapturous state. He even ends the poem not with a triumphant conclusion as in *Prometheus Unbound,* or even more mildly as in the three great lyrics, but casually, almost carelessly, almost like the open end of *The Eve of St. Agnes.* Above all, the poem marks Shelley's arrival at the ability to sustain poetry in an unbroken arch of verbal mastery, of being literally free from verbal compulsions, free to do with language whatever he wished.

That mastery appears again in his exploration of love and the failure of love, written in Pisa in January and February 1821, *Epipsychidion*, and in his elegy on Keats, *Adonais*, written in June 1821, as much a triumphant manifestation of poetic virtuosity as *The Witch of Atlas*. And *Adonais* is a praise, an exaltation, of poetry. Keats is to be lamented by all true poets because he was one of them, an evidence of the transforming power of the imagination and of the transforming power in nature that supports it. Those who evince in their lives and works that transforming power are the true immortals, who will live forever in the exalting realms of the human spirit. Yet in uttering this glorious ennoblement of the poetic power and its supreme importance for what in man and nature it makes manifest, Shelley accepts as never before his own alienation from a world that rejected and crucified, he thinks, both Keats and himself.

And so in his final work, the poem he was working on when he was drowned in July 1822, *The Triumph of Life*, published like *The Witch of Atlas* in Mary Shelley's 1824 edition of the *Posthumous Poems*, that alienation is fully explored. The poem is inspired in its construction by Petrarch and Dante, and "triumph" means such a triumph as Roman Emperors held in a victory procession. It is the triumph of life over the freedom and the joy of human life, the triumph of life as we know it in the contemporary world, a triumph of a crushing, destroying, value-negating force. The poem presents an incomparably vivid picture of the forces of oppression and destruction which keep the value-creating, regenerating, imagining forces from achieving their redeeming manifestation and fulfillment. It is impossible to know how Shelley would have ended the work, and it is idle to guess. Rather the poem must be recognized as introducing into the Romantic tradition more forcefully than any Romantic artist had yet done the opposite, the reverse, the negation of the ecstatic. That is, despair.

For if a cultural situation is such, as the Romantic situation was, that the individual is forced to create value from his own unique resources, unaided by any cultural tradition or any institution, such as a religion and a church, then the failure to create that value, first adumbrated in the last stanza of *Adonais*, especially after the enormous effort Shelley had made in the face of rejection, alienation, and discouragement, meant that the individual could only too easily be plunged into a bottomless pit, a hell of despair. That despair, barely hinted at before Shelley's *The Triumph of Life*, was to become one of the great, the central, the powerful visionary imaginative constructions of Romantic art. Before Shelley only Schopenhauer had dared to face it, and even he retreated into a consolation. Perhaps Shelley would have too, had he finished his final poem. But what we have, what he left us, is as uncompromising a realistic vision of the torture of human social and political existence as only the great realistic novelists of later in the century could endeavor to come to terms with and to present with all the resources of man's fictive powers.

ALPHONSE DE LAMARTINE (1790–1869)

The social class into which Lamartine was born was something of a French equivalent to Shelley's—the French *petite noblesse*. As recently as the seventeenth century Lamartine's ancestor had been a tanner at Cluny in southwest France. Gradually the family moved up on the social scale, and both the future poet's grandfather and father served in the armies of the Bourbon kings, though his father fully absorbed the principles and ideals of the Enlightenment. Lamartine was born in Macon, a town on the Saône not far north of Lyon. A couple of years later his father was imprisoned as an aristocrat, but in 1794 he was released. He moved his family to a nearby and very simple landed estate which his father, as third son, had inherited from the quite wealthy holdings of the family, even though neither of his older brothers married. So Lamartine grew up in conditions not far removed from those of the surrounding peasants and in a life very much like theirs. He was always a countryman at heart.

Still, his schooling was excellent, principally under the tutelage of the Jesuits, an education in which he absorbed the important literature of France and even England in the eighteenth century, admiring, for example, the poetry of Pope and most particularly that of "Ossian." He was very much a product of the late Enlightenment culture of emotional lability. Ten months in Italy in 1811 and 1812, mostly in Naples, gave him what he later insisted was an important and lasting experience of love for a Neapolitan girl of the people, but, more important, introduced him to a different culture, both of the educated Neapolitans and of the peasants. Moreover, he began to be increasingly under the imaginative control of Chateaubriand, of Senancour, and in 1818 and 1819 of Byron, whom he came to believe the greatest poet of the nineteenth century.

In the meantime the end of the Napoleonic regime and the restoration of the Bourbons appeared to offer some hope for a career. For a short time he served in the Royal Bodyguards, but when the king fled to Belgium Lamartine fled to Switzerland. The hundred days marked the end of his military service. The following years until 1820 were devoted first to a love affair with Julie Charles, begun when he was taking the cure at Aix-les-Bains and continued in Paris until her death in 1817. By this time and to a considerable extent under the force of his love he was beginning to take more seriously the writing of poetry, something he had done since his school days, more as an amusement than anything else. His manuscripts began to be circulated among his friends in Paris, and his reputation grew rapidly. At the urging of a friend he published in March 1820, *Meditations poetiques*—and like Byron awoke to find himself famous. His success opened up to him the diplomatic career he desired. His first appointment was as attaché to the French embassy in Naples; and in 1825 he obtained the post of secretary to the embassy at Florence.

The primary cultural importance of Lamartine's first collection was that Romanticism had at last and for virtually the first time penetrated the tired neoclassical defenses of French poetry. French Romanticism took a fresh start with this volume, and within a decade it was completely dominating the French cultural scene. The first poem in the collection, "L'isolement," brings into sharp focus one of the most important and most persistent themes of Romanticism and provides a more than adequate explanation and justification for it, the theme of Romantic love. The poem opens with a beautiful poetic transformation of a beautiful landscape—but then abruptly asserts, "I contemplate the earth like a wandering soul: / The sun of the living does not warm the dead." And, "A single being is absent, and everything is unpeopled." So he imagines a place beyond this sphere, a place where a "true sun shines from other skies." There he could recover hope and love. Thus the being whose absence empties the landscape of all desire is not merely a beloved but, as the emphasis on hope and love reveals, a source of value. The central romantic theme, the loss of value, is linked to the beloved as a source of value, love thus being, like hope, but one kind of value. Romantic love is revealed as a functional substitute for religion or equivalent to it, even as a religion itself.

Moreover, Lamartine links this loss of value to the inability to act. He ends his poem, just as Shelley ended "Ode to the West Wind," with a plea or prayer to be carried away like a dead leaf by a stormy northern gale. In both passages, though for different ends, there is a harrowed appeal to be the instrument of a power which would impel the speaker into a world of action, a power he cannot summon from within himself, from his own resources, so great, for Lamartine, is his sense of being an exile on this earth.

No Romantic notion has penetrated so deeply into the culture or spread so widely as this notion of Romantic love, the subject of endless popular songs which repeat precisely what Lamartine is uttering in this poem, which establishes, as it were, the condition for the whole volume of *Meditations poetiques* and for the *Nouvelles meditations poetiques* as well, published in 1823. For most of the rest of the poems in both volumes are ostensibly religious in subject. Hence arguments among critics have long bubbled on whether Lamartine was a sincere believer, or an agnostic, or perhaps even an atheist. But these arguments misunderstand the poems and Lamartine's objective. First, the poems are meditations, poetic meditations. The meditation is a very old pattern of religious rhetoric, something not quite a prayer, a searching, as it were, for an understanding of the attributes of deity and of the attributes of belief, and a finding and response to those attributes. The basic pattern is one of wandering, but "L'isolement" is unusual in the volume for its carefully organized rhetorical structure, though, of course, such thorough organization characterizes most of Romantic art. But Lamartine wrote "poetic meditations." They are not wandering meditations on what is known but rather random probings into a possible relation of man and god. It is not that the existence of god is a subject of doubt but rather that the way to god is in question. A traditional religious meditation is an exemplification of a belief. Lamartine is concerned, rather, with the effort not to achieve belief, which is not the question, but with experimentation in discovering how to experience belief.

The contrast between the two comes out sharply in his later notes to two poems, one ostensibly the answer to the other. The first, the sixth of the twenty-four poems in the original edition, is "Le desespoir" (Despair) and develops precisely the theme of hopelessness presented initially in "L'isolement." The answer is "La providence à l'homme," an exercise in rational theology. But in notes to the poems added many years later Lamartine repudiates the answer, for, he says, the first poem is from the heart, the second only from the head, only a bit of rationalism, not, he implies, something he can take very seriously. This is what he means by calling meditations "poetic." They are meditations on the problem of how to experience the *value* of belief, and that is what makes them examples of Romanticism.

Poems on such subjects as the church, the "temple," the crucifix, the holy week, the dying Christian are instances of the effort to use the *materia* of the Church as instruments for achieving the experience of the value of belief. They are very much to the point of what Lamartine is trying to do, for they are concerned with the fact that it is no longer true for the speaker, for the poet, for Lamartine, that these *materia* are still magic, that these *materia sacra* (they are to be found in all religions) are still capable of conferring value merely by eliciting the culturally maintained and redundant responding to them. If they are to be again efficacious they must become symbols or emblems in the value pragmatics of the alienated and isolated individual, symbols or emblems the power of which he must recreate from his own resources.

This comes out most effectively in one of the most beautiful of the poems in the second collection of 1823, "La liberté, ou Une nuit à Rome." It is a meditation on the Colosseum in moonlight, a topic which after *Childe Harold, Canto IV* was to become one of the most popular of the nineteenth century. Lamartine rivals Byron himself, and his poem is more beautiful. But it ends with a vision of the Cross in the Colosseum as twisted and bent as is a ship's mast by a tempest. And this image is followed at once by an address to the Spirit of Liberty, of ancient origin, to be sure, but the prime condition of the new century, the condition, or at least the political condition, in which the individual can recreate the value of existence.

It is clear, then, that by calling his meditations "poetic" Lamartine is in typical Romantic fashion calling upon poetry to perform the task that, in the past, religious institutions have performed. And this comes out even more clearly in several poems of an entirely new sort. They consist of a series of short poems in various measures and stanzas. They are in fact cycles, the form which we have already met as so typical of Romanticism, and which we shall meet again and again in the course of the century in all the arts, even architecture. In the most important of these, "Les préludes" (from which Liszt was to take the title and to an extent the idea for his most famous tone poem) Lamartine is dramatizing what was beginning to be and in time would become one of the most salient and powerful themes of Romanticism, instability, a theme that in the twentieth century was to affect and even revolutionize the very concept of scientific theory. The poem addresses itself to the many and repetitive efforts we make to *begin*, to accomplish a beginning, the implication being that no conclusion can ever relieve one of the need once more to begin, and begin again.

But what is most striking and particularly significant for the further development of Romantic culture, what, perhaps, most appealed to Liszt, is that in a note added in a later edition Lamartine called the poem "une sonate a poésie." Perhaps he had in mind the sonatas of Beethoven; perhaps he used the word without any specific reference. Evidently he refers in the title to the musical meaning of "prelude." But what his explanatory phrase brings out, and what Liszt was to bring out in his tone or symphonic poem, is the drama of music, its superior power to transform into art the emotional discontinuities, the sudden breaks, sudden redirections, abrupt interruptions of our actual emotional and cognitive experience, a distinction which exists only for the purposes of analysis but is not to be found in human experiencing itself. Lamartine's phrase illuminates what we have already encountered in this volume and in *The Birth of Romanticism*, the movement of all the arts towards the condition of music, the emergence of music as the model art of the nineteenth century, the art which of all the works of art of the Romantic tradition and of the nineteenth century has survived in fullest vitality, which even today we encounter constantly from thousands of radio stations. It is not that Lamartine set out to write the poetic equivalent of music but rather that by the time he wrote this note in the middle of the century he had come to recognize what he had done, had come to understand his own poetic genius. The two volumes published in the early 1820s are illuminating dramatizations of the struggles of many isolated and alienated Romantics of the first Romanticized generation to recreate from their own resources not religion but the meaningfulness of religion, to recreate that religious value which religious rhetoric, symbols, and institutions could no longer provide.

HEINRICH HEINE (1797–1856)

By far the most important German poet of the first Romanticized generation was Heinrich Heine, born in Düsseldorf of a Jewish mother and father. The father was a business failure, but Heinrich's paternal uncle was an enormously successful banker in Hamburg whom his nephew exploited and abused all his life—and for whom nevertheless he had a profound affection. The most important influence on Heine's childhood and early adolescence was the French occupation of Düsseldorf from 1795 to 1801 and again from 1806 to 1815, for some part of the time under the direct supervision of Napoleon. More than any other German city Düsseldorf experienced the spread of Enlightenment ideas by the French Revolutionary and Napoleonic armies. But with the fall of Napoleon the city and its Duchy of Berg passed under the rule of the reactionary Prussia. To Heine, as to many of the citizens of that part of Western Germany most under the influence of France and the Enlightenment, French culture was more important than German. It is not surprising that in 1831 Heine left Germany for Paris and stayed there the rest of his life. Unfortunately one of the consequences of the French occupation was Napoleon's Continental System, the blockade of Europe against English economic power; the result was severe economic depression and the bankruptcy of Heine's father.

Heine was educated in Düsseldorf schools, the second he attended being a Catholic school, the best in the city. Later he attended the French lycée converted in 1814 into a Prussian Gymnasium. He also attended a business school until January 1815. And then arose the question of what to do with him. The problem was compounded by the spread of possibilities, for one of the lasting effects of the Enlightenment throughout Germany was the emancipation of the Jews, their release from the Ghetto. Salomon Heine as well as the philosopher Moses Mendelssohn (1729–1786) showed what a Jew could now do. But the emancipation brought forth perplexing and exasperating problems. To what extent should traditional Jewish culture be maintained? To what extent should it be abandoned? Should Jews be converted to Christianity? Many were, and eventually Heinrich Heine was, since to make one's way in the German world being a Jew was a disadvantage, particularly if one hoped to become a lawyer or a university professor, for a time Heine's unrealistic hope, if not ambition. The reason for that hope was that his uncle's attempt to make a successful businessman out of him in Hamburg proved a failure, though in truth we know little about the matter. It was decided that Heine should attend a university in order to gain access to some kind of career other than business. This was Uncle's idea, for Salomon had taken over completely the responsibility for his nephew's welfare. It is worth noting that Heine's brothers and a sister went on to successful careers, and for his sister even splendidly successful, and all in the pattern of Jewish assimilation into German life, culture, and religion.

The most promising possibility appeared to be the law, and Heine started his university studies in 1819 at the University of Bonn, where he encountered various professors important to him for what he was really interested in, literature and history. The most significant was August Wilhelm Schlegel, whom later he was to treat quite savagely. After a year at Bonn Heine decided to transfer to the University of Göttingen, then reputed to be the best university in Germany and particularly strong in law. In a very short time he came to hate both Göttingen and the law. He got involved in a duel and for a time was suspended. So in March 1821, he went to the University of Berlin. In that growing city (still with only about two hundred thousand inhabitants, large for the early nineteenth century) he found not only a university but for the first time an intellectual and cultural milieu, dominated by some of the most brilliant minds of Germany, including Hegel, whom Heine probably much later came to understand, at least to a certain extent. More important was the circle of intellectuals around Varnhagen von Ense and his wife Rahel, born a Jewess, one of the most intelligent and cultivated women in all Germany. She was one of those who helped establish the worship of Goethe, an adulation Heine was expected to participate in. Nor was he then unwilling, for in 1819 Goethe had published *West-Östlicher Divan*, a collection of poems inspired by the Persian poet Hafiz. These are among Goethe's finest lyrics and as close as he ever came to the mood of some aspects of German Romanticism. Above all, it was the extreme elegance and "deceptive simplicity" of these poems in four-line stanzas that were to have the greatest importance for Heine, who had already begun to write poetry and was beginning to take himself seriously as a poet.

But the problem of earning a living remained. In May 1823, he left Berlin for the little town of Lüneberg, where his mother and father had taken refuge, supported by Uncle Salomon, and remained there until the following January, when he returned to Göttingen and slogged away at the detested law. In September he made his famous walking trip in the nearby Harz mountains, and finally in May 1825, he obtained his law degree. In that month he began instruction as a Christian and was baptized on 28 June 1825. But he made no effort to undertake a career as a lawyer. On the contrary, he had already tasted enough literary success to be convinced that only as a writer could he make a living in a way that was bearable to him. And these early successes established his fame and greatness as a poet and prose writer.

His early poems were unremarkable enough, hardly different from what any number of other young men were writing, imitations of the poetry of the early German Romantics. Actually his first prose writings, *Letters from Berlin* (1822) and *On Poland* (1823), both published in journals, were more promising. Thus his first volume of poems, *Gedichte*, published in 1821, included little of interest, but in April 1823, appeared *Tragödien, nebst einem lyrischen Intermezzo* (*Tragedies, together with a Lyric Intermezzo*). The tragedies were *Almansor*, written in 1820 and 1821, and *William Ratcliff*, written in a few weeks in January 1822. The *Intermezzo* consisted of sixty-five short poems written from 1821 to 1823. The two tragedies are not of great interest (*Almansor* had one disastrous public performance), but the lyric poems made him famous and became among the most popular of German poems. The theme of all three sections of the volume is love, but examined in an extraordinarily fresh and novel way.

Almansor takes place in Spain, perhaps a decade after Ferdinand

and Isabella had conquered Granada and driven the Moors from Spain. The theme is that of two lovers separated from childhood by the conquest, the flight of some Moors to Africa, and the conversion of others to Christianity. The two lovers, caught between the two cultures, are destroyed. *William Ratcliff* is stranger. The setting is Scotland, evidence of the wide popularity of Walter Scott, and the plot relates how Ratcliff, his love for Maria spurned contemptuously, kills her several fiancés and finally her and himself. The themes of the two tragedies interlock in a curious way. In the Spanish tragedy the lovers are destroyed by the hypocrisy and violence of the society in which they attempt to exist. In the Scottish tragedy Heine explores, though crudely, the intimate connection between love and self-respect, the ascription of value to oneself. The rejection of love is experienced as denigration and humiliation, the only possible response being revenge, murder, and suicide. Love destroyed by the sociocultural order was not new in Romanticism, but the destructiveness of love itself and the profound and deeply felt and experienced relation between love and value were new.

In the nineteenth and twentieth centuries, a period in which literary studies were dominated not merely by a biographical approach but by an apparent conviction that all literature worthy of the name is autobiographical, the *Intermezzo* was interpreted as a direct consequence and expression of Heine's rejection by his cousin Amalie and his later unrequited love for her sister Therese. The second of these is dubious, and the first hardly less so. Yet there is some evidence, and if these affairs did take place Heine used his experiences for a new kind of love poetry. The work is not an expression of love but an examination of it and of its consequences and of the consequences of its failure. The sixty-five poems imply a narrative. The speaker celebrates his falling in love, discovers that his love is not returned, explores all the consequences, and at the end endeavors to bury the "old, bad songs, the evil, dreadful dreams," to sink them in the ocean, to rid himself of his love and of his suffering.

The form of the work is the cycle, which as we have seen is one of the emergent forms of Romanticism. Heine had two predecessors for such a lyric cycle, each of the various sections of Goethe's *West-Östlicher Divan* and *Die Schöne Müllerin*, published in 1821, by Wilhelm Müller (1794–1827). In 1823 Franz Schubert (1797–1828) used Müller's cycle of poems for the first great Romantic song cycle and published it in 1824. In 1823 Müller published his second cycle, *Die Winterreise*, which Schubert set to music in 1827, published in 1828.

In 1840 Robert Schumann (1810–1856) continued this tradition by setting sixteen of the *Intermezzo* lyrics as *Dichterliebe* (*A Poet's Love*), published in 1844.

From Müller, Heine took something of the form and the spirit of *Die schöne Müllerin*, which tells the story of a disappointed and frustrated love and the resultant suicide of the lover. Like Goethe's poems the form is that of the German folk song, and Heine himself spoke of his poems as folk songs for the sophisticated and cultured, an apparent and superficial simplicity which on meditation revealed a subtle analytic poetry. For these poems are indeed analytic. The significant matter is not whether or not Heine expresses the failure of his love for Amalie but rather that he chose to use his experience, probably fairly unimportant to him, in order to explore the experience of being in love and above all to undermine the cultural and literary tradition of concealing love's true and destructive character. The theme is not love but the knowledge of love. As an emergent cultural phenomenon Heine's poems belong to the Romantic current visible from the beginning of Romanticism, the current known as realism—that semiotic strategy which is devoted to undermining the traditional and regnant culture. But in these poems it emerges more powerfully than it had yet appeared, and they are at the beginning of the realistic, sophisticated, disillusioned analysis of eroticism which has continued to the present, via Freud, and has drained it of transcendental meaning. The other Romantic tradition of eroticism was an endeavor to promulgate and maintain that transcendental character—at times even transcendent—the redemptive interpretation of eroticism, love as a functional substitute for religion. But transcendentalism shorn of its redemptive character reveals erotic love as an interpretation of the beloved to be the source of the lover's self-valuation, and hence the dependence of the lover upon the beloved for the sense of and ascription of his own value.

And precisely this dependent sense of value which transcendental eroticism conceals is Heine's primarily realistic and analytic interest, one which is often revealed by turning the tables on the beloved and, as so often happens when love is frustrated, refused, and disappointed, turning the power of denigration, that is, denial and withdrawal of value-ascription, against the beloved. The significance of that denigration is that it is the effort of the lover to recover from his dependence upon the beloved for the sense of his own value. This, of course, is central to the Romantic enterprise, as we have seen so often, for precisely that sense of one's own value, arrived at by one's own resources independently of culture and its institutions, is a central problem of Romanticism, almost its primary problem. The search for independence from the beloved is the meaning of the final poem of *Intermezzo*, the determination to bury in forgetfulness the whole experience and its consequence, the poems. Thus it may be said that the problem with which *Intermezzo* is concerned is the problem of how to free oneself from love, how to escape from it without destroying oneself. And that escape, the poems teach, is possible only through experiencing to the full every emotion, every feeling, judgement, pain, suffering, fear, ecstasy, consolation, despair, frustration, humor, irony, illusory fulfillment, hatred, bitterness, denigration of self and beloved—the destructiveness of erotic love—that being in love not merely offers but makes inescapable.

The technique Heine uses is known in popular humor as the punch line, the sudden twist or turn at the end of the poem which puts the experience it is exploring in an entirely new light, the line which shifts the reader from illusion to reality, the line which often reveals eroticism as simply ridiculous, absurd, and demeaning. And in this mode of disillusion poem after poem becomes perfection itself, often enough only eight short lines of perfection, but nevertheless perfection. The poems led a continuous life in European culture, because every mood and subtlety of being in love is to be found in these sixty-five lyrics. For the first time the destructiveness of erotic love to both lover and beloved is brought to light and fully explored. The importance of *Intermezzo* for the development of Romanticism is its synthesis or fusion of analytic realism with the emerging strategy of the virtuoso.

In May 1826, Heine published *Reisebilder I* (*Travel Pictures I*). It contained the work in prose and poetry from the fall of 1823 to the summer of 1825. First came *Die Heimkehr* (*The Return to Home*), originally nearly a hundred short lyrics and five narrative poems, three in ballad form. Second was *Die Harzreise* (*The Trip in the Harz [Mountains]*), the narrative of his walking tour through the Harz in September 1824, written from October 1824 to January 1825. Third came *Die Nordsee* (*The North Sea*), twelve longer poems in free verse, written in the summer of 1825. Of the short lyrics in *Die Heimkehr* it is not necessary to speak, since they continue the theme of the cognitive analysis of love from *Intermezzo*, except for the fact that if anything they are more elegant, subtle, and beautiful—more perfect—than the earlier lyrics. One of the narrative poems is of particular interest, for it is the first appearance of the lyric ironic punch line in narrative. "Donna Clara" deals with a love affair between a Spanish lady and gentleman. Clara keeps returning to her dislike and even detestation of Moors and Jews in spite of the efforts of the gentleman to turn her away from her prejudiced obsessions. Finally, in exasperation, he informs her that he is the son of the Rabbi Israel of Saragossa. This device Heine was to perfect and use with marvelous and even sensational effect in his narrative poems of the Paris period of his life, after 1831.

The most important section of the new book was *Die Harzreise*, which has been enormously popular from the time it was published. (It first appeared in mutilated form in January and February 1826.) In its pages Heine offered a new kind of travel writing, a Romantic kind. To be sure it offered traditional travel writing information about inns and mines and churches and scenery and valleys and mountains, particularly the famous Brocken, the haunt of witches on Midsummer's Eve, made even more famous by Goethe's *Faust I*. But like its partial model, Goethe's *Die Italienische Reise* (*The Italian Journey*), actually put together from letters and diaries and published in 1816 and 1817, Heine's book is as much about himself and his own personality as about anything else. But it differs profoundly from Goethe's book. In typical Enlightenment and non-Romantic modality Goethe was concerned with presenting a coherent construct of himself. But the charm of Heine's travel books is precisely the opposite. He offers instead a continuously varying version of himself, or, more precisely, a presentation of his constantly varying responses, a picture of a modern, unstable, ever-varying personality. It was the opposite of what still dominates personalized travel writing, the responses to different scenes of a stable and coherent personality. Rather, what Heine responds to elicits varying aspects and factors of a complex and incoherent personality, one characterized by discontinuities rather than continuities. The book retains its charm today and is even enhanced because now it is consistent with the extreme modern notion of personality as a randomly assembled package of interpreted and accepted and misinterpreted and violated and negated cultural instructions.

It is of interest and importance to the development of Romanticism that in these same early years of the 1820s there was an English equivalent to what Heine achieved in *Die Harzreise*. From 1820 to 1823 Charles Lamb published a series of essays in *The London Magazine*. They were collected and published as *The Essays of Elia* in two series, 1823 and 1833. Like Heine, Lamb elaborated a discontinuous personality package, both within each essay and from essay to essay. The reality of what he accomplished is often enough concealed and distorted by the word "whimsical," as if this conception of personality were odd and out of the ordinary, when in fact it is the norm of the personality package. There are a few more than fifty of Lamb's Elia essays, which thus constitute a series or Romantic cycle from which the reader, or at least the alert reader, creates an apprehension of the discontinuous complexity of Lamb's personality. And this gives us a clue to the source of the same kind of personality in Heine's travel book. In the *Intermezzo* and in *Die Heimkehr* Heine also presents a personality in discontinuous variability, one which the reader must assemble as best he can in an apprehension, if he is careful, of an infinitely varying, unstable, and subtly discontinuous individual, one which even wishes to reject and bury his experiences, to transcend them. *Die Harzreise* Heine himself broke off and called a fragment, adding a postlude which has almost nothing to do with the journey itself. From the point of view given by Lamb's essays and by the two series of Heine's lyrics, *Die Harzreise* can itself be fittingly understood as a series of separable passages forming not a continuous account of a journey but a cycle of responses to changing landscapes and people and groups of people, as with the incomparable account of the drunken students in the inn on the Brocken. One modern critic has attempted to connect all of Heine's early writings, up to the time he left for Paris, as the attempt to create a "persona," a self-portrait coherent and acceptable to the portraitist. But that judgment is a misapprehension of what Heine was trying to do, which was far more Romantic and therefore far more modern.

Instead, these ten years or so of poetry and prose were an attempt *not* to create a coherent "persona," to avoid that trap which converts us all into the commonplace, to escape exactly what his Uncle Salomon wanted him to be. In the endeavor to have a constant and acceptable value-ascribing notion of ourselves we become continuously less interesting as we grow older. Only those who accept the personality as an incoherent package can avoid that fate. Heine avoided that fate, and has bewildered his commentators and critics ever since, convinced as they have been that their task was to create a coherent explanatory construct of Heine's life and writings. From the time of Lamb and Heine the Romantic tradition has continuously been concerned with accepting and exploiting the personality as fundamentally incoherent, inconsistent, and, simply, messy.

What Heine had accomplished in his poetry and prose through *Die Harzreise* made it possible for him to create something truly innovative and culturally emergent in the poems of *Die Nordsee*. This is again a cycle of poems, and again devoted to Heine's comprehension of himself as variable, incoherent, discontinuous. And the poems, as is to be expected, show an even greater ease in this self-manifestation than he had yet achieved. They were original in two further ways. First, they are almost the first important series of German poems about the sea, inspired as they were by Heine's summer vacations in Nordeney and

Helgoland. And second, they are in free verse. The kind of poetry he had already written and was to write in the future consisted for the most part of short lines in four-line stanzas. In these, constant instability is maintained by a fairly consistent alternation between lines that end with a stressed syllable and lines that end with an unstressed syllable, an alternation between aggressive rhythm and a rhythm that reduces its aggressiveness into a passive acceptance of hindrance to aggressiveness and of stabilized and conventionalized cultural guidance. Moreover, the rhythm is almost always duple, that is, alternating between stressed and unstressed syllables. The first thing to be noticed about the rhythm of the new poems is that the alternating rhythm is abandoned for rhythms that vary between duple and triple (one stressed syllable to two unstressed syllables) in an unpredictable modality. Thus the fairly reliable rhythmic stability of the early verse is abandoned for something more flexible as well as more unstable. This instability is further multiplied by the unpredictability of line length, both in the number of syllables per line and the number of stresses.

This instability and unpredictability brings out the peculiar advantage and power of free verse. Traditional verse is, to be sure, organized in phrases, but there is an implied regularity to the phrase, either one phrase per line, as in most of Heine's previous verse, or two phrases per line separated by a caesura the implication of which is that it normally comes in the middle of the line. In free verse, particularly as Heine practices it, there is no predictability for the caesura, which may or may not appear. There is no norm, just as there is no norm for the line, which may be short or long without caesura, or may have several caesuras. In short, the measure of the verse is organized around the phrase, and this makes it, if it is read with sensitivity and understanding, highly effective. For each phrase, whether long or short, requires in the reading a constantly varying release of energy and signifies a constantly varying length of a span or arc of behavior. Free verse is a semiotic transformation of such arcs. What it constructs is a portrait of the instability of energy release and by implication the instability of personality itself. It is not surprising, therefore, that in the later twentieth century the most popular nineteenth-century poets as models have been those who wrote in free verse, such as Whitman, though there have been many others, and that Heine's free verse should have been an increasingly popular model for verse writing.

Indeed, writing in anything but free verse has now become rare, for today there is a full acceptance at higher cultural levels of what Heine and Lamb were almost the first to understand and establish the literary norms of, the instability and incoherence of the human personality. Today the personality has indeed been analytically dismantled. Of this analysis Freud has been a major purveyor, for Freud is in the very center of the emergent thrust of the Romantic tradition.

ALEXANDER PUSHKIN (1798–1837)

Alexander Pushkin was born in an old aristocratic family which had lost most of its wealth, though his mother and father continued to attempt to live in a high style they could no longer afford. From childhood he was exposed to the total disparity between social pretensions and miserable income, a discord that may perhaps account for his subsequent compulsive and foolish gambling. It must be acknowledged, to be sure, that compulsive, idiotic gambling was endemic in the upper classes of Europe throughout the eighteenth century and well into the nineteenth. His mother disliked her second son, but his father and his uncle at least had the merit of being writers. Young Pushkin was given access to his father's library, and by the time he was twelve he was extremely well read and had perhaps already conceived the ambition of becoming a poet. And in fact he became the first Russian writer of importance to attempt to support himself by his writing. His reading, of course, was predominantly in French literature, since the Russian aristocracy not only had little literature in their own language but were so Francophile as to speak French better than Russian, and certainly to write it better. One of Pushkin's major achievements was to establish Russian as a viable and flexible literary language. But that was in the future. For the time being he was, culturally and literarily speaking, a product of the French pre-Revolutionary Enlightenment.

That cultural situation was hardly changed by his 1811 entrance into a newly founded lycée, placed in a wing of the great palace at Tarskoe Selo, near St. Petersburg. The idea for that new school was the czar's. Alexander I's notion was the creation of an educational institution for the children of the nobility, who would in time become the officers of the Russian state. Pushkin was probably admitted because only the lesser and impoverished nobility was interested; the superior nobility knew that better education could be found in various private schools in St. Petersburg and by employing tutors. While Pushkin was at Tarskoe Selo two events of the highest importance for his future and Russia's took place. First was Napoleon's invasion of Russia and his overwhelming defeat and the destruction of his army. That gave Russians a new cultural and national and political self-confidence. That was in 1812. The second event happened in 1814 and 1815. The defeat of

Napoleon meant the occupation of Paris by the allied armies. The result was that Russian army officers encountered an advanced, sophisticated, and liberal Western culture. They returned to Russia enflamed with the notion of converting the autocracy into a liberal monarchy or even a republic. And it was this group that Pushkin encountered and mingled with when he left the lycée in 1817 and was appointed to the lowest grade of the Russian bureaucracy in the Ministry of Foreign Affairs. In a very short time he became well known for his liberal verses, circulated in typical Russian fashion (typical even today) in manuscript and by memorization. In fact these early poems were so liberal that in 1820 he was exiled to Bessarabia in extreme southeastern Russia. Because of the intercession of various friends and influential individuals he at least escaped, though narrowly, being sent to Siberia.

A month before he was exiled he had finished his first major work, *Ruslan and Lyudmila,* published not long after he left St. Petersburg. It was an immediate and sensational success, not surprisingly, for it was no more culturally emergent than his political liberalism. It was modeled on Ariosto and on Voltaire's *La Pucelle,* and the only remotely modern touch was that it made fun of the late eighteenth-century Gothicism, the *Romantik,* which had minimally penetrated Russian literary life and culture. The material was derived from Russian folktales, but the treatment was purely Western. To be sure, the poem is of the utmost elegance, wit, half-mocking eroticism, and superb prosodic competence. Its continued popularity led to Glinka's opera, produced in 1842, the first of a number of operas derived from and directly transformed from Pushkin's works, an attestation of the fact that in the 1830s he began to be recognized as a Russian classic and the founder of modern Russian literature. This vein of mock or comic epic Pushkin was to continue to explore for several years. In 1821 he wrote *Gavriiliada* and *Tsar Nikita and his Forty Daughters,* both technically accomplished, both still in an eighteenth-century manner, and both mildly obscene. The first was not published until after his death and the second was preserved only by its memorization by Pushkin's brother, Lev. The *Gavriiliada* circulated in manuscript and created such scandal that Pushkin denied its authorship, but in 1828 he had to confess to the czar. Nicholas I, happily, suppressed the whole affair. The poem ends with Mary's self-congratulations that she had been had by Satan, by the archangel Gabriel, and by God, all in one day. The other poem relates how the forty daughters of Tsar Nikita, born without an essential anatomical factor (to be as coy as Pushkin), were properly and completely outfitted. Both of these poems were written after Pushkin had already been swept away by Byron's verse tales and had started to write his own Byronic narratives.

The two poems are symptomatic of what is so often encountered in the nineteenth century—an individual who simultaneously displays both the culture of the Enlightenment and that of Romanticism. Cultural strata, as we have seen, are to be found in the incoherent behavior of the same individual.

A chance encounter in Ekaterinoslav in southern Russia (now Dnepropetrovsk) was responsible for Pushkin's discovery of Byron. He arrived there sick and soon became sicker. He was rescued by General Raevsky and his family, and the kindly General Inzov, to whose staff Pushkin had been assigned and who was made responsible for Pushkin's proper behavior, permitted him to travel with the Raevsky family to the Caucasus. The family was devoted to Byron, who began to be available to Russians in French prose translations as early as 1817. Moreover, one of the Raevsky sons had self-consciously become a Byronic character whom Pushkin in a later poem, after he had escaped his influence, was to call the Demon. On the way back from the Caucasus Pushkin and the Raevsky group visited the Crimea, and in September by way of Odessa Pushkin rejoined General Inzov in Kishinev. There he was to stay until July 1823. During these years he composed his Byronic poems, *The Prisoner of the Caucasus* (published in 1822), *The Bandit Brothers* (fragments published in 1825), *The Fountain of Bakhchisaray* (published in 1824), and *The Gypsies* (published in 1827). And there also he began writing *Evgeny Onegin*.

None of these Byronic poems is very important, though from *The Prisoner* to *The Gypsies* there is certainly an improvement. It would be inaccurate to state that Pushkin was merely imitating Byron or doing what he could with a fashion that was sweeping Europe. The alienated Byronic hero was the most popular Romantic figure and was to reappear in various avatars throughout the century. And it is not difficult to understand why, for the Byronic hero is the most easily grasped emblem of the failure of a culture to maintain the individual's sense of the value of existence and of his own value. So Pushkin's struggle with the figure is an attempt to understand him, to come to terms with what may be best understood as the figure's cultural usefulness, as well as the limitations of that usefulness and the need to transcend the figure's limitations. This effort by Pushkin must be related to the constant Russian problem, the need to assimilate the West and at the same time to maintain Russia's separateness from the West, to maintain Russianness. That split in Russian culture, still obtaining today, was to manifest itself in the conflict between the Westerners and Slavophiles. Up to his encounter with Byron, Pushkin was man of the Enlightenment and of the Enlightenment's interpretation and understanding of Renaissance and

Baroque culture. It would have been impossible for one of his intelligence and sensitivity not to recognize the Byronic challenge to that culture, its witness to and affirmation of that culture's failure. For Pushkin had himself felt the failure of that culture, its inability to withstand the increasing oppressiveness of Alexander I, his own exile, and the revelation of the superficiality of the liberalism in which he had exulted in the St. Petersburg years of 1817 to 1820, when he was just as concerned with playing the part of the brilliant young man about town.

In his exile he was in a way repeating Childe Harold's flight from England and Byron's own exile. Yet the exiles of the protagonists of the Southern Poems, as they are known, occur in a situation quite different from the situation of Byron's own heroes. The prisoner of the Caucasus is a Russian captive who admires the noble and primitive life of his Circassian captors and endeavors, through love of a Circassian girl, to enter that culture. But he fails to do so, as the girl understands. She frees him, he escapes, and she thows herself into the river. *The Bandit Brothers* is negligible. In *The Fountain of Bakhchisaray* Maria, a captured Polish girl, cannot respond to the love of Girey, the Tatar Khan, whose palace, Bakchisaray, is in the very center of the Crimea. Her rival, Zarema, a Georgian girl, the favorite of the Khan before the arrival of Maria, manages to get Maria killed and is herself killed. Returning from war, the khan builds the fountain in memory of Maria. Neither Girey nor Maria can reach each other across the cultural abyss that divides them. In *The Gypsies* Aleko, sought for some unnamed crime (a very Byronic motive), takes refuge with the wandering gypsies and becomes the lover of Zemfira. At first Aleko adapts successfully to the free gypsy life, but when Zemfira, tiring of him, takes another lover he kills both of them. Zemfira's father, asserting that Aleko cannot understand gypsy ways, expels him from the tribe, abandoning him on the steppes of southern Russia. Thus the theme of these poems is less exile than culture conflict. The poems are Pushkin's strategy for displacing and thus understanding the culture conflict he felt between Russia and the West and also the conflict between his eighteenth-century culture and the Byronic rejection of that culture.

He wrote *The Gypsies* from 1823 to 1825, revising it until 1827; it was published in May of that year. But he also started *Evgeny Onegin* in the fall of 1823, finishing in that year the first chapter and publishing it on 10 February 1825. By the time *The Gypsies* was published he had completed the first five chapters of *Onegin*. Chapter II appeared in 1826, Chapter III in 1827, and Chapters IV and V in 1828. Thus while he was working on the Aleko poem he was also working on the Onegin poem.

And culture conflict and culture transcendence are central themes of the major work. Although he did not finish the poem until 1830, publishing Chapter VI in 1828, VII in 1830, VIII in 1832, and the complete poem in 1833, on 23 March, it is to the point to consider the whole poem in this chapter, for the problem of the poem emerged early in the work.

Before endeavoring to grasp the central issues of *Onegin*, however, it is necessary to consider two other works written while he was working on his major poem, *Boris Godunov*, a historical drama or dramatic poem written in 1824 and 1825 but because of the czar's opposition not published until 1830, and *Count Nulin*, written in a few days in 1825 and published in 1828.

The influence of Shakespeare on *Boris Godunov* is obvious, and Pushkin himself pointed it out. But there is a more important influence, that of Walter Scott, whose novels Pushkin began to read in French as early as his stay in Kishinev. Because, it is reasonably certain, of Scott's historicism, Pushkin based his dramatic poem on the most up-to-date Russian history, indeed, the first history of Russia that deserves the name, Nikolai Karamzin's *History of the Russian State*, published in twelve volumes from 1818 to 1826. The early volumes contain the story of Boris Godunov. So dependent is Pushkin on Karamzin that the poem, not to speak of the extracts from it used in Mussorgsky's opera, produced in 1873, is barely comprehensible to the Western reader without elaborate notes. Here is visible what we have seen before, the conjunction of historicism and the reverse of the historicist coin, realism. The work is set in the Russian Time of Troubles, between the end of the dynasty of Rurik and the establishment of the Romanov dynasty. A pretender to the throne, having persuaded the Polish monarch and nobility to help him, not because they believe him to be the true heir but simply because his pretensions give them a chance and excuse to attack Russia, succeeds in defeating Boris' armies and, Boris having conveniently died, seizes the throne and has Boris' children killed.

The drama is concerned with the successful attack of the Catholic West on Orthodox Russia. What for a Russian lies in back of and propels the foreground events is the sense of culture conflict between Russia and the West, the sense that Russia is always under the threat of attack by the West, both by the West's armies and by its culture, a feeling that exists today in spite of the irony that Marxism was a Western importation. Thus Pushkin generalized the problem of culture conflict which he felt so deeply and which had so affected his life. His awareness of culture as the source of personality, understandable through historical awareness, is almost Hegelian in its intensity, though Hegel had not yet had much impact on Russian culture, at least not the impact it was to have in the 1830s.

Boris Godunov has a wonderful realism, particularly in the crowd scenes, modeled on Shakespeare but if anything an improvement. Yet the other side of historicism's coin, realism, which was playing an immensely important role in *Onegin,* is most clearly understood in *Count Nulin.* To grasp the peculiar significance of this poem it is necessary to return to July 1823, when Pushkin was transferred from Kishinev and the control of General Inzov to Odessa and the control of General Vorontsov. Here he was able once more to enjoy what he had missed so since he had been forced to leave St. Petersburg—theater, ballet, and above all opera. Odessa then had an excellent opera company which produced what all of Europe was raging about, the operas of Rossini. Pushkin too embraced the enthusiasm for Rossini. For the first time he encountered the elegance, the charm, the ebullience, the aggressive brilliance which, as we have seen, was Rossini's peculiar contribution to the Romantic tradition, and it is easy to believe that this encounter with Rossini's style had an impact upon Pushkin's. But the Odessa world of pleasure was not to be available to Pushkin for long. He did not get along at all with his superior and mentor, partly because he either seduced or appeared to seduce or appeared to be trying to seduce Vorontsov's wife. It took no great trouble for the powerful and experienced general to get Pushkin dismissed from service and exiled, in his father's care, to a family estate, Mikhaylovskoe, deep in the country west of Moscow and south of St. Petersburg in the neighborhood of the ancient city of Pskov. He arrived there in August 1824. Now he was truly in exile, officially and for the time being with no possibility of leaving. The result? He was even more productive than he had been in the detested Kishinev. He also had a new life to examine, the life of the petty Russian noble living on his estate, the life of the Russian country squire.

By the time Pushkin left Odessa he had completed the first two chapters of *Onegin* and part of Chapter III. At Mikhaylovskoe he completed that chapter and by January 1826 had completed Chapter IV. Between Chapters III and IV he composed *Boris Godunov* and *Count Nulin,* which he wrote on 13 and 24 December 1825, that is, between the first completion of Chapter IV and the revision completed in January 1826. *Nulin* can be regarded as a direct outgrowth or consequence of Chapter IV, that part of *Onegin* specifically devoted to country life. Count Nulin is traveling through the countryside when his carriage breaks down. He is offered shelter in a nearby country house. The master is out hunting, and the charming mistress entertains the count to dinner and flirts with him. Nulin interprets this as a direct invitation. He invades her bedroom. Instead of surrendering the lady gives him a good slap in the face. But the next morning all is peaceful and cheerful, the master having returned, and Count Nulin goes on his way. Here two themes of realism are intertwined. What would have happened, Pushkin asked himself, if Lucrece—he was reading Shakespeare's poem—had given Tarquin a good slap? The other aspect of realism consists of the perfectly observed and recorded detail of life in a country manor. Not a word is wasted. A whole way of life is effortlessly summoned. The poem has the perfection of Alexander Pope's *The Rape of the Lock,* composed with at least the equal of Pope's mastery. The literary source for that realism was Byron's *Don Juan,* Pushkin himself avowing that *Onegin* was in the genre of Byron's poem. Another source was Scott, where he found it allied with the historicism which he employed in *Boris Godunov.* Pushkin is the source of the realism of the nineteenth-century Russian novelists.

Pushkin called *Evgeny Onegin* a "novel in verse," but it is hardly a novel in the ordinary sense. In Chapter I, for example, only a few stanzas are devoted to the plot. And this is very nearly the proportion throughout the poem. For the bulk is devoted to commentary by Pushkin on what little does happen. Pushkin himself is a character in the poem and presents himself as a friend of Onegin, whom he meets in St. Petersburg in Chapter I and was to meet again at Odessa in the discarded Chapter VIII, "Onegin's Journey." The story or plot amounts to this: Onegin inherits the estate of his uncle and settles down there. A young neighbor, fresh from a German university, Lenski, becomes his friend. Lenski is in love with Olga, the younger daughter of a nearby family. The older daughter is Tatiana, who falls in love with Onegin and writes him of her passion. He tells her that marriage is not for him. At a birthday ball for Olga Onegin flirts with her, infuriating Lenski, who challenges him to a duel. The duel takes place, against Onegin's wishes, but he is propelled by custom. Onegin kills Lenski. He leaves on his travels. Olga marries a young officer. Tatiana's mother takes her to Moscow to enter society and find a husband. Tatiana marries a famous and rich general. Onegin returns, is astonished to find the shy country girl transformed into an elegant society lady, falls in love with her, writes to her of his love, is rebuffed—and that ends the poem.

There is some indication that Pushkin thought of continuing the poem, perhaps having Onegin join the Decembrists, that group of young liberal officers who in December 1825 attempted a rebellion against Nicholas I, who had just assumed the throne. It was the first important Russian political event of the nineteenth century, for it was the first effort to free Russia from the czarist autocracy. The Decembrists, some executed and some exiled to Siberia, have been Russian liberal heroes ever since. But as we shall see, in spite of the brilliance of the fragments of the continuation that have been recovered, Pushkin was wise to abandon his plan. No doubt he was inspired by the unfulfilled plan of Byron to have Don Juan end up in the French Revolution, again a plan that would have done extreme violence to the marvelous incomplete poem we now have.

For Pushkin does not write *Onegin* to tell a story. The first glimpse of what he was after is the fact that the poem begins in 1819 and ends in the spring of 1825. Though concerned with recent history it is nevertheless a historical poem. The only real excuse for continuing it to the Decembrist revolt, the stanzas of which were composed in 1830, was to continue and emphasize the historicist theme. But that would have been inappropriate, for the history that Pushkin is concerned with is the history of personality change and the part culture plays in personality transformation and self-transcendence. This is why Pushkin places himself in the poem as not only the narrator of what happened to Onegin but, far more important, to explain why it happened. Thus Pushkin dramatizes his function as the author of the poem—the analytic comprehension of Onegin's life. And that analysis is dramatized by means of presenting the reader with information about Onegin's reading.

Chapter I is devoted to Onegin's life in St. Petersburg as a fashionable young man about town. But he is weary of everything, of balls, of operas, of ballet girls, of mistresses. So he is not at all loath to bury himself in the remote countryside. There he reeducates himself, or perhaps educates himself for the first time. He reads the works of eighteenth-century liberal writers and even endeavors to apply some of those liberal ideas to his serfs. This is his first transformation. His second comes from his friendship with Lenski, fresh from the West, filled with late eighteenth-century Schillerian idealism. But Onegin sees the sentimentality behind this. Hence his rejection of Tatiana is reasonable, for she has been exposed to and victimized by the sentimental authors of the eighteenth century, particularly by Samuel Richardson and his tales of Clarissa Harlowe and Sir Charles Grandison. But his world-weary attitude toward Tatiana is partly mysterious—until Tatiana visits his manor house after he has left. She persuades the housekeeper to let her into his study, and there she discovers what he has been reading. It is above all others Byron. Onegin's reading has transformed him from a late eighteenth-century liberal into a modern Byronic figure, the most culturally advanced figure available to him—and to Pushkin during his early years at Kishinev. And as a Byronic, typically Romantic, wanderer Onegin goes on his travels through Russia, even as far as the Caucasus and of course the Crimea and Odessa, just as Pushkin had only a couple of years before Onegin set out on his journey in those admirable stanzas which Pushkin decided to cancel. Romantic wandering is the symbolization of what the Romantics discovered to be so important to cultural transcendence and to self-transcendence, randomization of thinking. For Pushkin was to invent a more subtle and more profound investigation of that randomization.

And now Onegin comes to Moscow, encounters Tatiana as a mature and beautiful society lady, married to a famous general, and falls in love with her. She refuses to answer his letters. So he takes up reading again, but this time a mishmash of seventeenth-, eighteenth-, and nineteenth-century authors. Instead of symbolizing randomization Pushkin presents it directly, and with extraordinary perspicacity presents its consequence—cognitive overload, the precondition to significant cognitive breakthrough or innovation. The effect is a release of Onegin's imagination in what have been called the finest and most penetrating stanzas in the poem. His imagination is indeed released. He almost goes mad. He becomes not a poet but, Pushkin tells us, like a poet, one free from commitment to social roles. And so he goes straightforwardly to Tatiana. He finds her reading his letters, and in tears. Proudly she rejects him on the grounds of her honor as the wife of a respectable man. She accepts completely the role, the self-conception, that society and the culture have imposed upon her, but she is still in love with Onegin. She has experienced—and this is the contrastive point Pushkin is making—no transformation, no self-transcendence. But Onegin has, through the release of the imagination, through becoming like a poet, and that grasp of the nature of the poet saves him from insanity.

So Pushkin asserts the capacity of self-transformation, of self-transcendence to free oneself from and escape from the roles that society and culture, including literary and philosophical culture, entice us to accept and so stabilize our personalities. That is why Onegin's love for Tatiana is completely frustrated not by a woman but by sociocultural rules and behavioral modes. Once the individual is thoroughly alienated by the transcending release of the imagination, only in that release can value be sought for and experienced. *Evgeny Onegin* was Pushkin's demonstration of what Onegin—who had gone through the stages Pushkin himself had gone through—finally learned. But because Onegin was not a poet, there was nothing he could do with his release into freedom and value. That is why Pushkin abandons him to the sound of the General's approaching footsteps. But Pushkin *was* a poet.

He could use that freedom. He could embody and exemplify that value in his poem. The technical accomplishment of *Evgeny Onegin* can be appreciated only by someone who knows Russian, and knows it well. It is prodigious, Rossinian in its virtuosity. Like others of his generation Pushkin had discovered that a superb artistic virtuosity, a competence beyond anything that had yet been achieved, was the most powerful mode for establishing and experiencing value created from one's own resources. And that is what "creativity," in the Romantic tradition, really means. Pushkin had achieved this in isolation and exile and, as we shall see in subsequent chapters, continued to achieve it under the burden of political oppression.

FRANZ GRILLPARZER (1791–1872)

For many years it has been said over and over again that Romanticism is fundamentally undramatic, and that that is why the major Romantic writers were able to produce only closet dramas which, though often of considerable or even high literary and poetic value, were unsuccessful on the stage. This notion, however, ignores the enormously successful opera of Romanticism, beginning with Rossini and including two of the most theatrically successful composers who have ever lived, Verdi and Wagner. It is also to ignore the superb plays, successful in the living theater even today, of the Viennese Franz Grillparzer.

To understand Grillparzer's success it is useful to make a distinction between the dramatic and the theatrical. The former term is used in response to music, to fiction, to poetry, to behavioral interaction, and so on. Whether there is a meaning common to all these uses is a problem that may be postponed for the time being, until we come to the music of Schubert. The second term, theatrical, can be limited in its appropriateness to what is effective, for whatever reason, on the stage. And this is a very complicated matter, for when we consider the stage semiotically the condition that leaps to our attention is that the stage simultaneously uses a number of semiotic systems. Literature can exploit different and various semiotic systems only by transforming them into language. It has only one semiotic system at its disposal, with the exception of intonation when poetry and prose are read aloud and with the very minor and relatively unimportant exception of poetry printed as a visual design. In stage situations the following semiotic systems can be easily discriminated: language (that is, the script), intonation (that is, all the various signs available in verbal utterance), facial expression, movements of the extremities of the body, movements of the trunk and of the body as a whole, makeup, costume, movements of the complete costumed and made-up body through the space of the stage, rapidity of such movements and of the movements of segments of the body, as well as of speaking, the enormously various semiotic possibilities of the setting, particularly of the significance of space, and the equally varied possibilities of the properties (such as furniture, lamps, books, bibelots, pictures, and so, as well as costume properties), lighting, and music. For a literary genius to expect his play to be theatrically successful is obviously more than a little absurd, unless—and this is the telling point—he has had a vast experience in the theater, preferably an experience that involves not merely being a spectator but actually working in the theater in some capacity or other. He must be not only a master of language but must be equally sensitive to all the visual and aural semiotic possibilities and practices of the actual theater. A good theatrical director is one who can correlate and make effective all the semiotic possibilities of the production he is bringing into theatrical viability.

Once we have realized the semiotic complexity and the almost unlimited resources of the stage it becomes easy to understand why the history of the theater has brought forth so few plays worth reading outside of the theater—as, that is, literature, verbal semiosis without the rich integration into the complex semiotic situation of the stage. The vast majority of successful theater pieces are of no artistic interest outside of the theater situation. Indeed, it is surprising that, almost by accident, the theater has produced at the most a couple of hundred literary masterpieces. The Greeks, quite understandably, were interested in preserving only a very few of the innumerable plays Greek culture produced. It is not surprising that there has been but one Shakespeare. But it is surprising that there has been even one. Successful theater can exist without a good script, or even any, as in the ballet. The term "playwright" is well chosen, "a builder of plays," and to be a successful playwright requires vast theater experience.

Now it is true that Grillparzer did not have any theatrical experience from the inside, though his uncle was for a time secretary to the Burgtheater. His father was a lawyer, rather withdrawn and forbidding, but his mother was a Sonnleithner, a family conspicuous in Vienna for its musical and general cultural interests and activities. The Napoleonic wars created considerable economic difficulties in Vienna, and Grillparzer's family felt grave financial problems, especially after the father's death in 1809. After Grillparzer left the university he spent a few years as a private tutor. At last in 1814 he at least gained a living by becoming a civil servant in the customs department.

He had already started to write plays. His first major effort, *Blanka von Castilien*, rejected by the Burgtheater, was modelled on Schiller's *Die Braut von Messina*, itself an only moderately successful effort to create modern tragedy on the model of Greek tragedy. His next attempt, however, was a sensational success. It was a totally different kind of play. Instead of being based on a literary tragedy only mildly successful on the stage, it was modelled on the plays of the popular theater. The best clue to Grillparzer's grasp and conception of theatrical drama is to be found in his remark that though Goethe was a great poet he was worthless as a playwright. The clue to the success of *Die Ahnfrau* (*The Ancestress*) is to be found in Grillparzer's assiduous attendance at the most popular theater of all, the theater for which Mozart had written *The Magic Flute*, the theater in the Leopoldstadt. From that popular theater and other similar theaters in the outskirts of Vienna were to emerge Grillparzer's theatrical contemporaries, both enormously successful in this theater world of magic, ghost, spirits, fairies, and theatrical spectacle, Ferdinand Raimund (1790–1836) and Johann Nestroy (1802–1862). Both of these men were able to raise this popular theater to a much higher cultural level without ever changing its basic character. Grillparzer himself was to write a serious play in the style of the popular theater, *Der Traum ein Leben* (*A Dream is Life*), first produced in 1824. *Die Ahnfrau* is a ghost play. The ancestress, killed by her husband for infidelity, is condemned to haunt the family until all her descendants are dead. Grillparzer wrote the play in a few weeks in 1816 and it was produced on 31 January 1817.

It was a sensational success, not only in Vienna but throughout Germany. It is not to be taken, of course, very seriously, and culturally it is far more a work of late eighteenth-century Enlightenment "Gothicism" than of Romanticism. Nevertheless it was a work of great importance for Grillparzer's future, for in it he demonstrated with total success that he had learned the difference between theater and drama, that he had grasped the fact that in the theater the visual is more important than the verbal, and that only in the greatest plays are they equal. One happy effect of the success of the rather notorious *Die Ahnfrau* was that he was granted a regular salary by the burgtheater and acquired a powerful ministerial patron who was able to put pressure on Grillparzer's government department to grant him various favors, time off to work on his plays and to travel.

The success of his first produced play stimulated him to try again, and once again he made as rapid a change from his second play as his second play had been from his first. For his third play he turned to Greece, not its mythology but to, one might say, its literary history, to the story of Sappho and her suicide for love of Phaon. For some years Grillparzer had made a careful study of the seventeenth-century Spanish drama of Lope da Vega and Calderon, as well as of Shakespeare and especially Racine, for whom he had an unlimited admiration. All of these influences as well as the popular theater went into *Sappho*. Once again it was a success from the time it was first performed on April 21, 1818.

It is clear that what Grillparzer set out to do was to so construct a play that an explanation for Sappho's suicide would be forthcoming. Yet modern commentators have often been puzzled as to why Grillparzer's Sappho leaps from the Leucadian cliff. Sappho has fallen in love with Phaon. She wishes to live an ordinary life as well as that of an exalted artist. But Phaon, a harmless young man who is overpowered by Sappho but too awestruck to think of her as a woman, a much older woman, falls in love with her slave Melitta. The two lovers escape the island, with Sappho's permission, and Sappho leaps to her death. As the exalted artist she is also the Romantic alienated artist. She dies because her desire to reconcile two divergent modes of living is impossible of achievement. The life of poet and the life of ordinary woman are irreconcilable. Phaon's love for an ordinary girl has shown Sappho that she cannot cross the abyss that art places between the individual and ordinary life, but she can no longer tolerate the absolute aloneness of her existence as poet. Her suicide is a response to her perception of an irresolvable dilemma.

The importance of *Sappho* to the development of Romanticism is very great. The Romantics we have examined so far in this volume and in *The Birth of Romanticism* have been concerned with creating a new culture, a new style of art and even of life. Grillparzer is the first we have encountered who quite deliberately set out to rescue and preserve for Romanticism the cultural resources of the past, and to make those resources usable. That effort was a factor in Romanticism's historical consciousness, and it was to be a continuing problem and ambition for the Romantic tradition. Grillparzer's first step we have already seen, learning the lesson of the popular theater. Often in the history of Romanticism the artist has turned for renewal and for insight into the vital center of his art to the art of the people, the art of peasants, the culture of the laborer. This undertaking can be best understood as a factor in the realism in Romantic tradition, a realism which we have seen to be endemic from the very beginning of Romanticism. In essence, Grillparzer had asked himself, What is the reality of the theater? And that reality he had found in the popular theater. Thus *Sappho* is not only a highly readable play; it is also an effective and immediately successful theater piece. As one reads it, it comes to vivid visual life as the plays of, for example, Schiller let alone Goethe do not, or do so rarely. Grillparzer had learned from the Leopoldstadt the lesson of props, of careful and detailed stage directions, of telling the director and the actors where and how to move. Thus the play has the feeling of freshness and the modern. This effect is aided by the versification, which often violates its basic pattern, and by the diction, which includes words and expressions not hitherto admitted on the serious stage. In reading it one can hardly help visualizing it. For the ideal reader of a play is one who performs the role of director. *Sappho* is effective and realistic because it is a theater piece, that is, an interaction of bodies, and because it uses props not as decor but as factors in the flow of action—roses and a dagger.

The second step in rescuing for the purposes—even the salvation— of the present was in the choice of a famous and often used subject, which Grillparzer presented in almost classic manner—unity of time, place, and treatment—another example of rescuing the past. Yet the play has nothing of the stateliness of the high drama of the seventeenth and eighteenth centuries. It was successful because it looked at an old and well-known, even well-worn, story through modern eyes. Thus the past is revitalized, but the present is given new vitality by revealing its continuity with and relation to the past. Grillparzer had the extraordinary ability to make the remote past seem contemporary. He does so by renewing the classic drama with the truly theatrical resources of the popular stage.

For his next effort he turned to the often treated story of Medea, inspired by seeing a performance of Cherubini's opera *Médée* (see *The Birth of Romanticism*). In the theater, in both plays and opera, the legend of Medea had traditionally been limited to her rejection by Jason, her murder of her children, and her flight. Grillparzer, however, began with the arrival of Phrixus in Colchis, bearing the Golden Fleece. Instead of a single play he wrote a trilogy, *Das goldene Vliess* (*The Golden Fleece*), consisting of *Das Gastfreund* (*The Host*), *Die Argonauten*, and *Medea*. He worked on the trilogy in 1819 and 1820, interrupted by the suicide of his mother. It was produced on 26 and 27 March 1821, and was less successful than his two preceding plays. Cherubini and his eighteenth- and seventeenth-century predecessors were concerned in Baroque and Enlightenment manner with the passions of Medea. Grillparzer was concerned with understanding Medea, with explaining her. Thus he tells the whole story, using once again the resources of the truly theatrical. The rapidity of the action, the irregularity of the versification of the Colchians as opposed to the regularity of that of the Greeks and of Medea part of the time when she is in Greece, the effective use of props and costumes, the stage directions—all these give the trilogy not the atmosphere of a legend but as with *Sappho* the sense that we are reading or at a performance looking at something that once had really happened, at history, not legend. Medea, for example, does not end in the traditional manner by flying off in chariot drawn by dragons. Rather, having repossessed the fleece, she bears it off to Delphi to return it to the sacred place whence Phrixus had stolen it. She proves herself morally superior to Jason, the barbarian morally superior to the civilized Greek. At the end she reveals to Jason that his quest for the fleece was only a valueless illusion—a shadow, a dream.

And the explanation that Grillparzer implies for Medea is that her behavior is the result of what today we would call culture shock, the conflict between two utterly different cultural modes. In its way the conflict is the repetition on a larger and more transcendentally generalized scale the conflict that Sappho felt. But Medea does not commit suicide, though she is tempted. Rather, she goes to submit herself to the priests of Delphi, either to become a sacrifice or an outcast. The irresolvable dilemma of Sappho which she resolved by the morally inferior way of suicide has become a cultural dilemma for Medea, one which leads her not to flee from life but to face honestly and with full suffering what she has done, betrayed as she was by Jason, and to recognize the valuelessness of human life. Medea's love for the worthless Jason has led her to despair, wrath, and murder, and finally to a position that is beyond suicide. She failed to understand herself; she failed to understand Jason; and so she has come to understand the destructive potential of humanity. The understanding of Medea that Grillparzer offers is the understanding of human transformation, not self-transcendence but the opposite, self-victimization.

Another category of subsumption makes it possible to comprehend Grillparzer's trilogy at a profounder and, one might say, more Romantic level. That is the category of tragedy. The tragic is a category that has spread from the theater to all of human life, and for good reason. In spite of all the thrashings about of literary criticism and aestheticians, a wall can never be erected between art and life. If that wall were possible art would be no more than a trivial amusement. Art is a response to all of experience, not just to art. When it comes to the spread of the terms tragic and tragedy, we are most likely to utter them in response to a perception and judgment that an individual's aggressive competence has met a hindrance so severe that it has failed and in extreme cases the individual so defeated has died. That is why for centuries it was believed that the only proper protagonist for a tragedy was a great man, preferably a king. Such an individual is supremely competent, or rather his competence is most evident, because he wields and controls supreme political and economic power. Thus Lear is defeated first by his failure to act competently in response to his own perception of his weakness, his failing competence, by the family, by struggles within the family, by the state, that extension of the family, by intrastate rivalry, and finally by interstate conflict, and even by nature itself.

In the eighteenth century, however, it began to be perceived that the middle-class man, the bourgeois, could also be a tragic figure. Grill-parzer's greatness is his discovery in *Das goldene Vliess* of what was to become the source of tragedy in the Romantic tradition, based from the beginning on the alienation of the individual from his culture. In his trilogy the explanation of Medea's tragedy is that that which is most fully human, culture or learned behavior, is in its embodiment in the individual the source of his failure, of his defeat. This point he brings out through Jason, who embodies the failure of Greek civilization. Thus what destroys Medea is not merely the conflict between two cultures but culture itself. Her abject surrender to the priests to whom she leaves the decision about what to do with her is the failure of her personal interpretation and modification of the two cultures she has encountered, the barbarian and the Greek. The play is left with the bitter paradox that the defeated sense of her own value and of the value of existence can be overcome only by submission to the highest level of cultural sanctioning. The ultimate source of the tragic is the failure of the human enterprise itself. The only answer to that predicament is, as Medea says to Jason, to endure the failure.

For his next play Grillparzer turned from treating legend as history to history itself, *König Ottokars Glück und Ende* (*King Otokar's Success and End*), written in 1823 and first performed on 19 February 1825. Like Pushkin's *Boris Godunov* it is more readily understood by citizens of the country in which it was written than by other than Austrians and Germans, for it is concerned with the coming of the Hapsburgs, by origin a Rhineland family, to their possession of Austria. Ottokar was a thirteenth-century king of Bohemia who conquered Austria and the provinces south of it, Styria, Carinthia, and Carniola. The work is the longest of Grillparzer's plays, encompassing twenty years of history. It is also the most Shakespearian, directly influenced by Shakespeare's history plays. It is even more theatrical than they are, having some resemblance to what was soon to emerge, the Romantic historical opera, with its pageants, costumes, and grand encounters of kings and emperors. In spite of its almost too favorable portrait of Rudolf von Haps-burg it was at first denied performance by the increasingly severe and arbitrary censorship of Metternichean Austria. Fortunately it came to the attention of the Empress, who liked it, and production followed. But it was strangely unsuccessful, partly because of the enmity it aroused among the Bohemian population of the Austrian empire. Grillparzer even received threatening letters.

Actually Grillparzer was inspired to write the work by the death of Napoleon in 1821. It is a prime example of Romantic historical analogism, the examination of a contemporary problem by abstracting it from its immediate situation and displacing it into a more comprehensible situation of the past. Grillparzer was interested in exploring and analyzing Napoleon's failure by examining the similar failure of a similar conqueror, though the latter's conquests were on small scale. They were, however, grand for the thirteenth century. What Grillparzer does is to contract the all-embracing explanatory vision of *Das goldene Vliess*, the fundamental failure of human aggressive competence, but one with many analogies, down to a specific historical circumstance. Napoleon and Ottokar were not the only conquerors who were defeated by their very success. What defeats such conquerors, and Ottokar in particular, is confidence in the visibility of their rapid successes. In Grillparzer's play, as in Napoleon's career, that confidence is shown by the conqueror's willingness to sweep all opposition out of his way, to shove brutally anyone out of his way who seems at all a hindrance, beginning with his wife, whom he had married in order to gain control of her inheritance. He is defeated by Rudolf von Hapsburg, who acts more circumspectly, more morally, but only in the sense that he is aware that the viability of success depends upon the cooperation and good will of others. Ottokar is destroyed by blindly accepting what may be called the ideology of certainty and the seduction of success. In thus analyzing the failure of the conqueror, Grillparzer wrote the first great Romantic historical drama.

FRANZ SCHUBERT (1797–1828)

In 1820 Grillparzer encountered in the home of his relation, Ignaz von Sonnleithner, a wonderful young composer, Franz Schubert, whose friend Leopold von Sonnleithner was the son of Ignaz. The occasion was a performance of Schubert's cantata *Prometheus* (D. 451), now lost. The performance was an indication that Schubert was beginning to be known in the musical circles of Vienna, although almost entirely through his songs. He had already been discovered in 1817 by the opera baritone, Franz Vogl, then fifty years old, who became his friend and performed his songs for most of the rest of his life, nearly until his death in 1840. Later in 1820, on 14 June, Schubert's *Singspiel Die Zwillings-brüder* (*The Twin Brothers*, D. 647) was to be performed at the Kärtnertor theater. It was to be the first performed of Schubert's many efforts to write for the stage and except for the incidental music for *Rosamunde* (1823) the last. Yet his greatest achievement was to bring to songs and above all to instrumental music a profoundly innovative high drama.

It was Schubert's good fortune and terribly difficult problem to have been born in a city in which Beethoven was already recognized as the heir of Haydn and Mozart. While he was still an adolescent, Schubert felt that after Beethoven there was nothing to be done. His problem was not to surpass Beethoven in his own line—that would be impossible— but to strike off on a different line, to transcend or at least escape from Beethoven in a direction in which Beethoven had scarcely moved. And young Schubert had the genius and the training. His father was a schoolmaster with his own school. To save money Schubert's brothers and he himself, at times, taught in the father's school. Nevertheless the child's musical genius was recognized by his intelligent father, who taught him the violin, and his eldest brother, Ignaz, who taught him the piano. In short order he told them he had nothing more to learn from them, and so in 1806 or 1807 he was placed under the tuition of Michael Holzer. He soon learned all he could from that respectable but occasionally drunk organist. Fortunately he was accepted as a choirboy in the imperial court chapel, an appointment that meant that he was admitted to the Imperial Royal and City College, where his musical ex-perience and studies were continued, as well as an excellent general education. Eventually the responsibility for his musical development was taken over by Anton Salieri, the friend of Haydn and rival of Mozart (whom he did not poison) and even minor tutor to Beethoven. Even after Schubert left the college in 1813 to take up training to be a teacher, Salieri continued to supervise Schubert's work until the end of 1816.

Schubert taught in his father's school until 1817, when encouraged by his friend Franz von Schober, for a year he attempted an independent life. But early in 1818 he had to return to teaching for six months. Then, however, he accepted the position of music master to the children of Count Johann Esterhazy. After a summer in Hungary he returned to Vienna and began to live with his friend Johann Mayrhofer, a poet many of whose lyrics Schubert set to music. In January 1819 he com-posed *Die Zwillingsbrüder*. That summer he traveled with Vogl and in the winter he worked on his Mass No. 5 (D. 678), not finished until 1822. Early in 1820 he began to work on the unfinished setting of a poetic drama *Lazarus* (D. 689). In June his *Singspiel* received a few per-formances, the result of which was that he was commissioned to write the music to accompany the words for the melodrama *Die Zauberharfe* (*The Magic Harp*, D. 644), presented in August 1820. This was an important work for his future. For the first time he began to write dramatically for the orchestra, and so successfully that the overture is now performed as the overture to the popular *Rosamunde* music. The first immediate result of this venture was a composition of December 1820, a movement and a fragment of another for string quartet, known as the *Quartettsatz* (D. 703). It is the emergence of the mature Schubert, the way out of the trap of Beethoven, Mozart, and Haydn. Through Mayrhofer and other friends he had become familiar with the new Romantic literature of Germany, and soon he was to start reading Scott. He had grasped the task of the Romantics.

To understand this emergence, this genuine cultural transcendence, it is necessary to examine what he had so far accomplished. In bulk it was considerable, though almost none of it was published until much later in the century, long after his death, some not until the 1890s. For voices he had composed four masses, and several dozen pieces of sacred music. He had composed an opera and three *Singspiele* and a half dozen or so fragments of both genres. There were dozens of choral works and dozens of chamber works besides the quartets. And there were several dozen sonatas, fragments of sonatas, individual pieces, dances, and fantasies for piano, both two-hand and four-hand. Had Schubert died in 1820 it is quite possible that little of this mass of music would ever have been published. His instrumental works were a late blossoming of the Viennese classical style of the last years of the eighteenth century. There were dozens of other composers who were writing music of the same sort, though lacking in what had emerged in these works, otherwise not very interesting though certainly not negligible, a wonderful capacity for melodic invention and an even more remarkable grasp of tonality emerging in his truly original capacity for frequent and surprising modulations. Only in the latter could there be said to be something of Romanticism, and perhaps even that can be traced more or less successfully to the late eighteenth-century culture of emotional lability.

Yet to this mass of excellent journeyman work there was one massive exception—songs. Schubert wrote over six hundred songs, including various versions of a number of them, and over half were written from 1811 through 1819. His devotion to the possibilities of the German *Lied* emerged early. In 1814 he wrote thirty-four songs, but in 1815 he wrote one hundred and seventy-eight. And almost at once he started to write masterpieces. The first was "Gretchen am Spinnrade" (Gretchen at the Spinning Wheel, D. 118), the wonderful lyric "Meine Ruh ist hin" (My peace is gone) from Goethe's *Faust, Part I*. That was on 19 October 1814.

Just a year later in October 1815, he set a second Goethe masterpiece, "Erlkönig" (D. 328), a song if anything greater than the poem. In 1816 he wrote one hundred and twenty-six songs, but in 1817 only sixty-eight. Thereafter his song production dropped off to less than an average of a couple of dozen a year except for the two great years of the song cycles, *Die schöne Müllerin*, 1823, and *Winterreise*, 1827. He began by setting lyrics of late eighteenth-century poets, Schiller, Matthisson, and Hölty. But even in 1815 he began to experiment with lyrics by the minor Romantic de la Motte Fouqué, and in 1814 with poems by Goethe, to whom he was to return again and again. Shortly after this he started to set the poem of his friends Mayrhofer and von Schober. In 1815 he began the experiment of writing a group of songs by the same poet, an adumbration of his later cycles. One was Theodor Körner, born in 1791, four years younger than Mayrhofer. Others were Hölty, Kosegarten, Schiller, Goethe, Klopstock, Claudius, all eighteenth-century poets. By 1818, however, he was moving to more recent poets, Friedrich von Schlegel, Grillparzer, and especially Novalis, and thenceforth most of his poets were minor and major Romantic poets, including Heine in his last year of composing. Not all of these songs were masterpieces and many are of little interest, as appears only too clearly in the massive recording of four hundred sixty songs by Dietrich Fischer-Dieskau. Yet there are dozens, even several hundred, superb songs, and many are indeed masterpieces. In the tremendous compositional effort of 1815 and 1816 Schubert created a new kind of song, and it was from these that emerged the great instrumental works of the 1820s, the last seven years of his life. For in these songs his effort was to explore a kind of music and create a body of music that no previous composer had so attempted to grasp and understand. In his songs Schubert discovered what was to be his great achievement, the mastery of musical drama.

But to grasp what he achieved we must first have a general notion of what the terms "drama" and "dramatic" involve or subsume, and how that drama is manifest in music. The Greek root of "drama" means "to act," and from that was derived the Greek word for action on the stage. Just as the word "tragic" has moved from the theater out to actual life, so the word "drama" has moved from the theater in the same direction and back, as it were, to its origin—action. And again for this extension of the term there is a very good reason. What the theater does as a complex of semiotic systems is to abstract some pattern of action from the general life of humanity, a pattern that is a categorial pattern, since it can successfully subsume any number of actual living behavioral patterns. Thus the tragic, as defined in the preceding section, is but one instance of the dramatic—action that results in defeat. The dramatic, a more inclusive category, is action itself in its essence. Now action can be considered as the response to culture, that is, instructions for behavior, instructions that turn behavior into performance, another word derived from the theater and now applied to all human behavior.

But the individual does not merely respond to cultural instructions. He interprets them, and he interprets them in either of two ways, as hindrance or as guidance. We are likely to use the term "dramatic" if a smoothly ongoing performance, that is, one which the individual interprets as guidance, is suddenly interrupted, deflected, frustrated by something in the performance situation which the acting individual interprets as hindrance. Moreover, we are most inclined to use the word "dramatic" when that hindrance is overcome, when not the individual is defeated but the situation is defeated. Thus the first successful attempt to reach the top of Mount Everest was widely categorized as "dramatic." The overcoming of the situation is the antithesis of the tragic, of course, and thus in the widest and fullest sense of the word can be categorized as "comic." To be sure, we no longer use the word in that sense, but to gain its original and fullest sense we have but to think of Dante's *Divine Comedy*, the effort to subsume in a universal pattern all human experiences of defeat and ultimately "comic" triumph, the entry into paradise, the world of total and perfect and unambiguous guidance, a world governed by "the love that moves the sun and the other stars." This is the dramatic on an enormous scale, but most unimportant and even trivial overcoming of a hindrance, such as kicking a stone out of the way, is equally "dramatic." And from the Dantesque sense of "comedy" can be derived the modern notion of the "comic" as the "funny," for one of the important meanings of laughter is the sense of triumph at the overcoming of an obstacle or hindrance. At the end of Mozart's *Don Giovanni* the music is the music of laughter, for the Don has been defeated. In short, we use "dramatic" when the essence of human performance is radically revealed.

When it comes to the dramatic in music, it is readily apparent that Western music since the early seventeenth century has had an unparalleled semiotic means for subsuming the dramatic, and that means is the distinction between major and minor, the former subsuming instances of guidance, the latter those of hindrance. Thus Strauss's *Elektra* ends with the death of the heroine and immediately thereafter an immense chord in C major. She has died, but she has been victorious in overcoming the terrible situation in which she was plunged by the murder of her father by her mother and her mother's lover. Likewise the sense of exaltation one is inclined to experience at the end of some tragedies, the sense, it may be, Aristotle was trying to grasp with his term "catharsis," is the triumphant arrival at *understanding* the defeat of the protagonist, an understanding that Grillparzer's Medea offers directly to the audience. Thus in this antithesis between major and minor, Western music arrived at a musically unique capacity to subsume semiotically all patterns of action, both defeat and triumph, and of course simple ongoing successful action under the control of a cultural guidance, as in nontheatrical dance music, which is almost always in the major and both controls and subsumes successful guided performance.

Yet this schema is not quite complete. Where in human action does the dramatic emerge? We may observe and discriminate three factors in any action—the actor, of course; the situation, or that element in the situation to which the actor is responding; and the actor's interpretation of the situation. Clearly no drama emerges from the simple encounter of actor with situation. Rather, it emerges from, and only from, the actor's *interpretation* of the situation. It is interpretation which determines whether or not some semiotic aspect of the situation is either guidance or hindrance. What gives drama its interest, whether in the theater or in life itself, is the ever varying and fluctuating interpretational activity of the actor. Emotion is the consequence not of the impact of actor on situation but of the effect of the actor's interpretation of the situation. Likewise the observer of the situation, as in the theater, responds emotionally as he interprets the actor as interpreting the situation as one of guidance or of hindrance.

From this analysis it is possible to state more precisely than was possible in Appendix I of *The Birth of Romanticism* what music as semiosis accomplishes. In theater music, the singing voice or instruments support, illuminate (sometimes ironically) the actor's interpretation as revealed in the verbal semiosis. From the fully formed theatrical situation in which the factors of the situation are presented by visual semiosis it is possible to move to the song, in which the situation is presented either directly or indirectly, that is, by implication, by verbal semiosis. Here the music again supports, either straightforwardly or ironically, the interpretation. The next step is to apply this analysis to purely instrumental music in which there is neither actor nor singer nor situation. In such musical circumstances it is, then, possible to propose that what music does is to present a semiotic construct of the process, the ongoing flow, the activity, the behavior of interpretational activity. Thus "abstract" music is less a semiotic construct of emotion than it is a semiotic construct of the activity which elicits emotional responses. And this is why it can elicit emotional response in the listener. This analysis of the semiotic character of abstract (that is, nonsituational) music makes it easier to understand those who maintain that music is without meaning, is not meaningful, for it reveals music as a semiotic construct of the creation of meaning, which is exactly what interpretation amounts to.

This is what Schubert understood and what made him both a great and a highly innovative Romantic composer, one whose self-appointed task was to go beyond, to transcend culturally, what the foremost composer of his day had achieved. We can see, in fact, precisely when Schubert grasped this when we look at "Gretchen am Spinnrade." First, the song takes place in a fully developed and already well-known theatrical situation, Gretchen's realization in Goethe's *Faust I* that Faust had abandoned her. (*Faust: Ein Fragment* was published in 1790; *Faust: Erster Teil* was published in 1808. Schubert's knowledge of Goethe's drama is evidence of his cultural sophistication when he was not yet eighteen and of his excellent education. Next, the poem, clearly to be sung in a production of the work, is Gretchen's interpretation of her abandoned situation, her unhappiness, and her memories of happiness, culminating in Schubert's setting with a high note, almost a cry, on "his kiss." Thus Schubert's first great song is the setting of a verbalization created for the theater. An indicator of the interpretational activity of the dramatized Gretchen is the accompaniment, a semiotic transformation, to be sure, of the sound of a spinning wheel. There are many such in the nineteenth century, but they are invariably in the major. In Schubert's song, however, the "sound" of the spinning wheel is in the minor. To Gretchen it is at once a hindrance—an ordinary household duty has become a hindrance—and in its continuity at the same time a semiotic transformation of her obsession, her despairing and abandoned love for Faust.

Schubert's next major triumph in songwriting came a year later in "Erlkönig," from another poem by Goethe. Here again is a fully developed dramatic situation, a father's furious struggle to reach the safety of his home, to escape from the lethal efforts of the supernatural king of the elves. In this song Schubert attempts something more complex, something almost verging on opera, for there are three actors, each of which interprets the situation, the father, the child, and the elf-king. And to these three voices are added the voice of the narrator. To each of these Schubert gives a differing melody and tonality, and supporting them is the narrator's interpretation of the beating of the horse's hooves as a desperate urge towards safety, an urge encountering hindrance and at the end overcome by it. Schubert has created in this song a miniature opera. In songs in which there is no narrative but only a response to and interpretation of a highly generalized situation—most of the songs, in fact—there is what Schubert learned from narrative songs with a well-defined situation: the interpretative response to the situation, no matter how generalized, simply nature, for example, or the mere prospect of death.

By 1820 Schubert had written more than four hundred seventy songs as well as dozens of settings for groups of voices, mixed, male, and female. He had mastered the musical dramatization of a poetical interpretation of a situation either implied or presented by verbal narration. The next step was the most important, for now he discovered how to transfer that dramatization to instrumental, abstract music. As already suggested, the first trial was the *Quartettsatz*. Up to this point his most successful piece of chamber music was the well-loved *Die Forelle (The Trout)* piano quintet, written probably in autumn 1819 (D. 667, published in 1829 as Opus 114). Unquestionably a delightful and accomplished work, it was nevertheless surpassed by the *Quartettsatz*, a single movement with a fragment of another. It is not easy to determine what place that completed movement might have had in a completed quartet, for it conforms to none of the standard movement types, except possibly the rondo. It consists of an alternation between an almost violent outburst and the effort of a gently rising theme in the major to transcend or escape from the violence. But that effort to escape, if that is what it is, invariably collapses into the initial turmoil. The final effort to arrive at a radiant transfiguration promises to succeed in a final reconciliation, but once again it collapses into the briefest renewal of the turmoil, terminated by two powerful chords. The movement is the drama of the effort to rise above an unendurable situation, and the ultimate failure of that effort.

Schubert's next major effort to realize his sense of musical drama, won with such prolonged effort, was the Symphony No. 7, or No. 8, depending on whether one counts as a symphony a piano sketch in two movements of 1818, but best known as the "Unfinished Symphony," written in October 1822 (D. 759, published in 1867). Perhaps like the *Quartettsatz* the work was left incomplete because Schubert was not yet sure of what he was attempting to do, or at least unsure of precisely how to do it. Yet the Unfinished Symphony seems almost a miraculous event in the history of the symphony. Surely few symphonies are better known or more loved. Its immediate appeal, from the time of its discovery to the present, is that Schubert has—to use traditional terms—introduced lyricism into what was traditionally an epic convention. The eighteenth-century symphony—continued in spite of his Romanticism by Beethoven—was that in which the first movement of the symphony, as well as frequently the third and almost always the last, was built up by developing a chain of motives, such a chain comprising what was known as a theme. But Schubert instead introduces a boldly assertive melody, the kind of melody one would find in a song, that is, a full-fledged melody instead of a chain of motives. And this was to become the predominating practice in the nineteenth-century symphony. Structurally this innovation meant that the movement is a chain of songs, rather like the act of an opera, instead of the manipulation of motives for the primary purpose of the formation of a symphonic structure. It has been asserted by purists, those who take the eighteenth-century symphony as paradigmatic, that Schubert's innovation was a perversion of the very character of the symphonic form. But such a judgement is hardly more than a pointless bit of musical Platonizing, erecting an ideal into a reality. Rather, what Schubert did was to turn the symphonic movement into a series of sustained interpretational constructs, analogous to the characters in a play or a novel. And this analogy is reasonable. It is only crude or approximate to think of actors or characters in a play or a novel or individuals in life as being in conflict or agreement. Rather, it is more precise and more accurate to think not of the interaction of actors but of the interaction of interpretations. And just as a theme is modified as the musical work emerges, so do interpretations modify under the impact of hindrance and guidance. Thus the first movement of the Unfinished Symphony opens with a softly uttered theme deep in the bass, a melody that moves upwards with difficulty, implying that it encounters an opposition, then in tragic manner collapses and falls farther into the bass and into silence. The rest of the movement dramatizes a series of struggles to transcend or escape from this initial failure—but without success. The movement ends with a more forceful statement of the failure of the initial effort, and several powerful chords in the minor assert that inability to escape from a debilitating situation.

The second movement is constructed similarly. Just as the first movement is not in a remarkably fast tempo, so the second movement, equally untraditionally, is hardly less rapid in movement than the first. Furthermore, it departs from the eighteenth-century second or slow movement, traditionally an operatic aria, a long sustained melody capable of elaborate decoration. Instead, in the Unfinished Symphony the structure of the second movement is very like the first, a series of songs, of sustained characterizations, the general mood of which is uplifting, as it were, is hopeful, but hardly joyous and is far from ecstatic. It is a mood of frequently disturbed and troubled mild happiness, an often shadowed loveliness.

Why Schubert did not continue with this work is, of course, not known, since nothing was known of the work until several decades after his death. Instead in the next month, November 1822, he turned to a work he was able to complete, a work of daring and novelty, the Fantasy in C Major, known as the *Wandererfantasie* after a theme taken from a song of 1816 (D. 760, published in 1823 as Opus 15). The fantasia is an old musical pattern, but Schubert does something remarkably novel with it. First is the great length, matching the slow movement of Beethoven's "Hammerklavier" sonata (see the preceding chapter), which he must have known since its publication in 1819. Moreover, in the spirit of the Romanticism of the 1820s it is a frankly virtuoso work. The construction is also novel, having some resemblance to a four-movement sonata, in that it is divided into segments, though played continuously. On the other hand, it is quite different from the sonata since it is constructed on the dramatic exploitation of a liminted number of recurring themes. One dominating theme, with which the work opens, is a first experiment, as it were, with repeated chords, suggesting a determination without an object or purpose, an aggression without an aim. The rest of the work is concerned with exploring the possibilities of escaping from and transcending what is perhaps best thought of as an obsessive trap. In one episode the tempo is slowed down and the aggressive attack becomes a despairing minor. In another episode a lyric escape is attempted. Finally a fugal development breaks the pattern, and the fantasia ends in an explosion of release, roaring up and down the length of the keyboard and culminating in powerful and triumphant chords.

The next important work was the Piano Sonata in A Minor, composed in February 1823 (D. 784, published in 1839 as Opus 143). It was the first completed work in the sonata pattern since the *Trout* quintet of 1819, and it was the first in a series of such works that continued to the end of his life, piano sonatas, string quartets, piano trios, and so on, fourteen superb works, plus the great C Major Symphony of 1825. The A Minor Sonata begins with a melody on single notes which proposes an effort to break out of a limiting situation and the initial failure to do so. The opening impulse is almost extinguished, but a lyrical upward-moving impulse successfully propels the action forward. The great moment of liberation comes in the development, or argument. A sudden magic modulation into a distant major is like the sun going up or the parting of a curtain to reveal a glorious landscape, for the melodic line climbs rapidly upward. It is a moment of radiant exaltation, and the result is that at the end of the movement the initial hindrance has been overcome in a passage of supreme loveliness. Yet in the course of this movement the fundamental pattern of the sonata emerges, a pattern developed further in the second movement. It consists of reaching a moment of tranquil loveliness interrupted by violent minor chords or, in the second movement, an almost cataclysmic outburst of aggressive frustration. This is accomplished in a remarkably dramatic manner. The opening melody is one of tranquil loveliness, almost as simple as a folk song. It radiates confidence that is soon fulfilled and assuaged. Then when it ends and before it begins again is heard a peculiar little motive in the bass, a kind of soft mutter that moves up and down and back to its starting point. Yet after a time that motive is uttered with greater volume and power, moves upward, and releases an aggressive torrent of powerfully hindered sound in the minor. But then the mood of the principal theme returns. In the third and last movement the pattern is one of a bare alternation between release of energy in virtuoso brilliance and a completely unrelated melody of relaxed loveliness and delicious harmonization. Schubert pushes here to new extremes the possible polarity of the rondo pattern.

During these early years of the 1820s Schubert continued his efforts to achieve an operatic success. In 1821 and 1822 over a period of five months he composed a full-length opera, *Alfonso und Estrella* (D. 732, not performed until 24 June 1854 and published only in 1892). Though it contains much lovely music it lacks the dramatic power that was beginning to emerge in his instrumental music. In March and April 1823, he composed a one-act *Singspiel, Die Verschworenen*, his cleverest and most successful work for the stage, but it was not performed until 1861 (D. 787, published 1889). From 25 May to 2 October he made another attempt at an opera with spoken dialogue, *Fierrabras* (D. 796, published in 1886 and performed in 1897). Once again the charm of the music lacked the dramatic power he had already accomplished in the works we have examined. Not surprisingly, however, that sense of drama emerges in a work which has been called a kind of opera, though rather unconvincingly, the great song cycle *Die schöne Müllerin (The Fair Maid of the Mill)*, written in October and November of 1823 (D. 795, published in 1824 as Opus 25).

The author of the cycle of poems from which Schubert was to select the texts for his song cycle was Wilhelm Müller, born in 1794 and dying in 1827, while Schubert was setting his second cycle of Müller's poems, *Winterreise*. Müller fought in the Freedom Wars in 1813 and 1814, and in 1819 became teacher in the Gymnasium in Dessau and later became the librarian at the ducal court. He published the *Müllerin* poems in the first edition of his *Gedichte aus den hinterlassenen Papieren eines reisenden Waldhornisten (Poems from the Posthumous Papers of a Traveling Hornplayer)* and in the second edition of 1824 the poems from which Schubert selected the texts for *Winterreise*, the first half of which he found in 1823 in a journal, *Urania*. Müller wrote the *Müllerin* poems as a parody of the sentimental lyrics of the time, but Schubert turned them into serious lyrics in part by his selection but mostly by his setting. The texts he chose comprise a narrative.

A young miller in his wandering years gets a job at a mill he has come to and falls in love with the miller's daughter, discovers that she is in love with a huntsman, and drowns himself in the millstream. The drama emerges in the contrasts from song to song and particularly in Schubert's masterly modulations. Throughout the cycle the accompaniment (which requires a first-rate pianist) suggests the sound of the millstream, too much so, according to Fischer-Dieskau, but the device is a repetition and development of the sound of the spinning wheel in Schubert's first great song; that is, it is the young miller's obsession. In the first eighteen poems he speaks, in No. 19 the voices are successively an anonymous narrator (for the first time), the brook itself, and the protagonist, begging the brook to sing him to rest. In No. 20, the last song, the voice is the brook's. Throughout, the drama is intimate, subjective, the feelings, or more precisely, the varying interpretations by the youth of his feelings and of the changing situation from hope to rejection and sadness and suicidal despair. But in every poem subtlety controls the drama, revealing, perhaps, why Schubert's attempts at theater drama were most unsuccessful, since through his songs he had located the true source of drama in one's feeling and one's interpretation of those feelings. And that is why, it would appear, that he could create a powerful drama in instrumental music which he was unable to create for the theater. Nowhere in the cycle does the young miller directly encounter another human being whom he must interpret, and that is the essence of the drama of the theater. Rather, Schubert's drama is the Romantic drama of encounter with one's self. *Die schöne Müllerin* is important not merely for itself—it is after all a great masterpiece—but for what it reveals about Schubert's entering into, grasp of, and development of one of the great and central themes of Romanticism, analytic self-exploration.

In October he received the commission to write the incidental music for a play by Helmine von Chézy. It was his last effort for the stage, and evidently he was not very interested. He did not trouble to write an overture but used that for *Alfonso und Estrella*, though today the 1820 overture to *Die Zauberharfe* is known as the overture to *Rosamunde*. The play was given on 20 December 1823 (Theater on the Wien), and was repeated only once. The music, however, was admired and the entr'actes and ballet music are now very popular (D. 797, published 1821). But on the whole the year 1823 was painful, for he had become very ill from syphilis and for a time was hospitalized. In February 1824 he was in despair, both because of his ruined health and the breakup of a circle of friends. Nevertheless in February began one of his most creative periods. He spent the summer once again with the Esterhazys in Zseliz and returned in September in much better health. His accomplishments during this period of nearly two years are astonishing. To mention only the most important ones, those in a full sonata form, he began in February and March 1824 with two string quartets, one in A minor (D. 804, published in 1824), and a second in D minor (D. 810, published in 1838). This is the famous *Tod und das Mädchen* quartet, so called from the fact that Schubert used as theme for a set of variations in the second movement the opening melody from the song of that title, written in February 1817. It was followed in June by a duet for piano known as the Grand Duo Sonata (D. 812, published in 1838), and several other large-scale works for piano duet. In April 1825 came an unfinished piano sonata in C major with a particularly splendid first movement (D. 840, published in 1861), and in May another piano sonata, in A minor (D. 845, published in 1826 as Opus 42). In August he wrote a further piano sonata in D major (D. 850, published in 1826 as Opus 53). And probably at this time he wrote the first piano trio, in B-flat major (D. 898, published in 1836 as Opus 99). But the culmination of this year's work was the "Great" Symphony in C Major (D. 944, published in 1840). When he wrote this symphony has been much debated, but recently it has been argued on various grounds, particularly grounds of style, that it belongs to 1825. Certainly in mood, if that is any test, it matches the high happiness of this summer in the Austrian mountains.

Splendid as all these works are, and some of the individual movements are among the most beautiful he ever wrote, such as the slow movement to the Piano Trio (D. 898), they do not go much beyond what he already accomplished. Indeed, none of the piano sonatas has the high drama of the Sonata in A Minor composed in 1823. There is a certain facility about these works, in their frequently virtuoso aspects, which has led them to be compared with the piano music of Johann Nepomuk Hummel (1773–1837), an exemplar of late eighteenth-century Viennese classicism. Thus in some ways Schubert's music of these years was to a certain extent a regression to his music before 1820. Certainly, however, the first two movements at least of the Piano Trio are an exception, and the slow movement in particular has something of the dramatic intensity and sense of barely endured struggle that was soon to emerge in the music of Chopin and Schumann.

The explanation for this partial failure to pursue the possibilities of musical Romanticism is to be found, it may be, in the Symphony in C.

The first and most notable thing about it is its great length, called, as we are told so often, "heavenly lengths" by Schumann. Still, it is possible to get a little weary of it and to begin to feel that it is excessively long for the material presented and that it is indeed a less advanced work than the Unfinished Symphony of 1822. This disillusion can be traced to a device that appears constantly, and sometimes continuously, in all four movements, the reiteration of the same notes, something he first experimented with in the *Wandererfantasie*, though in that work he did not carry this almost obsession nearly so far. This reiteration, now loud, now soft, now a single repeated note, now repeated chords, moves neither up nor down except in the fourth movement. There in the second theme it is most conspicuous and in the series of phrases of reiterated notes moves in each phrase down the scale. What this repetition indicates is a stability, either present or pursued. The first movement opens with a horn call that moves upward, and the three notes of that upward thrust alternate with the repetitions of the first theme and provide the movement's drama. The second movement ends in the minor, to be sure, but the sense of a full acceptance of guidance, what is usually known as "happiness," dominates the remaining two movements. The symphony ends with four powerful notes that move downward in a chordal series, a reversal of the upward thrust of the opening, an affirmation of the desired stability, a withdrawal of aggressive ambition or impulse.

So the whole symphony is a reduction of the dramatic tension of the work of 1823, just as the third and fourth movements of the trio are like eighteenth-century music in that they offer simple charm in place of the tension and struggle and intensity of the first and particularly second movements. It is a pattern regressive from Beethoven's major symphonies. Thus this period in Schubert's life may perhaps—though one hesitates to make so flat a biographical deduction—have been an expression of his relief in thinking that he had recovered from his illness, his attack of syphilis, or even an effort to avoid facing the facts about his condition. His infection was to kill him in a few years. But putting aside this speculation we are left with a pattern that so often recurs in the Romantic tradition, the retreat from the analytic difficulties and demands of Romanticism into the synthetic and even ease of the Enlightenment. Yet Schubert's retreat was, in true Romantic fashion, to be but temporary. In many of his works but especially in *Die Winterreise* he recovered and even surpassed the dramatic intensity and power he had earlier achieved. In the great song cycle it shows that he understood, as he never had before, what the Romantic tradition has so profoundly analyzed and understood—suffering.

Meditations on the Consequences of Romanticism

I

The central consequence of the impact of Romanticism comes out with extraordinary vividness in the work of three artists of the 1820s, two of the oldest Romantics and the youngest. In the early 1820s or perhaps in 1820 itself Goya painted for his own house a series of paintings unparalleled in the history of European paintings. The Black Paintings are so called in a double sense, one because black is dominant in a number of the paintings, and two, black in a metaphorical sense—gloom, pessimism, despair, horror. Many of them, perhaps most, are mysterious, indecipherable except for the gloom and horror. One, however, is so clear that it is possible Goya wanted it to be the key to the whole set. Two men are buried up to their knees in mud, or perhaps sunk in the ground, possibly because of what they are doing. For they are flailing at each other with huge clubs. The fact that the landscape is almost without feature, is even a desert, emphasizes the absolute futility of their combat. It is an unforgettable image of the basic fact of the human enterprise, the endless and self-destructive fight of each man against another. The most haunting painting of all shows an empty space diagonally crossed by a featureless barrier. Above the barrier is visible the head of a dog, gazing upward. Why he is there and why he is gazing can scarcely be known. But the design can obviously be understood as a visual metaphor, the kind Goya so often painted, of pure uncomprehending longing for significance. Like all the Black Paintings both of these strip away meaning and value from human life. The paintings are mysterious because life is mysterious. It is not surprising that between these paintings and his death in 1828 Goya was to paint a superb series of bullfights, the natural continuation of the Black Paintings. No such paintings were to be painted before well into the twentieth century. The Black Paintings of Goya are irresistible instances of the culturally transcending impact of Romanticism, as well as the Romantic's realism, his search for value that led him to the most uncompromising and unconsoling vision of human life. It is not surprising that the Black Paintings are nearly contemporary with Schopenhauer's remarkable vision.

2

Equally transcending the 1820s are the last works of Beethoven, the final sonatas, the *Requiem*, the Ninth Symphony, the *Diabelli Variations*, and above all the last six quartets, or seven, if one includes the Great Fugue as a separate work. Nothing like these, especially the quartets, had ever been written before, even by Beethoven, or better, especially by Beethoven. In the Great Fugue, originally written for the last movement but rejected by the publisher and a rondo substituted for it, is rather like the Black Paintings. Aside from being almost unplayable it is as ugly as music can be. What all these works are about is tension, the exploration of tension, and the extraordinary efforts it takes to overcome tension, to transcend it, and to enter into a condition of reconciliation and peace. That escape from unbearable tension was once provided by the church and by other consoling beliefs and ideologies; but these were no longer available. The individual must achieve that transcendence of human hopelessness and suffering, must create value, by his own unaided efforts out of his own unique experiences. We have seen this kind of effort before, but never before with such forthright directness as in these last works of Beethoven. The perfect instance of the contrast between struggle and the escape from struggle which to Beethoven, evidently, could be achieved only in music is in the last sonata, Opus 111. Perhaps that is why it is the last sonata. The first movement is all struggle and tension, but the second and last movement is precisely the reverse, a transcendence of struggle into a calm that achieves by the time this long movement is over an ecstatic, life-transcending bliss. It is the kind of music that hitherto had been achieved only in a religious context. But Beethoven achieved it by his own powers, and in doing so transcended even what he had achieved in music. But the struggle was far from over for him. In his last quartet, Opus 185, he went so far as to verbalize what he was trying to achieve in music. "Must it be?" he writes in the score, and answers with, "It must be!" Evidently before his death Beethoven arrived at a triumphant and humorous acceptance of his bitter life, of the conditions of human existence. Once again, that cultural transcendence was achieved by his own power as an artist. It is not surprising that not long after, there appears the first verbally successful—in the sense that it lasted for decades—of the Romantic's notion of art as the source of value—Art for Art's Sake, art as the supreme value, as indeed the only source of value, because all else had failed, all religions, all ideologies. Moreover, the work of Goya and Beethoven in the 1820s was proof that the Romantic artist was going increasingly to be faced, sometimes to a crippling degree, with a hitherto unknown freedom of artistic invention.

3

This unparalleled freedom affected the brilliant young painter Richard Parkes Bonington, an Englishman who spent his most important years in France. At first in water colors and then in oils he achieved in his landscapes a freshness and purity of vision that even today is breathtaking. In the sudden transcendence of traditional painting he surpassed what had been so far achieved by Constable and Turner, whose work seems by comparison studied, even, marvelous as their works were, labored. Paris was ready for Bonington. When he was still an art student his watercolors began to sell rapidly, and he was to have a profound and lasting influence on the subsequent path of French painting. It was not merely Eugène Delacroix, Bonington's friend, who was released by him. Delacroix, of course, was a follower or at least a continuator of Géricault, from whom he derived much of the Romantic intensity of the subjects of his painting, his Romantic realism, but the difference is not merely that Delacroix was inspired by Rubens and at one point by the exhibition of some of Constable's paintings in Paris. Delacroix's burst into color, already evident in the paintings of the mid-1820s, and the freedom of his brush, so that the brushstroke itself becomes an emblem or sign of the artist's passion, springs from the examples and impact of Bonington. Bonington was the first instance of what was to prove the peculiar destiny and character of nineteenth-century painting, and above all of landscape painting, from which modern art emerged, the sense that one so often has, even with minor painters, that they were inventing painting, at least thinking about painting from its very foundations. Because of

Bonington the tradition of landscape painting was to have the quality of freshness of observation, of seeing the world in a way that transcended the platitudes of perception and the conventions of painting that in poetry Wordsworth had achieved so early in Romanticism.

4

That very quality of what one might almost call the invention of perception appears in the early landscapes, those of his trip to Italy, of Camille Corot, older than both Bonington and Delacroix but starting later than they did. Here again it is hard not to see the influence of Bonington. To come on one of Corot's Italian landscapes after going through galleries of his predecessors is always a shock, the shock of walking from darkness into light. Corot fused the freshness of Bonington with an even greater realism. Above all for the first time he captures the intensity of light of the Mediterranean region, just as his pictures are, at first glance, of an almost innocent and naive realism—but only at first glance. Clearly, as we have seen often enough, agitation and tension are understandably a mark of the Romantic tradition, and were to remain so even to the present day. But also from Wordsworth on there is to be found the escape from that agitation into a radiant ease of being. In other artists, and in time even in painting, late in the century that ease was to be transformed into the ecstatic.

5

Contributors to that development and for many decades the most analytic of painters were the Barbizon artists: Constant Troyon, Jules Dupré, Théodore Rousseau, Narcisse Diaz de La Peña. To these can be added the somewhat different Jean François Millet and Charles François Daubigny, who emerged much later than the four central Barbizon painters. One may also add Rosa Bonheur, whose excellence is only beginning once again to be recognized. Of the Barbizons first it may be said that as soon as their paintings became known in other countries, those countries' traditions were transformed. Hardly a country in Europe did not experience their impact, sometimes initially by a visit, as in Holland, of a restless painter to Paris, where he saw their work and responded by transforming his own style. To call the Barbizon "landscape" artists and let it go at that is seriously to misunderstand them. Rather, they grasped what Bonington, Corot, and Delacroix had accomplished, a transformation of painting, and their response was to analyze that transformation and to seek in that analysis the very grounds of painting as an art. Landscape painting was the ideal medium for such a venture. Figure painting, even in Delacroix, historical painting, religious painting—all of these are too limited in their possibilities. The human figure and the disposition of figures in historical or religious anecdotes restricts the investigation of the nature of painting. To be sure, there were in the 1820s and the 1830s and 1840s excellent painters in most of the countries of Europe who devoted themselves to historical realism, eventually to be transformed into a realism of the contemporary world. But these are really offshoots of Romanticism, or blind alleys. It was the Barbizons who were on the central path and led to the impressionists and through them to the culturally transcending painting of the first decade of the twentieth century, the Moderns as we still call them. No other term has yet emerged, though the somewhat absurd term "postmodernism" indicates the necessity for such a term.

The advantage of landscape for the analysis of paintings is that there are almost no limits to the disposition of the elements of the design. The sky can occupy as much of the painting as one wishes. There can be a lot of trees or a few. There can be as many cows standing in as many rivers or pools as one wants. People can be ignored, except for miniscule figures, staffage, included to place the painting in time and space, invariably contemporary and easily accessible space. But the figures are generally so small that they add little to the design except certain accents or at times foci for the organization and line and spatial disposition. Landscape painting offers precisely that freedom of disposition which is essential for analytical exploration of what painting consists of. Consequently the Barbizons analyzed the possibilities of color. Rousseau was perhaps the most effective in color analysis. In his paintings of cattle Troyon most effectively analyzed the disposition of size and shape which is the source of a painting's monumentality. And all of the Barbizons show a remarkable diversity and experimentation in the compositional transformations of the real landscapes they were responding to. It was, in a sense, a new kind of studio painting which preserved the appearance of open-air painting, for no matter how transformed, their immediately responsive source was the open-air sketch. And they went farther than this. By the late 1840s and in the 1850s they were exploring what might be called the emotional symbolism of painting, actually what I have called elsewhere "regulatory signs," regulation of the level and character of aggression. Thus in many of these later paintings, frequently of an almost lurid sunset scene, in the foreground there is an open area or forest clearing; beyond that is a dense, dark forest, a tangled wood. But through that tangle there is an opening, sometimes a path or a woodland road, which leads to the light beyond the dark wood. It is a symbol of self-transcendence. The eye of the observer is guided to move from a relatively commonplace space through a difficult and oppressive experience to a world of light, of transforming and transcending value, beyond that experience. Likewise in all the Barbizon school there is a new, exploratory, analytical sense of color. And always there is, in traditional terms, a certain lack of finish, that is, an awareness forced upon the observer that these paintings are the result of the artists' application of loaded brush to canvas. Indeed, in the very late and little known paintings of Daubigny, paintings of the 1870s, the brush stroke emerges as not merely evidence of the painters' imaginative activity but as part of the very design of the painting. In this emergence of the brush stroke, in itself analytical, painting moves from imitation not to expression so much as to painting as a construct, as a creation. And above all it is a sign of the artist as a secular redeemer, as art as the source of human value, and to the painter as the instrument of that value-creation. This aspect of the Barbizons, the brush stroke, is exactly parallel to what in these same years Turner was doing, nor was it too different from what, though to a lesser degree, Delacroix was also doing. It was far different from the tradition of Ingres and the historical realism painters, who aimed synthetically at creating not a picture but a scene. Thus when Ingres was a history painter, as in fact he defined himself, he became relatively uninteresting and the more uninteresting and unconvincing as he grew older. But in his portraits, which he thought less serious than history paintings, he could in his own terms, perhaps, irresponsibly play with costume and furniture in a way that revealed the painting as more of a construct than an imitation. It was, then, the Barbizon painters who found the route for the true consequences of the Romantic tradition. In the second half of the century no school of painting that was vital and led to new developments, new cultural transcendencies, new analyses of the nature of painting, was not under the influence of the Barbizons.

6

Still, the glory of the Romantic tradition of painting was Turner, who has at last come into his own with the publication of a complete catalogue of oil paintings and the building of the Turner Wing at the Tate Gallery. Extraordinary as were Turner's paintings of the first quarter of the century, those of the second quarter were even more astounding. The paintings he exhibited are almost unbelievably beautiful, but those he did not exhibit went even farther in the direction in which he was moving, a direction he maintained hardly without deviation. At the very end he was painting pure color fields, though the titles still suggested something in nature. What was he responding to, and what controlled his responses? In spite of Ruskin's claims that Turner was always truthfully responding to nature, even though Ruskin was aware that "imitation" was not the task of painting simply because it was impossible, as one examines Turner's work chronologically it becomes increasingly obvious that he was responding to his own paintings. One usually uses the word "tradition" to talk about a series of painters or artists of any kind, but the word is still appropriate when limited to Turner's work. Grasping fully the task of the Romantics to create value by means of cultural transcendence, he set out to transcend himself. He grasped that cultural transcendence, since its empirical existence is in human behavior, means transcendence of one's self, and transcendence of the self-transcendence. And this he achieved. He created his own tradition, and he went beyond it. What he was devoted to was not responding to nature, no matter how impressionistically or how truthfully, but responding to his own paintings as paintings. He was at the dead center of the consequences of Romanticism because he subjected painting and the very act of painting, the application of color-loaded brush to canvas, to deconstructing, disintegrating analysis such as no painter before or since has ever achieved. For that reason alone it is not idle to claim for Turner that he was the greatest painter who has ever lived, the most intelligent and the most intellectual. His imaginative inventiveness in thinking of things to do with a brush on canvas or paper was endless. No painter has ever understood better the act of painting, of painting as a mode of human behavior. Of all the painters of the Romantic tradition he was the purest Romantic virtuoso.

7

A writer almost as much a virtuoso in prose as Turner in painting or Liszt in music is Thomas Carlyle. His principal masterpiece—there were certainly others—is *Sartor Resartus*, "The Tailor Retailored," or "Man as symbol-maker made conscious of himself as symbol-maker." The book has two themes, a theory of semiosis and a theory of Romantic self-transcendence. "Symbol" is a term the Romantic tradition wrestled with for more than a century. It is still wrestling with it. From the usual point of view—that of immanency of meaning in language—it can scarcely be understood or explained, although all kinds of efforts have been made to do so. From the position of behavioral semiosis it presents no problem. The meaning of a sign is the response to that sign. Hence one can only say that the response is or is not appropriate, not that it is true or false. What the notion of symbol gets at is that a sign can elicit more than one response, and that more than one response is appropriate. Carlyle's position is a kind of idealistic-empirical pragmatism. Man makes clothes to control his behavior. In the same way, man invests the totally incomprehensible and mysterious world with meaning in order to control his behavior. Lacking the modern notion of culture and refusing, sensibly, to guess about the origins of signs, Carlyle simply says that their source is the unconscious mind and ultimately God. But his position is not merely idealistic. It is also empirical. Man, he says, is the toolmaking animal, a definition often used by subsequent anthropologists, who, however, usually failed to understand that for Carlyle the tool is a sign, that signs and symbols, whichever term one prefers, are man's primary tools. They are his instruments for work, for creating order out of what man can only see as chaos. And this conception of "sign" anticipates Wittgenstein, who eventually came to the same conclusion.

Carlyle seeks the source of the symbol-making power as he seeks to explain self-transcendence (in particular, both transcendence *of* the self and culture-transcendence). He sees self-transcendence as having moved from Enlightenment culture through a period of negation, of denial of value, to what he calls the Everlasting Yea—the affirmation of the value of one's self, of human existence, and of the world. With immense subtlety Carlyle proposes that the Everlasting Nay, the denial of all value, is escaped from by wandering during what he calls the Center of Indifference, between the Nay and the Yea. He has seen that an unacceptable position can be escaped from and in time transcended by randomizing one's behavior. The Center of Indifference is the period of disengagement from all human patterns of culture, from every kind of commitment. With that freedom man can wander, can explore the possibilities of randomness, that exploration to be achieved by exploiting alienation. It was a discovery in human behavior of the utmost originality, and it was to be rediscovered by psychoanalysis, which in free association and the associative exploration of what is remembered of dreams uses precisely the technique of randomization in order to enable the patient to escape from his self-created trap. There is also another link to later psychoanalytic thinking in Carlyle's presentation of the coming of the Everlasting Yea. For this the individual is not alienated but, rather, isolated from man and his culture, an isolation which Carlyle signifies by placing his hero, "God-Born Devil's Dung," on the top of a mountain, a highly traditional placement for religious revelation. Carlyle's hero simply quite suddenly and without preparation or transition from his indifference experiences value, feels himself God-born. By an unconscious act the world is suddenly suffused with meaning and value. Thus Carlyle is convinced that all symbol making, all semiosis, has an unconscious source. In that, of course, he goes far beyond psychoanalysis and in a more adequate direction.

8

Carlyle was a virtuoso of prose style, a virtuoso of syntax and of metaphor, a virtuoso of rhetoric. In the same 1830s in which he created his style there was emerging on the other side of the Channel a virtuoso of narrative, one who pursued the analysis of social structure in a path parallel to Carlyle's pursuit of the analysis of meaning. Honoré de Balzac was, like Carlyle, a late starter. Indeed he had written much before he knew what he was doing. He was above all a virtuoso of fiction, a virtuoso of narrative technique, an immense innovator in novel writing. When in the late 1830s he realized what he was doing, he called his enterprise, after Dante, *The Human Comedy*, by which he meant not the comic but the dramatic, as Dante had before him. Even though he died before he finished his vast project, he came close enough to completion to make it quite clear what he was doing. And that was no less than a sociological analysis in fictional form of the history and the social structure of France between the defeat of Napoleon and the French Revolution of 1830. Thus though the historical period he used was recent, nevertheless he was engaged, inspired by Scott, in historical realism. He saw personality as the expression or deposit or outcome of culture and social structure. But he also, in true Romantic fashion, saw culture and social structure as profoundly affected by the innovating and heroic personality. The creative and destructive, the good and the bad, the interaction of self and society was Balzac's theme. In the very decade in which the term "sociology" was invented he created the first great modern sociology. Moreover, because his theme was the interaction of society and personality, he created the first truly modern psychology, even though he presented it in the mode of fictional exemplification. So subtle and profound were his perceptions and his analysis that even today, especially in the French provinces, one can encounter again and again personalities who seem to have stepped out of the pages of Balzac. More than any preceding novelist he saw drama as the conflict between individuals' varying interpretation of situations. With Balzac the realism that is discoverable in the very beginning of the Romantic tradition burst into the fullest incandescence. What was implicit in Scott, the contrast of cultures and societies, became in Balzac explicit. In Balzac, Scott's intuitive exploration of a society's varying cultures became analytically self-conscious. Balzac stripped away and dismantled the pretensions of his society, which like the pretensions of all societies conceals a society from itself. When one understands Balzac's accomplishments one can understand the accomplishments of his two greatest imitators and followers, Zola and Faulkner, and how they too were working in the Romantic tradition of cultural dimantlement, of social analysis.

9

In the very years in which Balzac was beginning to create his intuitive sociology August Comte was laying the foundations for his theoretically controlled scientific sociology. He saw human history in developmental terms. Though he hardly used the term he conceived of historical development as the development of culture, virtually in its most modern sense. By "society" he very nearly means "culture," just as he saw the sciences as social phenomena. What made him fully Romantic in the profoundest sense was his proposal that culture (society, history) develops in three stages, and that each of the sciences, though originating in different historical epochs, goes through the same three stages—the religious stage, the metaphysical stage, and the positive stage. So he called his philosophy the Positive Philosophy. The essence of that philosophy was that man had now arrived at a cultural stage in which he can understand and control his world, including his social world, by a theoretically controlled comprehension of facts. With such a positive philosophy, it would now be possible to develop the last science necessary for human success, the science of sociology, the theoretically controlled understanding of the facts of human behavior, including the sciences as social facts. To be sure, there was still in his thinking an Enlightenment redemptionism—its source being religious redemption—which was still common to most thinkers of this period, including Marx, who like Comte never rid himself of that redemptionism, never freed himself of what is an essentially religious assumption. Nevertheless the achievement of Comte was directly in the line of one of the most important consequences of Romanticism, already appearing here and there early in the century, the analytic dismantlement of the superstructure of Western culture. For Comte, Western man could now be free of religion and free of metaphysics, free to understand the world as it really is. Eventually Comte realized that one of the most important characteristics of humanity and society is the experience of value, and he grasped that that function had been carried out by religion. With religion no longer tenable something was needed to effect the function of religion, some value-creating and value-affirming behavioral mode. He proposed, therefore, that a new kind of saint be recognized, the kind he called great men, above all, great thinkers. The worship of great men would thus ensure the continuous entry of value into human life, the continuous maintenance of value. Comte's idea was analogous to and contemporary with the full establishment of the idea of art for art's sake, art and the value experience of art as the primary source of human value, the fullest flourishing of the artist as prophet and priest.

I O

Music in the 1830s and the 1840s produced the most famous, the most typical, and the purest instances of the Romantic virtuoso. To be sure, that virtuoso spirit was to be found in other arts as well. In poetry young Tennyson became a virtuoso of sound in poetry, while the slightly younger Browning became a virtuoso of syntax, inspired, it would appear, to a considerable degree by Carlyle. His most remarkable effort was *Sordello*, in which he pushed syntactical distortion almost to the point of incomprehensibility. Only more than twenty years later did his complete revision of the punctuation, still hardly consistent or perfect, make the work comparatively readable. Both poets at first wrote in the vein of historical realism, and both in later years moved into contemporary realism. Browning shared with Balzac, in whose fiction he was intensely interested, the depiction of extravagant and fantastic personalities. Browning and Balzac are thus like Dickens, whose fictions combined Romantic virtuoso extravagance with a virtually unendurable nineteenth-century version of Enlightenment sentimentality and decaying religion.

Nevertheless the most complete exemplar of the Romantic virtuoso was a great pianist, Franz Liszt, who became in time a great composer. For years his virtuoso legend has overshadowed his achievements as a composer, and only recently has his achievement as a composer begun to be appreciated. His model and inspiration was the violinist Nicolo Paganini, whose talents were so fantastic that he was reputed to be in league with the devil, whom he rather resembled. His music was written almost solely to display his accomplishments as a violinist, but otherwise is not very interesting, except to violinists. His performances, however, made him the epitome and emblem of the emerging awareness of the Romantic virtuoso. Liszt, already a child prodigy, determined to be his equivalent in pianism and even arranged some of Paganini's compositions for piano. Liszt's prodigious gifts and accomplishments were such that Chopin, himself an exquisite pianist, asserted that he had never heard his Preludes performed properly until he heard Liszt play them. Among Liszt's most extraordinary and demanding works for the piano are his Transcendental Etudes. The title claimed them to go beyond anything yet achieved in piano technique. And indeed they formed the foundation for virtuoso technique for decades afterwards. It would be a mistake to think that these and other Liszt works exist solely for displaying the technique required to play them. They signified something more, and the contemporaries of Liszt understood them very well. Though they would not have so expressed it, these Etudes stood for the human possibility of cultural transcendence, of going beyond what human beings had yet achieved and at a higher level. From the virtuoso movement—it was so widespread that it deserves that title, though of course as a movement it was never organized—flowers the transcendental sports movements, first manifest in the mountain-climbing achievements of the second half of the century. And so with other sports, the establishment of the Olympic games, the formal institutions of world records, set up so that they might be surpassed. Still, in the 1830s and 1840s it was music that was the purest example of the virtuoso ideal. It was the period of the *bel canto* operas, works especially of Bellini and Donizetti, a theater which combined historicism with the appearance of the Paganini ideal in the voices of operatic singers and in the style of the music written for them. For the first time opera became a popular art, the cinema of the nineteenth century, and for a hundred years well into the twentieth century, opera singers were adored all over Europe and the Americas. In what are improperly thought of as the decorative cantilenas of operatic arias, there was presented again the virtuosic ideal, but here put into the service of emotional expression, signs of passion which transcend the power of language, even words set to music. That is why Rossini began to write out the "ornaments" rather than leaving them to the taste, the imagination, and the powers of the singer. The characters in these operas are best understood as analogous to the extravagant personalities in the work of Browning, Dickens, and Balzac. Their essential realism appears in the high level of interactional aggression around which the stories of the operas are constructed.

I I

That exaltation of being, the essence of the virtuoso tradition, is to be found not merely in the historical Italian and French operas but also in the earlier operas of Richard Wagner. In these legendary operas, *The Flying Dutchman, Tannhäuser,* and *Lohengrin,* the heroes are extravagant, exalted, and doomed. Even Lohengrin is doomed to be forever alienated from ordinary humanity. In all three Wagner explored the character—and consequences of Romantic alienation. A redemption from that alienation was to be the theme of *The Ring of the Nibelung,* but before it was finished the virtuoso stage of the consequences of Romanticism, with its extravagant and its still hoped-for feeling for Enlightenment redemptionism, for the redemption of society, had come to an end. That was the effect of the revolutions of 1848.

The *Ring* was doubly analytic, textually and musically. In the 1840s Wagner, like most other German intellectuals, was profoundly influenced and moved by Hegel. He thought the *Phenomenology* the greatest book ever written, though like everyone before and since he found some passages entirely inscrutable. Moreover, the *Ring* makes it more than plausible that he also knew *The Philosophy of Right* (or *Law*), perhaps the most transparent book that Hegel ever wrote. In it he demonstrates that each level of society, from the individual through the family to the king, the highest level of society's hierarchical structure, exists to resolve the internal conflicts of the next lower level; but in so doing it develops internal conflicts of its own which it cannot resolve but must be resolved at the next higher level. The king's resolutions of conflict are sustained by the force of the army. Thus Hegel sees society as stabilized by physical power, or force. Nevertheless he entertains the possibility that the constitutional monarch was not the final ordering of society: if it were, society would be internally self-sustaining. Power or force is the indication that a more satisfactory social structure is not only possible but necessary. Wagner wrote the text of the *Ring* to reveal how the Romantic, culturally transcending hero would bring about the reconciliation of Gods (the power of Wotan exercised by the subsidiary powers governing social roles) and men. The love of Siegfried and Brünnhilde in its consummation before the gods would herald the resolution of the internal conflicts of the social structure. Thus in the Romantic tradition there still continued the secular redemptionism of the Enlightenment and the preceding sacred redemptionism of Christianity on which the secular Enlightenment had modeled itself. Wagner's thinking was thus analogous to Marx's, also a version of Hegelian optimism. But the shock of the failure of the 1848–1849 revolutions led Wagner to the pessimism of Schopenhauer and the revision of the conclusion of the *Ring*. This led him to reconceive of the gods as ideological illusions. The forging of the gold of the Rhine into the ring was the extraction from nature of economic surplus. That is the destructive element in society which Wotan must control but cannot. In the new ending the death of gods and heroes and the return of the ring to the Rhine leaves man with none of his redemptive ideological illusions, either of power or of wealth. At the very end, in the orchestra, the illusion of conflict-resolving love makes a final aggressive surge and then fades into nothingness. Analogously Marx was unable to reconcile the contradiction between his Enlightenment redemptive vision and his analysis of society. In spite of the financial help Engels gave him he was unable to finish *Capital* and left only fragments. Wagner directly and Marx by failure and implication pursued the analytic dismantlement of Western culture farther than anyone had yet.

Love as the ultimate or perhaps fundamental illusion is the point of Wagner's next work, *Tristan and Isolde*. In *Götterdämmerung* a magic potion causes Siegfried to fall in love with Gutrune. In *Tristan* a magic potion does not cause Tristan and Isolde to fall in love but does surrender them to love's illusory power. That it is a destructive illusion is shown by Tristan's death and Isolde's conviction that he is still alive, while she herself vanishes into the *Weltall*, the world without distinctions, the world of nothingness, of pure illusion. On the simple realistic level she is mad. Yet in his next work, *The Mastersingers*, Wagner finds a way out of the dilemma. There he sees that even if we can act only by means of illusions, we can after all act—and do great things. In this text, illusions become instruments. Wagner has virtually moved into a pragmatism of the American sort, and not far from the time when American pragmatism itself was beginning to emerge. In *Parsifal* he shows how religious myths and instrumental illusions can indeed produce great results, the escape from erotic love by the fusion of masculinity and femininity, and the consequent—freeing women from their bondage of being either house slaves or whores. That Wagner himself thought that he had solved the problem originally posed in *The Flying Dutchman*, how the alienated can achieve value, is indicated by his decision henceforth to write no more operas but instead to write symphonies. His death intervened.

Musically Wagner's analytic power is as remarkable as it is in his texts. The form this took was the leitmotiv, a device which has been widely misunderstood. The first evidence for what Wagner had accomplished with this device is *Das Rheingold*. That first music drama of the *Ring* has in its music an extraordinary freshness, as if Wagner had invented music anew. And in a sense he did. Each motive is not the equivalent of a verbal phrase, or of a name, but is a musical cell capable of endless development and variation in combination with other musical cells. Each is a tiny, self-subsistent melody. In the motives, Wagner has analyzed music into minimal melodies. The endless flow of music, his "endless melody," emerges from joining these melodic cells, not fragments, by means of nonrecurrent melodic miniatures. Nietzsche was to grasp something of this when he claimed that Wagner's art was the art of the miniature, though he failed to grasp what Wagner had achieved or to what use Wagner had put the motives. Richard Strauss, like so many others who have attempted to use Wagner's device, was not successful. Unlike Wagner's, his motives tend to be uninteresting and unmemorable in themselves; Wagner's are always beautiful and memorable melodic miniatures. Strauss's genius lay, rather, not in using the motives as Wagner did but in inventing great soaring extended melodies in traditional operatic fashion. To be sure, Wagner could do that too when he wanted to, but the endless melody constituted on recurrent motives at its most successful, as in *The Mastersingers*, gives one the experience that an entire act is but a single immense melody. Thus it has been something of a mistake to name the motives, though not always. For example, the Sword Motive, first appearing in *Das Rheingold*, and then recurring most powerfully and beautifully in the first act of *Die Walküre*, is not badly named but is rather inadequately named. A more appropriate name, if it has to be named, is "summons to masculine aggressive competence." It is really time that the whole question be reopened, and that names (which are indeed convenient) be assigned only on the basis of *every* appearance of the motive in the entire *Ring*. Wagner had such an immense attraction for subsequent composers—and still does—because he had analytically reduced the flow of musical structure to its fundamental element, the melodic phrase of musical meaning; and because on that basis he created for music a new freedom, analogous to the freedom of Hans Sachs's pragmatism. The leitmotiv system is indeed a pragmatic or instrumental use of the concentration of melody into a miniature, into the essence of melody.

1 2

When Wagner was beginning to work on the *Ring*, in the new country of the United States of America Herman Melville was writing *Moby Dick*, a novel remarkably analogous to the *Ring*. This was all the stranger because Melville's earlier works had been more Enlightenment than anything else. The two novels based on his experience in the Pacific islands are splendid instances of Enlightenment primitivism. *Mardi* was an allegorical exploration of various Enlightenment themes, ideas, and ideologies and the rejection of all of them. As the novel ends, Taji is still seeking the lost maiden Yillah, the emblem of pure value, unadulterated by institutions and beliefs. Thus did Melville rapidly repeat the Romantic experience, as did so many others in the century. In *Moby Dick* he suddenly leaps forward to the post-1848 position in Europe, aided and perhaps enabled by *Sartor Resartus*, a work which made his historical position in Western European culture clear to him. The novel is filled with allusions to Carlyle, and indeed many of the tricks and strategies of Melville's style in this work are clearly derived from Carlyle. Yet he also goes beyond *Sartor Resartus*, which ends with a promise of a redemptive or at least progressive revolution as the hero leaves Germany for France when he hears of the French Revolution of 1830. There is no such quasi-redemptive hint in Melville's novel, the end of which is as uncompromising as the revised end of Wagner's work. Ahab, having lost a leg to the great white whale, is determined not to seek revenge but to create from a meaningless accident a meaningfulness for both the universe and himself as part of that universe and as also independent of it, as at once thrall to materiality and transcendingly free of it.

The instrument of his destruction, in the end itself destroyed and swallowed up by the sea, is the *Pequod*, the whaling ship, the analogue to the ring of the Nibelung. Both are emblems of economic forces. Only Ishmael, the narrator, survives to tell the story; only the isolated and alienated Romantic can stand apart from this failure of human belief to find meaning and value on the other side of the mask which man himself has imposed upon the world, determined to find meaning where there is none. In his next novel, *Pierre*, Melville told the story all over again. The idealistic hero, believing in the transcendental Romanticism of such earlier writers as Emerson and Thoreau, is destroyed by moving from the idyllic pastoralism of his home to the realities of nineteenth-century urban economics, the city's struggle for existence, to which he cannot accommodate himself. Years later in *Billy Budd* Melville set forth the anti-explanatory, anti-ideological ideology of developed Romanticism. In a terrible irony Billy accepts his execution as just and blesses his executioner. Melville deliberately omits the only scene which could explain this, Billy's interview with his captain, Starry Vere.

I 3

Both *Moby Dick* and *Pierre* are instances of the movement in the Romantic tradition from historical realism to contemporary realism. The Goncourt brothers were the first to recognize what had happened and where the post-1848 realism came from. The realistic novel, they said, is an historical novel about the present. The historical novel, beginning with Scott, had taught novelists to base their work on research, and the rapid development of historiography in the nineteenth century was of inestimable advantage. That development was made possible by the opening of national archives to scholars. The resulting works of historiography were mines of information for the historical novelist. Moreover, the very same tendency in the Romantic tradition to engage the mind with the real that led to Romantic realism and Romantic historicism had an impact on historiography itself, just as the historical novel inspired historiographers. Macaulay was inspired by Scott's novels when he set out to write his history of England and wished to reach Scott's audience. Thus the historical novel was transformed into the realistic novel by the transference of the examination of the past from a distance to the examination of the present from a similar distance, that is, a detached or objective orientation. It is also instructive that some of the earliest realist novels and even some later ones, well into the twentieth century, were written by men who had started out as journalists. This is true even of Dickens; the realistic elements in his novels, no matter how transformed and mutilated by his sentimentality and his sensationalism, can be traced to his journalist training and practice. One of the clichés of American realistic fiction is the journalist who is determined to write the Great American Novel.

To be sure, that post-1848 realistic objectivity, the new realism, found its greatest examination in the work of a man who was not a journalist, Gustave Flaubert. *Madame Bovary* shows very much the same development as does Pierre—from the pre-1848 redemptive idealism to the post-1848 objective realism. Emma Bovary is educated by nuns and imbibes from them Catholicism's response to the Enlightenment and Romanticism, converting both into an erotic sentimentalism. The swooning St. Teresa, overcome by her loving adoration of the figure for whom she was to be the Bride of Christ, became one of the principal Catholic ideals, especially in the education, if one can call it that, of Catholic girls. This fusion of religion and eroticism occasioned the emergence of an erotic redemptionism remarkably like the redemptive eroticism, or even sexuality, of Romanticism, such as is seen in *The Flying Dutchman* and in Tennyson's *In Memoriam*. So Emma longed for a higher existence than that afforded by her husband in a dull French provincial town, in itself a combination of Flaubert's own experience and what he had learned from Balzac. Her notion of redeeming love, of redemptive eroticism, led her to accept the illusion that a shameless seducer, of a higher social class than hers, a member of the aristocracy (for which she had a sentimental middle-class adoration), would love her forever and transform her life, flying with her to an imaginary Italy. Having invested all of her sense of her own value in this one relation, when she is deceived she has little choice but suicide. Thus redemptive love as a destructive illusion is found in Melville, in Flaubert, in Wagner, in Mérimée, in Turgenev, and in— among many others—Sacher-Masoch. In all of these, love is revealed as at best a temporary source of value, temporary because unreliable, and unreliable because illusory.

This theme Flaubert was to repeat in *Salammbô* and *A Sentimental Education*. The first of these, set in ancient Carthage, is particularly interesting in showing the link between historical realism and contemporary realism, as did another of Flaubert's novels, *The Temptation of Saint Anthony*. *Salammbô* employs realist objectivity and realist technique in evoking the brutality, the viciousness, and the horror of an ancient civilization and, by implication, civilization itself. *A Sentimental Education* again shows the illusionistic failure of erotic love, an illusion so destructive that at the end the protagonist finds consolation only in a sentimentally distorted memory of an adolescent experience. Finally, in *Bouvard and Pecuchet* Flaubert made an inventory of the cultural resources of the nineteenth century bourgeois civilization and revealed its failure. Thus the great theme of Romantic alienation continued to show its power.

I 4

The most completely Romantic poet of the mid-nineteenth century was Charles Baudelaire, who in response to the events of 1848 went through the transition from a socially redemptive Romanticism, like Marx's and Carlyle's, to an antiredemptive realism. The title of his great book of poetry, *The Flowers of Evil,* is a pretty strong direction on how to respond to what he was writing. The flower is a traditional emblem for value; thus the title may be interpreted as "value derived from negative value," all the culturally defined sources of guilt. He was using not precisely a Romantic tradition but an idea like that which Shelley used when he equated evil with an eagle and good with a serpent. Baudelaire was, because of the failure of the 1848 revolution, in a cultural position that Romantics as early as Wordsworth had experienced, but more completely and more intensely. After having in an opening poem established alienation as a theme of the collection, he turned to contemporary realism. He had of course seen in Balzac and Stendhal (whose *The Red and the Black* showed alienation as the consequence of the failure of eroticism, the army, and the church) of the possibilities of the use of contemporary life in fiction. In the drawings of Constantin Guys he saw the possibility of contemporary life for poetry, closer to art than to fiction. His great theme was spleen versus the ideal, that is, depression or loss of value as opposed to the source of value, the ideal. Thus in the ugly modern city and in the erotic perverse he was determined to find a new source of value. His total alienation from the value sources of his society forced him to seek value in what his society had rejected as sources of value. The first task was to face directly and honestly what society preferred to ignore, thus emphasizing that the creation of value is the task of the isolated and alienated individual or "self." And in facing the socially rejected and condemned he concluded that the only possibility was "something new," to be derived from the old captain death himself. The most appropriate interpretation is that he meant not death but the awareness of death as absolutely final. Thus realism is the rejection of all transcendental consolations. That strategy for achieving something is the voyage. That was like Carlyle's Center of Indifference, the randomization of behavior, the escape from the sociocultural restrictions of behavior, from the culturally established and socially enforced mode of controlling and limiting behavior. For more than a hundred years Baudelaire like Flaubert was one of the great liberating figures of the consequences of Romanticism.

15

On the other side of the Atlantic an equally liberating figure emerged at the same time, Walt Whitman. *Leaves of Grass* was to go through immense expansion and revision from 1855 to 1892, but the heart of it was the original book, and the heart of that was the section he later named "Song of Myself." This original book was so long buried in later editions that it was recovered only after World War II. Whitman was considerably more positive than Baudelaire, though he too sought acceptance of what men call evil and corrupt, but after all he did not live in Europe under the Second Empire. Certainly one of his themes was an Americanism which he opposed to the failure of Europe in 1848. Nevertheless that Americanism was only a small part of what he was trying to say and do. It gave him, as it were, courage and an excuse for his experimentation, but his efforts were directly in the Romantic tradition.

Indeed, his work to the very end was an extraordinary effort to realize a central Romantic theme, adumbrated as early as "The Ancient Mariner" and first made manifest in *Sartor Resartus*. It is what Baudelaire calls for in his final poem. It is the wandering exposure to new possibilities. It is randomization of behavior. Whitman, with the Romantic tradition behind him, though of course he did not know Baudelaire though he certainly knew Carlyle, saw in that randomization of the imagination, if not of behavior, the strategy for the creation of value. That was his realism, and it is significant that for years before he became a poet he was a journalist. Randomization is what he offered his reader, often in the form of catalogues or lists, sometimes of categorial coherence, often utterly miscellaneous in their content. He simply set forth in his unique, loosely rhythmic, long lines, everything that men do that he could think of, every occupation, every mode of existence, every form of love that he dared mention or hint at. It was a time, it must remembered, when information about life and the world outside of one's own immediate circle was hardly available, except for a tiny number of the rich who were able to move about and travel. The awareness of the world outside of one's own immediate circumstances was just beginning to be available. In the same 1850s Hawthorne wrote *The House of the Seven Gables*, in which photography and the railroad are shown as liberating forces, the liberty of information. One of the merits of Dickens and Balzac was that they opened up England and France to the awareness of the vast majority of their readers. Realism itself—and this is one of the reasons it triumphed and still does—offered that randomizing knowledge. It is instructive to remember that in the 1950s the coming of television meant to the uneducated and nonreading housewife an immense expansion of her world. We know from the studies of the impact of television that it was felt as powerful liberation. The nature films of Walt Disney, though suffering from a Dickensian cuteness and sentimentality, continue to be shown on television to generation after generation, and for the same reason. The official and conventional justification for such knowledge only conceals their real function as randomization.

A further aspect of that randomization was at mid-century beginning on its vast proliferation—travel literature. Such literature had of course existed since the early Middle Ages, but now what was but a brook became a river and soon a Niagara. So surfeited are we today with knowledge about any aspect of the world and its peoples we could wish to have that Whitman's catalogues can seem pointless and dull; but read with an awareness of their novelty at the time and especially with a realization of the Romantic tradition of randomization as a strategy of cultural transcendence they are still powerful and beautiful. One of his titles that was to have lasting appeal was "Song of the Open Road," and it is evident from other poems that Whitman read widely in travel literature. Yet his poetic procedure was not mere cataloguing, mere randomizing. Nothing could be more explicit than his determination to celebrate that randomization, to insist that it is the source of value, that it is indeed the primary if not the only source of value. With Whitman the secularization of value creation is for the first time complete and uncompromising. In beginning his poem with "I celebrate myself," he arrived at the full realization that the creation of value is the task of the individual, that this "self" is the behavior of value creation from one's own resources. Thus Whitman claims that he is at one with all selves, with whom he wishes to share his liberation. And that liberation was peculiarly intense because behind the mask of randomization lay what he was really doing, not an analytic but a randomizing dismantlement of the superstructure of Western culture. He did what Baudelaire wanted to do and was trying to do. Thus like Baudelaire he was one of the great liberating figures of the Romantic consequences.

Moreover, he was vastly aided by a central development in Romanticism, the tradition of the virtuoso. One's understanding of what he was trying to do is helped, for example, when his fascination with the Romantic opera is taken into account. In one poem he calls a section an "aria," and the subdivision of "Song of Myself" and of his late poems as well are each best understood as the poetic equivalent of the virtuoso aria of Romantic opera. Indeed, the syntactical repetition of line after line has a striking resemblance to, and no doubt is derived from, music. Each series of subdivisions is a series of arias, is a libretto for unwritten music. It is not surprising that in England, where his work was first appreciated, several of his poems were later set to music by Frederick Delius and Ralph Vaughan Williams. Music thus helped him in what was clearly his aim, the reduction or dismantlement of conventional prosody to what he considered a much more fundamental poetic mode.

1 6

The nearest equivalent in Europe to Whitman was not a poet but a painter, Gustave Courbet. His first successful paintings were self-portraits, himself isolated in a landscape, Romantic self-definitions. He soon moved on to what he himself called "realism," pictures of rural life, burial scenes, on a large scale, evocations of the life of rural France, small towns and peasantry. He painted scenes of peasant labor, stone breaking, winnowing wheat, spinning. In time he turned to forest scenes, scenes of stags, himself isolated against the ocean, rivers rushing out from caverns, small-town girls walking in the countryside. His grandest picture, on a very large scale, was *The Artist and his Muse*. This was an almost Whitmanesque self-portrait, showing himself in his studio with some of his pictures forming the background, and the foreground inhabited by the figures of his poetic imagination—old men, countrymen, beggars, fashionable figures, and even Baudelaire himself. It is a sublime emblem of the Romantic artist surrounded by the realities which he has grasped with his artistic imagination, his poetic creativity. That is why his muse is naked. And again in Whitmanesque manner it is a random assemblage. Like Whitman he grasped randomness as a path to artistic freedom and cultural transcendence.

1 7

In the same post-1848 years emerged as a painter an artist who had already made a great reputation as a political caricaturist, the greatest who has ever worked in the European tradition, Honoré Daumier. In these years he created a style of painting so radical and so innovative that it was not understood for some decades. Now he is recognized as one of the greatest of French painters. The only work that anticipated him was the late painting of Goya, beginning with the Black Paintings, which he could not have known. Daumier's style, however, was even more radical than that of Goya. To be sure, he belonged in subject matter to the realists, scenes of laundrywomen, judges, physicians, all kinds of scenes from the streets and public buildings of Paris, and even a realist vision of Ecce Homo, and a marvelous series inspired by Don Quixote, who in his madness that rose above and transformed mundane realities was a Romantic hero and had been for decades. Stylistically Daumier was eclectic, deriving his ideas about painting from many sources, from Roman bas-reliefs to Rubens and Delacroix. However, the principal source of his style was his own political lithographs. These are so powerful and effective because he mastered the essence of caricature, the selection of the telling attribute of the figure being caricatured, the selection and the exaggeration. But Daumier's superiority as a caricaturist was that the selection was of the highest importance and the exaggeration was minimal. His caricatures are great because they are reductionist. And that reductionism, that dismantlement of the European tradition of painting, that invasion of painting by lithographed caricature, that seeking for the visual essence, that equal determination, like Goya's and Turner's, to discover the painterly essence, the essence of applying brush to canvas, is what made him so misunderstood at his time and so heroic a figure today. Like Turner he revealed that the direction that painting in the Romantic tradition and its consequences had to move in was not truthfulness to subject but truthfulness to paint, to the act of painting. Truthfulness to subject was the aim of the English Pre-Raphaelite painters, who departed from a full realism only in the direction of what they have been little known for, an extraordinary intensification of realism by means of intensified color, an intensification which was to find its equivalent in French painting only after another forty or fifty years, or even longer. Compared with their predecessors, the Pre-Raphaelites might with justice be said to have discovered color. Even so, however, their truthfulness to subject, like Courbet's, was not the direction in which painting was to move. The work of both was too conservative, too limited for the most part to the questioning of the subject matter of European painting—but too unquestioning of its mode.

1 8

Yet of all the artists who called themselves realists—and there were German, Russian, Polish, Scandinavian also, witnesses to the delta-like spread of the consequences of Romanticism—perhaps the finest, though little known in the United States, were the Italian Macchiaio-loi, so called because their first though not final style emphasized *mac-chie* or spots. It has been said, half seriously perhaps, that only the Italians have really known how to paint, a remark in which there is something of justice. Certainly an exploration of the collections in Italy of nineteenth-century paintings shows that the Italians of the century never lost the Italian genius for composition, drawing, and color. Perhaps the greatest of the Macchiaioloi and perhaps the greatest Italian painter of the nineteenth century was the one most fully aware of his realist break with Italian academicism and the most fully determined to be a painter of modern life, Giovanni Fattori. At least his equal was Silvestro Lega. If the constant mark of Romantic painting throughout the century was the sense of freshness, the sense of painting being newly invented, few have the freshness, the sense of immediacy of painterly response, of this group based in Florence in the 1850s and the 1860s. Even in color reproduction, almost the only way to see their paintings without going to Italy, the finest works of this group leap from the page with a convincingness that the other realist painters we have glanced at rarely achieve. The sense of immediacy emerges from the sense of the transformation of scene to canvas with the minimum of traditional artistic manipulation and convention. Their paintings come to you with an air of Whitmanesque freedom.

1 9

These years saw in music an extraordinary invention, one that can be recognized as an instance of the ideology of Romanticism. That was Franz Liszt's invention of the symphonic poem. There had been anticipations of the idea in works of Beethoven, Mendelssohn, Schumann, Berlioz, and Wagner, not only in his overtures but also in his Faust Overture, originally planned to be a three-movement Faust symphony, probably inspired by Berlioz. Still, the idea for such works did not crystallize until Liszt invented an appropriate and evocative name. His first musical poems were piano works written during his virtuoso period, various pieces in his *Years of Pilgrimage* and various arrangements of melodies from operas, which were less virtuoso arrangements than they were "Piano Poems" on the opera itself. Liszt's first symphonic poem was based on a poem by Hugo, the second took its title from a poem by Lamartine, another inspired by a poem by Schiller. Others were inspired by paintings and by historical events and classical myths. To these can be added his Faust Symphony and his Dante Symphony.

Smetana was one of the first to take up Liszt's idea, and he was followed by composers in France, Bohemia, and Russia. The idea reached its culmination in the symphonic poems of the German Richard Strauss. Symphonic poems continued to be written until the 1930s. Thus Liszt's invention coincided with the emergence and development of realistic fiction and realistic painting. Music's connection with the nonmusical had been in the past and was to be in the future principally in opera, in which text appeared to govern music but, more accurately, music governed the interpretation of text. In the symphonic poem music also governed the interpretation of the idea of a text, or of an event, or of a painting. Or rather, music set out to control the listener's response to the text or whatever was the "subject" of the symphonic poem. With the emergence of the symphonic poem, however, the connection between the musical and the nonmusical gets shifted noticeably from works' "subjects" to their *titles*— first in piano works and soon thereafter in works composed both for piano and violin. The fundamental drive behind these various works by so many composers, however, was achieved by Richard Strauss in his Domestic Symphony, an interpretation of a composer's day, including children and making love. Even before this, sections of *Thus Spake Zarathustra* and *A Hero's Life*, the hero of both being Strauss himself as a hero of musical innovation and creativity, there were sections almost as realistic as the Domestic Symphony and the later Alpine Symphony.

Thus the driving force behind the symphonic poem was the effort to establish a direct relation between music and nonmusic, between music and something that had actually happened, either in literary imagination or in historical reality. The symphonic poem was a manifestation of Romanticism's drive to reality. It is an interpretation of reality just as the realistic novel was such an interpretation. Beginning with the Goncourts and Flaubert and achieving its triumph with the immense Rougon-Maquart series of Zola, this phase of Romantic realism is best understood as analytic realism as opposed to what, though rather inadequately, might be called the intuitive realism of Balzac. That is, the selection of subject and detail was governed by a theory of society and behavior, even, as in Zola, by an ideology believed to be scientifically founded. Analytic realism is a more accurate title for what Zola and his followers (of which there were many throughout Europe and America, and still are), called "naturalism," a term which Zola addmittedly invented for publicity purposes. In fact he frequently used symbolic devices in his novels. So behind the symphonic poem was the effort to dismantle musical tradition so that the source of music, the same imagination that governs literature and the other arts, could be uncovered. It implied a theoretical advance in aesthetics, for it considered the arias not as imitating the world but as responding to it. It was the same realistic effort that governed Wagner's invention of the leitmotiv, a common source for art that Joyce was to seek in *Ulysses*.

2 0

The leading poets too moved into the new realism. In his next two volumes after 1850 Browning devoted two long dramatic monologues, his unique version of the realistic movement in Romanticism, to contemporary religious issues, Catholicism and Spiritualism, for neither of which he had much respect. His next work was a return to historical realism, but with more realism than historicism. The vast poem, *The Ring and the Book*, is an intensely analytic investigation into the notion of "truth," which emerges as each individual's unique interpretation of the world. The resulting notion of truth is very much like pragmatism, just as Wagner proposed a kind of pragmatism at about the same time. Tennyson also moved into contemporary realism with a study of insanity in *Maud*, and continued with more frequent realistic studies. And he too embarked on a vast quasi-historical analysis of the nature of illusion, *The Idylls of the King*. The same tendency for the realistic movement to investigate the nature of religious truth was found most powerfully in the work of the French poet, Leconte de Lisle. Like so many of his generation he too was disillusioned by the failure of the 1848 revolution. He moved completely away from conventional religion to an uncompromising atheism. His poems about Asia and the antique Mediterranean world were investigations into the character of the religious imagination. His poem on nothingness was a grim vision of a world without value, a valuelessness to which his analytic examinations of religious illusions led him. Value is to be experienced only in a stoic examination of the emptiness of claims to truth, but only when that vision is transformed into poetry. This claim that poetry, and art in general, was a revelation of the truth of human existence which the truths of science and of the nonpoetic could not achieve, that poetic truth has a unique existence, and that poetry has a unique semantic function, was to have a long life.

Thus a distinction was made between the "truth" of value and the "truth" of fact. The truth of fact was seen to have no redeeming function, no source of value. The truth of value, to be found only in art and poetry, was not to be demonstrated but only experienced. The redemptive task of art, observable in Romanticism in its beginnings, was thus by Leconte de Lisle, and eventually by endless others, given a greater power by the implication and sometimes the assertion that only the truth of value, the truth of aesthetic experience, was humanly significant. Thus art became a surrogate of religion, a consequence of Romanticism to last for decades, well into the twentieth century. It was not long before its great rival revealed itself as the socialistic redemption of society, an Enlightenment idea still of immense power in spite of its frequent failure.

2 I

The shift from analytic realism to what came to be known as aestheticism can be observed in the stylistic shift in the music of Brahms. He destroyed all of his youthful works, but even so his first publications were still in the manner of the virtuoso or transcendental Romanticism of Robert Schumann. But then suddenly in the early 1860s he moved to what is often though inaccurately known as his "classicism." To be sure, to a certain extent he modeled his work on the "classicism" of the late eighteenth century, but in fact only in its overall structure or plan. What he was primarily interested in doing was creating his own unique style, which at one time was judged to be almost academic but now can be seen as a determination to create pure musical beauty. An examination of Brahms makes it reasonable to change the idea of "aestheticism" into the notion of "stylism." The art for art's sake movement, the notion of the unique function of art, aestheticism—all these were really a search for style. So understood, the aesthetic movement can be recognized as one of the profoundest and most searching developments of the consequences of the Romantic tradition.

But style is not an attribute only of art. In fact, all behavior is styled. It functions by protecting man from the randomness his brain demands, by limiting the range of his behavior in a way that is metaphysically and morally indifferent. For style is a profounder concept than metaphysics and morality. As Leconte de Lisle had grasped, it maintains the individual by protecting him from the meaninglessness, the failure, of ordinary existence. It gives him an uncommitted continuity of self-perception. The connection between analytic realism and stylism is that stylism made it possible to contemplate without self-destruction what analytic realism was revealing. And that was the revelation of the pitiful resources for existence of Western culture. Together they encompass a further dismantlement of the superstructure of Western culture, its exposure, as Wagner and Tennyson and so many others grasped, as a structure of illusions. Stylism makes the notion of the self empirical and solid. It enables the individual to construct and maintain his sense of value, his own and the world's, without committing him to any religious or philosophical or moral position.

2 2

The close union of analytic realism and stylism can be seen vividly in the poetry of Algernon Swinburne, especially in his masterpiece, one of the marvels of English poetry, *Atalanta in Calydon*. In the 1860s he emerged as the first fully formed stylist in Western literature, parallel with Brahms' emergence as the first true stylist in music. Both sought for an extreme and frequently voluptuous beauty. But both also sought for an achieved intense and powerful passion controlled by style. Swinburne constructed his style from an extraordinary mastery of the resources of verse—assonance of various kinds, rhythm, and an extremely demanding syntax, built upon syntactical accretion. The result was a style, or a stylistic surface, so powerful, so intoxicating, that the reader tended to pay little attention to what Swinburne was saying. Two of his more powerful notions were the burden upon man of erotic love and the evil of belief in God. So that "Silence is most noble till the end." But he was saying more than that. Actually his work proceeded from an analysis of the incoherence and self-destructiveness of the individual to an analysis of the destructive incoherence of the family and to the destructiveness of the social structure. His was an alienation so severe that eventually he had to be held together, as it were, by the domesticity provided by a friend and quasi-guardian. Unfortunately that same friend interfered with Swinburne's desire to write fiction. His two novels were brilliant examples of the destructive interaction of individual and family and of individual and eroticism. Somewhat like Swinburne's work was *The Rubaiyat of Omar Khayyam* by Edward Fitzgerald, one of the most popular and most liberating poems of the century, one that is still liberating, with its climactic cry to God that he accept man's forgiveness, that God who "e'en with Paradise did devise the snake."

2 3

At the same time, across the Channel there was under way that almost revolutionary development in painting called, inaccurately, impressionism. A group of French painters, often though not always exhibiting together, had diverse origins in the studies of their predecessors. Some did indeed use the technique of impressionism, particularly of divisionism—letting the eye mix individual dots or streaks of color instead of mixing colors on the palette—but all had in common a rejection of academic painting and for subject matter either modern life, inspired by Baudelaire, or landscape, developing out of the Barbizon painters. The oldest and the more or less leader of the group was Édouard Manet. He was initially inspired by the Spanish school, particularly Velasquez, for instead of being the product of a studio he developed his own style by studying the old masters in the Louvre and by wandering in true Romantic randomizing fashion among the museums of Western Europe, thus being an early example of a stylist. Like Whitman, Manet intensified the Romantic tradition of the self as the source of value. As much as his painting, this independence from cultural conventions and this self-intensification appealed to the somewhat younger impressionists, who are in fact best understood as creating and belonging to that stage of Romanticism I have called analytic realism. In Manet's painting one is not only aware of the painting itself but also of the process by which the painting was produced. The "personality"—to use a most inadequate and somewhat misleading term—of Manet, like that of Baudelaire, was more salient than that of any of his predecessors. It was something other than the different masteries of tradition of Delacroix and Ingres. It was both a synthesis of a selected line of tradition and transcendence of it. Thus arose his ironic use of traditional devices and forms, some even of the Renaissance, in *Déjeuner sur l'Herbe,* for which a better title would be *Artists' and Models' Picnic in the Park,* the women being obviously the mistresses of the artists, or in *Olympia,* the grand horizontal in the pose of a Renaissance Venus, or in the highly realistic picture of a dead Christ, in a chair, with hairy chest and excessively solid angelic supporters and displayers.

Since the meaning of any sign is a response or more precisely what is judged by someone to be an appropriate response, irony is simply what is judged by convention to be an inappropriate response. The implication of these paintings is that the Renaissance artists were painting their mistresses (or the mistresses of their employers) in the guise of goddesses, and that religious paintings were less religious than religious publicity. Thus Manet transcended the past by revealing its dishonesty.

So "honest" painting became the aim of those inspired by Manet, some of whom really used impressionist and divisionist techniques. But whether they did or not they all were interested in the fundamental reality of painting, the response of the artist to the subject as revealed in the activity of his brush. Thus impressionism is less a matter of perception than it is an analysis of the whole process of painting including its final stage, the perception of the painting. The famous lack of finish which offended so many of the public, actually most of them, meant that at least in painting there was revealed what was implicit and often explicit in Romanticism from its very beginning: the responder to the work of art, the perceiver, the observer, the reader, the listener, is as creative an individual as the artist himself, that is, he too is a creator of value. The impressionists are popular today because they painted such pretty pictures of the kind of scene one encounters on vacations or on Sunday trips from the city. That is a recognition, though unwitting, of the other aspect of these painters, their stylism, their aestheticism, their interest in transforming any landscape into an object of beauty. The occasional use of factories, more often than not in the form of distant factory chimneys, is an instance both of their realism and of their stylism. Thus Pissarro ended up by painting the boulevards of Paris, from above and at a distance.

And so it is that the two dominant artistic cultures of the second half of the century, realism and stylism (or aestheticism), are intimately related, are two sides of the same coin. The union of these two aspects of the Romantic tradition was achieved later in the century by those painters, novelists, poets, sculptors, architects who were known as the "decadents." These artists, of whom Joris-Karl Huysmans was perhaps the first, combined an utmost elegance and beauty of stylistic surface with an often profound investigation and exposure of what the dominant bourgeois society preferred not to talk about, preferred to keep hidden, swept under the rug. Huysmans began as a "naturalist," a Zolaesque analytical realist, and imposed on this his stylism. His novel *The Cathedral* is less a novel than a guide to the artistic treasure house of Chartres Cathedral. Even his conversion to Catholicism was more a matter of style, of the attempt to create an armor for the self. It was the great artistic tradition, at least until the nineteenth century, of Catholicism that appealed in the same way to so many of the stylists. The greatest of the English stylists, Walter Pater, who proposed that the self armor itself by "burning with a hard gemlike flame," eventually became interested in religion and in religious ritual for aesthetic or stylistic reasons rather than religious ones.

2 4

In the 1880s the dominating interest of the leading impressionists, stylism, led to a transcendence of what they had done so far. The most conspicuous example of this new development was Claude Monet. So profound was his transcendence that his later work was not truly appreciated until after World War II. In the 1950s abstract expressionism precipitated a revival, indeed the first true recognition, of the late paintings of Turner; so it shortly led to a revival and again the first true appreciation of the work of Monet after the 1880s. In his work the realism was gradually overcome by what came to be known as expressionism. What Monet began to analyze was what hitherto only the Pre-Raphaelites, though not entirely successfully, had emphasized, color. Color may be said to have the same relation to configurations that music has to a text. It guides and controls the interpretation of the painting. Pater said that all art approaches the condition of music, and indeed the music of the nineteenth century has survived more massively than have the other arts.

In the early twentieth century, Kandinsky was to think of painting as visual music, and in doing so eliminated all but the most evanescent traces of subject matter. Eventually he and Malevich were to eliminate subject matter entirely. That process began in the 1880s when artists began to think of motif instead of subject. The painting is not "about" the landscape in the sense that the painter is responding to the landscape as landscape, but rather the landscape is now only a motif, an excuse and an opportunity for a painterly response. In time, of course, even that excuse was no longer needed. Thus by means of the culturally transcending path of color, painting became a construct, just as abstract music, of a moment in the interpretational process.

2 5

Two painters in particular evinced this new stage in the continually culturally transcending progression of the consequences of Romanticism. They are Paul Cézanne and Vincent van Gogh. The most powerful influence on the young Cézanne after his learning period was

Daumier. From him Cézanne learned that simplification which exposes the structure of a painting; and structure was thus what he emphasized for the rest of his life. From the impressionists he learned how to use color, and then he set forth on his own extraordinary and lonely path, achieving results which did not begin to be recognized until the 1890s and then by only a few painters and collectors of very advanced taste. In a well-known remark Cézanne said that he wanted to make paintings as solid as those in museums, but his solidity was of an entirely different sort, though he certainly achieved it. The essence of what he did was to use color to analyze pictorial space. He reduced realism to the felt or experienced reality of the picture itself rather than, in the impressionist manner, the reality of the process of painting. In doing so he did not hesitate to distort the appearance in order to reveal the structure that supported the appearance. Even the late Monet continued to be an illusionistic, that is, an "imitative" painter. The motif though only a motif was still undistorted, except by a flood of color that if anything heightened the illusory character of the work. For Cézanne, however, the painting is clearly and unmistakably a construct. Cézanne transcends both the ideal of beauty and the ideal of the real to reveal how perception constructs the world.

2 6

There is a certain resemblance between Cézanne's pictorial thought and not so much the thought of Nietzsche as the way he was at the time of constructing his philosophical works. Early in his career he did something the significance of which was scarcely to be recognized for nearly a hundred years after he did it. He tore language loose from the world. Just as Cézanne showed painting to be a semiotic construct, so Nietzsche showed language to be a semiotic construct. He created the notion that even philosophical language for all its pretensions cannot mirror nature, cannot say what the world is, and indeed in a peculiar sense cannot even say that it cannot say what the world is. Thus in his philosophical works he progressively destroyed, dismantled philosophy as an extended discourse. He wrote in short paragraphs and insisted that it was not what these paragraphs said that was important but rather what they did not say. He realized that the extended philosophic discourse seduces writer and reader into thinking that he has understood reality when in fact he has only understood philosophic discourse. And, Nietzsche thought, that did not amount to very much of importance. On the whole, philosophers have detested

Nietzsche because he revealed their profession as otiose, a partaking of the self-deception of culturally and socially committed human behavior. So he was not concerned with saying anything but rather with freeing himself and the reader from cultural illusions. That is what he meant by the famous transvaluation of all values. Nietzsche was the climax though not the completion of the consequences of Romanticism, for he first uttered what was implicit or at best barely hinted at in the work of his predecessors. The task of the Western European who has achieved freedom is cultural transcendence, which is indeed the achievement of freedom, a freedom that transforms him from a victim of culture to its master.

2 7

In the paintings of van Gogh there is something analogous to Nietzsche's leap to freedom. Magnificent as Cézanne's paintings are there is always, even to the end of his life, something excessively self-conscious about them, something almost painful; one is only too aware of the struggle, the severe intellectual struggle, that went into their making. Hence in some ways his most agreeably and immediately satisfying works are his water colors, particularly those that, perhaps mistakenly, we call unfinished. In these we see the delighted beginning of the enterprise, not the struggling fulfillment of it. So in his finished oil paintings he rarely offers the delightful, the simply sensuous satisfaction of painting and responding to painting, the fulfilling exercise of the process of painting. For that we turn advisedly to van Gogh. From a rather gloomy palette he was triggered by his encounter in Paris with the work of the impressionists into a way with the paint of painting and above all the use of color which transcended what they had done and were still doing. Thus he picks up something that emerged in the late works of Daubigny (who died in 1879), though perhaps he did not know it, the frank presentation of the brush stroke as a factor in the design or composition of the painting.

This is the source of the popular fascination with his painting for those who know little about art and care little. The brush stroke and in his drawings the pen stroke and the heightened use of color, together with the freedom of both as means of "self-expression" (unsatisfactory term), makes him into a "personality," makes it easy to grasp that a unique self is at work in unique self-creation. The self as the creator of value, present but subdued for nearly a hundred years of the Romantic tradition, in van Gogh leaps out powerfully, even

stridently, but certainly unmistakably. Thus he is the visual analogue
to Nietzsche. Nietzsche is a philosopher for people who know little
and care little (and quite advisedly) about formal, academic philosophy. Thus, just as the twentieth-century deconstructionists have
turned back to and built upon Nietzsche, so the popularity of van
Gogh was heightened immensely by the arrival of the abstract expressionism of the 1960s. Just as Nietzsche becomes more interesting
as the twentieth century moves to the twenty-first, so van Gogh seems
a greater artist than he seemed half a century ago. Though his paintings are carefully crafted and rarely violate the actuality of the scene
he was responding to, so that where he stood when he painted his
later pictures can be still identified, nevertheless they seem to be the
product of a bursting spontaneity that has surpassed the conventions
not only of painting but even of perception. And that greatness one
feels is the greatness of a man who mastered both the manner of his
perception and the manner of transforming that perception into a
painting. That is why so many of his paintings have the quality that
can only be called visionary.

2 8

Side by side with the late Monet and final works of Manet, with Cézanne and van Gogh, with Nietzsche and with Pater, there was another progression in the consequences of Romanticism, the
movement—perhaps tendency would be more accurate—known
then and still today as Symbolism. Like so many such terms—impressionism and cubism are examples—what it meant at the time is more
than a little vague. However, if we recognize that Carlyle's *Sartor Resartus* was a very important text for the Symbolists, the matter can be
a little clarified. A painting, the Symbolists maintained, should mean
something other than the object depicted or verbally presented. So far
this is consistent with the basic notion of Symbolism—that it is appropriate to respond to a sign in more than one way. The confusion
arose in *how* it should be responded to. Most common was the notion
that no matter what was presented as a sign, its symbolic function
should be an objectification of some internal state, emotional or intellectual or spiritual, whatever that might mean. There were, however, in the true Symbolist work no clues as to what that internal or
subjective condition might be. But already in the 1880s the paintings
of Monet became in this one sense Symbolist paintings. The series of
haystacks or the series of cathedrals were supposedly painted in re-

sponse to changing light, but this traditional explanation of these works is quite unconvincing. If there was any imitative relation to the perceived light, the colors Monet used were a powerful intensification of that light. They were so extreme a departure from the different colors of the object in changing light that it was obvious some other interest was at work in Monet's activity. Like theatrical lighting they evoked a mood, whether or not they were a symbol of a mood that Monet actually felt, whether or not they were what T. S. Eliot called them in an effort to define all poetry as Symbolist—"objective correlatives." But to the Symbolist such intensifications and distortions of the perceived color of the object were indeed objective correlatives.

This makes it apparent that what the Symbolists were really wrestling with was the whole problem of meaning. In later years and even into the second half of the twentieth century, one of the oddest results of Symbolism was the tradition of the "spiritual" in painting. This was one of the forces, perhaps the principal force, behind the development of abstract painting, not the kind of abstract painting that is an abstraction from the visual object, as in Picasso beginning in 1907, but pure abstraction. A painting thus could consist of almost randomly assembled and associated geometrical forms or, as in Malevich's *White on White*, of a very delicate distortion of a single square. Kandinsky started with organic configurations combined with a kind of scribbling but moved on to abstractions made of geometrically perfect shapes. What did these paintings *mean*? They were not, as has so often been thought, experiments in pure manipulation of shapes and colors. To many of the painters who did them, for a long time almost all of them, they were symbols of the spiritual, by which they meant simply symbols of the nonmaterial, the transcendent, the divine. The Symbolists, with the aid of Carlyle and his clothes philosophy and with some aid from Baudelaire's *correspondances* of the relation of the inner to the outer and the outer to the inner, had discovered that at least one kind of meaning is not immanent in the observed and observable world. They had discovered that that meaning is man-made, and in time they were to discover that meaning is a cultural product—without always realizing what they had done.

What they did was strikingly parallel to Nietzsche's tearing language loose from the world, that, metaphorically, it lives a life of its own independent of the world. And at the same time, the Viennese physicist Boltzmann asserted that scientific laws, theories, and hypotheses are all the same thing, that the highest of these forms, scientific laws, were verbal constructs, enabling man to deal with reality. Even in the 1860s Darwin had said that scientific laws are no more than mental conveniences. The extremest poet of this Symbolist stage of Romanticism was Mallarmé, who discovered meaninglessness. What these various parallel discoveries meant was that the analytic dismantlement of the superstructure of Western culture had reached the point at which it questioned meaning itself. In its most absolute form Symbolism abstracts meaningfulness from man's semiotic grasp of reality. Thus Mallarmé found value in the limitations of language, in what language cannot say. But this meant to him and to many painters, who discovered the limitations of pictorial semiosis, that language is the instrument of the spirit, not the invasion of the world upon the spirit, and that the spiritual noncognitive response to the world truly transcends reality.

At this point in its development, the Romantic tradition of art as redemption became part of the Symbolist movement, the Symbolist factor that was to last into the second half of the twentieth century. Art had become a quasi-religion, in the sense that it was the ultimate source of value. Now art literally became religion in exactly the same sense. This step was assisted by the widespread popularity of Theosophy, a religion that accepted all religions and all forms of religion as equally valid. For millennia language had identified the source of value as the divine, though this identification was actually, we can now see, no more than the recognition that culture (learned behavior) transmitted from generation to generation by semiotic behavior is the source of value. In the most basic sense value arises from obedience to cultural controls—or under certain circumstances the negation of those cultural controls, that is, when they are judged to be no longer viable or even defensible. What the painters were to claim is that the purest shapes and colors (color free from visible configurations) completely transcend the world and are therefore symbols of the divine, though it is enough to say that they are symbols of culture.

But that they could hardly say. The notion of culture in the modern sense had barely emerged, and for long was to be confined to anthropology, which had a great deal of trouble in defining it. There was in fact almost no way to explain pure abstraction except to say that it is a symbol of the divine, at least for intellectually and philosophically unsophisticated artists. After all, to call something divine is merely to claim for it the highest merit. And certainly the apprehension of such paintings and of the purest poems of Mallarmé and some others is to experience, if one is not completely puzzled and if one can surrender to them, an extraordinary sense of transcendental freedom, or if nothing else at least a sense of transcending the conventions of art and the conventions of perceiving the world. Furthermore, it is to the credit of these artists to realize that the notion that these works are symbols of the divine means that nothing else can be said about the divine, that from the notion of the divine no proposition can be deduced. So if we are to say what these paintings symbolized, and what the Symbolist movement was concerned with symbolizing, it is simply the experience of value. The great achievement of the whole Symbolist movement was the reduction of Western culture simply to the abstraction of meaningfulness from the world and to the fixing of the place of value within human experience.

2 9

During the last years of the century there was in Vienna a parallel to the Symbolist movement in the work of Sigmund Freud. He grew up in a Vienna in which building after building was erected in one of the historical styles. The historicization of culture in the nineteenth century, a central thread in the Romantic tradition and its consequences, was not merely to be found in literature and painting and opera. In every major city in Europe and America and South America, in lesser cities, and in the great houses that the old rich and the new rich built in town and country, historicism was omnipresent, unavoidable. Historicist architecture was a particularly salient instance of the effort of the Romantic artists to achieve a new style. A true Romantic architecture, it turned out, had to be based on a repudiation of past styles. So Romantic architecture in the nineteenth century struggled with modifying and adapting historical styles, endeavored to use the historical styles in order to create emblems of the Romantic self. This was true not only of major buildings but frequently of the middle-class villa, which would have on its facade scraps of Gothic or Romanesque or Renaissance or Baroque architectural decoration. In the last decade of the century the problem began to be resolved in two directions. One was the refinement of historical styles in the direction of the abandonment of the attempt to dramatize selfhood. Architecture came to be less assertive and more archeologically accurate. Architects began to create buildings which were not imitations of medieval structures but more coherent instances of a particular, not a generalized, Gothic or Renaissance or eighteenth-century style. The buildings were no longer mere emblems of the artist's self or even of the employer's but were only emblems of the economic competence of both. The architect, in effect, submitted to his employer. The other direction was to create a new style by synthesizing historically different and disparate styles.

The result was the style known as Art Nouveau. It was not a truly modern style but the first and necessary step towards a modern style. It was the epitome of that stage in the progression of the consequences of Romanticism for which I have proposed the term stylism rather than the usual term, aestheticism. The historicist styles were usually adjusted on some ground or other to the purpose of the building, but Art Nouveau was used for any building, commercial, ecclesiastical, domestic. The buildings were accompanied by Art Nouveau furnishings, pictures, dresses, jewelry, book bindings, posters, book designs, as well as vases and tableware, dishes and silver. And the style was truly international, found in every country of the European culture area, from Belgrade to Belém. It was the first convincing and successful answer to the question, "What is style?" That was its historical importance, and that is why what we still call Modern art emerged from it.

In the very years of the triumph of Art Nouveau and Symbolism Freud created a Symbolist-historicist model of personality and personality development. He discovered that if a patient were allowed to randomize his verbal behavior in conditions of absolutely protected privacy, certain distortions of ordinary meanings would assume a repetitious pattern. He then explained these emergent meanings by a historical construct, inspired not only by the historicism with which by the end of the century any educated person was surrounded but also by the German Romantic philosophers, whom of course he studied extensively when he was young, particularly the historically minded Hegel, or so it would seem. By this time, of course, Hegelianism had so penetrated German-speaking culture that it was possible to be quite Hegelian without reading a word of the master. Like Art Nouveau, Freudianism was not a truly modern psychology. Intellectually responsible commentators have towards the end of the twentieth century begun to call Freud a pseudoscientist and a charlatan. And these judgments may be quite just. After all, little is easier than the creation of emergent meanings out of any semiotic expression or deposit. The ascription of divine meanings to abstract paintings is an obvious example. Nevertheless, like Art Nouveau, he prepared the way for a modern conception of the personality, though it has been slow to emerge, by raising both the questions of the history of a personality and of the style of a personality, and by explaining the one by the other. He was a focus of the consequences of Romanticism.

Without knowing it, evidently, Freud created a notion of the personality as the individual's unique culture. It took Jung to realize that the personality is a modification or special case of the culture into which he is born. But both urged, in true Romantic fashion, that it is possible to transcend that personality or unique culture. Thus both proposed a technique other than the techniques offered by art to achieve self-transcendence, a Romantic ideal from the very beginning of Romanticism. And both become more acceptable if read not as science but as literature, as art. So both offered individual redemption through an innovated mode of literature. Both guided their patients in becoming literary-symbolic interpreters of their own verbalisms and nonverbal semiotic behaviors. The redeeming self-transcendence they offered was not the freedom that truth about oneself is said to give but the freedom that deconventionalized interpretation of oneself gives. Their limitations, of course, were that they had such limited interpretative modes and models at their disposal.

3 0

Just as Art Nouveau and psychoanalysis were triggers that released the individual who had absorbed the Romantic tradition into the next phase of Romanticism and its consequences, Modernism, so Debussy was the musical equivalent of Art Nouveau that triggered musical Modernism. Debussy's music was not itself Modern, just as Art Nouveau was not a Modern style, but like Art Nouveau, it was a stylistic leap. It was an original style, but unlike preceding styles in music as in architecture not a self-directed derivative from an older style. Rather, Debussy created a stylistic synthesis, highly innovative, from a combination of devices abstracted from traditional Western music, and also from Russian and Javanese, all held together by the violation of various musical conventions. He was, for example, one of the few composers, perhaps the only one, who understood Wagner's use of the leitmotiv. His choice of Maeterlinck's *Pelleas et Melisande* for his first and only completed opera indicates the close relation between Art Nouveau and Symbolism. What was most innovative, though it had been tried once or twice before, with unsuccessful results, is that he did not himself write a libretto derived from Maeterlinck's play but instead set the text as Maeterlinck had written it, except for the omission of a couple of minor scenes. In his close association between text and music, he cut down through the mass of operatic convention to the basis of music, intonation. The work is still too strange for the conventional operagoer. It is instructive that the greatest modern opera, *Wozzeck*, uses the same device of setting to music a play rather than a libretto. Both restore to the operatic stage a wonderful dramatic freshness scarcely known since Monteverdi's *Orfeo*, that freshness which is virtually the definitional trait of each stage in the unfolding of the consequences of Romanticism.

3 1

When Debussy was working on *Pelleas*, Richard Strauss wrote *Also Sprach Zarathustra*. It was an extraordinary orchestral tour de force, the *Tondichtung*, as he called the symphonic poem, carried to new possibilities, particularly of orchestral virtuosity and sheer length. Yet Strauss remained a nineteenth-century or pre-Debussy composer to the end of his life. The real message of Nietzsche's work he failed to grasp, for Strauss's music was self-assertion, though a Romantic one, rather than the more significant self-transcendence. He understood Nietzsche's message of the will to power in *Zarathustra* and in *Beyond Good and Evil* as providing an ethical justification for that very self-assertion. Nietzsche's point, however, was not simply the will to power, which he found, quite correctly, to be the fundamental trait of human behavior, but the use of the will to power to transcend one's culture and in doing so to transcend one's self. In asserting, though preceded long before by Hegel, that God is dead, Nietzsche denied the divine justification for the absolute validity of the existent culture: conventional notions of good and evil are mere justifications for historical accidents. Romanticism having used history must now escape from history. In calling for a transvaluation of all values Nietzsche was saying that the ultimate aim of the will to power is the creation of value, of saying, in an almost Carlylean way, "Yea" to all existence. His assertion that joy is deeper than sorrow is an assertion that the way to the creation of new value is through the midnight of absolute negation, a denial that is a call to life and freedom. Behind every great figure who created Modernism can always be found Nietzsche.

3 2

Nietzsche was the great releaser in what might be called the climax of the consequences of Romanticism. That climax was the self-realization and the self-revelation of what Romanticism had set out to achieve in the 1790s. This is the significance of the fact that almost simultaneously but unknown to each other Picasso, Loos, Schoenberg, Stein, Matisse, Mauthner all created nonhistorical styles, and did so by repudiating the European cultural tradition. Picasso accepted archaic and "primitive" art as equal in value to European art, and in doing so cut to the very basis of the art of painting. What is a painting about? It is about being a painting. Thus Picasso heralded what was to be the concern, the steadily increasing preoccupation of both literature and philosophy—language itself. So Picasso and Matisse set out to analyze painting down to the ultimate elements of painterly structure, just as Kandinsky at the same time set out to analyze it down to the ultimate elements of painting as gesture. Although Frank Lloyd Wright was a great architect and more advanced than Richard Strauss, he nevertheless remained an American version of Art Nouveau. But Adolf Loos in Vienna stripped architecture down to the point at which architecture barely emerges from building. In that, he was to be followed by the architects of the International Style. Not long after, Joyce began to work on *Ulysses*. He named his hero Stephen Dedalus after the first Christian martyr and the artificer of the Cretan labyrinth who also escaped from it. Thus he is a martyr to the provincial and second-hand Irish culture, the looking glass of a servant, and European culture in general, and as Dedalus he both creates the labyrinth of language and in that creation escapes from it, transcends it.

Just as Picasso's paintings are about painting, so Joyce's verbalizations are about verbalization, are about language. And simultaneously with Picasso's invention of the misnamed Cubism, Schoenberg abandoned tonality and set out to find a basis for music more profound than the diatonic conventions of European music. In *Pierrot Lunaire* almost all the themes of Romantic culture for a hundred years are either adumbrated or hinted at or boldly stated, even though the text was fifty years old. When it was first presented in Berlin in October 1912, it was incontrovertible evidence that Modernism had arrived, that it was here, that it was triumphing, and that that triumph was the triumph of Romanticism. And at much the same time, Gertrude Stein started publishing her incomprehensible stammerings. Inspired by Picasso's searches into painting, she went further than the Symbolists in stripping language of all meaning and all function except the function of simply being language. Only after decades of investigation into language has it been possible to understand what she was doing. Of all the analytic dismantlements of Western culture, taken almost to the edge in the years before the First World War, Stein's dismantlement was the most radical, the most complete.

3 3

The great achievement of those we still call Modern was to make vivid an acceptance of the meaning of "value" and its connection with the meaning of "self." Culture is the control of behavior, its empirical basis being the control of one individual by another. One primary behavioral control is guilt, since guilt is assigned when the individual disobeys or refuses the control of a cultural instruction. This fact makes it impossible to consider value successfully without also considering guilt. The reason is that value is successful obedience to a cultural instruction of control. Shame, on the other hand, is unsuccessful obedience. And guilt is assigned when the individual disobeys or refuses the control of a cultural instruction. The exception occurs and confusion arises when a culture is judged to contain, as indeed it always does, conflicting controls, basic cultural incoherence. Thus value can be assigned to the individual if, under certain circumstances, he refuses to obey certain cultural controls. Such refusal is the source of what we call creativity. What the Moderns did was to refuse so completely the cultural controls over both the form and semantic content of art that only a few individuals could at first ascribe value to them and to their works. What they did was to create their own cultural controls, a behavior made possible by alienation and also by the culture that made it value-laden to disobey certain cultural controls. That creation of one's own cultural controls is the "self." One may say, therefore, that only with the Moderns did the self emerge fully from the matrix of Romanticism.

3 4

These artists, and in time a philosopher or two, worked with the feeling that they were clearing the decks. More than one artist then and since has proposed burning the museums. It took some decades for pop art to emerge, but when it did it finally transcended the notion of art as redemption. It did so by ironic juxtapositions and fusions of art and popular art. Just as Modern Art in general revealed the consequence of Romanticism (or of the Romantic tradition, whichever one prefers) and used historicism not as an end but only as an instrument, so pop art revealed redemptionism as only an instrument, an instrument towards a higher end, the transcendence of culture by discovering what it is. In the same way in the 1970s it could be announced by the talented philosopher Richard Rorty that the idea of philosophy as a means of establishing truth had come to an end, that it merely sustains the ever changing, myriad-formed, polychromatic, high (remote from the empirical) modes of verbal explanation, that its task is not to settle anything but to keep thought from settling down, from innocuous desuetude, from exhaustion, and from drying up into ideological rigidity, thus becoming a justification for political tyranny. With Rorty's announcement what Nietzsche wanted for philosophy begins to emerge. Because it is not redemptive, art can be free to be anything—free to be trivial, transitory, amusing, evanescent. Because of the Romantic undertaking and its consequences, a few human beings can now revel in man's fundamental and ultimate and freeing affinity: the affinity for chaos.

Readiness is all.

Biographical Afterword

H. W. MATALENE

This biographical sketch is based on an interview that Morse Peckham gave me, his student at the University of Pennsylvania since 1960 and his friend and colleague at the University of South Carolina since 1969, in the spring of 1986. Doing the interview (and hearing Peckham's subsequent reaction to an earlier version of this essay) showed me how much he disliked the prospect of being "explained." His narrative to me about himself made it clear that I and my readers were not going to get much of his personal life to think about alongside his writings, and I remember his quip when a classmate at Princeton published the first scholarly biography of Ernest Hemingway: "Now that Carlos has gotten hold of poor Hemingway," he said, "death holds new terrors." He felt that "personalia" can only diminish public achievements, not explain them. His lack of interest in himself as a personality dawned on me in the fall of 1968, when I read the manuscript of his *Art and Pornography.* Amazed by his assertion that sex is among the *least* powerful of human needs, I asked him point-blank if he had ever had any sexual experience. "Oh yes, lots," he said, "and many kinds, but it's never been very happy." And without batting an eye, he went on clarifying his book's distinction between "sex" (as a physiological appetite) and "eroticism" (Western culture's magnification of this appetite, which, he felt, the slightest grain of introspective common sense shows to be puny indeed beside our needs for water, food, shelter, and healing). Much as he liked me and helped

Citations in the Biographical Afterword are to editions listed in section VIII of the Bibliography.

me, Peckham was not about to let himself be "explained" by any little Freudianistic platitude of a graduate student angling to reduce his intellectual life to his sex life.

Morse Peckham was born on 17 August 1914 in Yonkers, New York. His father was Dr. Ray Morse Peckham, whom the boy once heard called "the best optometrist who ever lived." His mother was Edith Roake Peckham, whose graduation from New Paltz Normal School gave her the family's best educational credentials. Peckham's older brother, Robert Hamilton Peckham, was his only sibling. Until 1928, the family lived on a lake in the country near Waterbury, Connecticut. Peckham later called these years "Wordsworthian." He was grateful for the "late nineteenth-century culture" of his parents, to whom intellectual accomplishments of all kinds were everything, and money and social position next to nothing.

In 1921, he missed several months of school as a result of illness. During this interim, the boy wandered around Waterbury, watching adults earn livings, and laying in the basis of a historical-materialist world-view that he later called "more 'Marxist' than Marx himself." His mother settled him for naps by reading him Tennyson, and he listened in on her meetings with a friend who would drop by to read Balzac with her. He went to a rural school, and since no other children lived nearby, he learned to amuse himself. At ten, he was moving chessmen around on a toy stage to help himself visualize the action as he played at reading Shakespeare. After his father took him to a concert, he was moved to ask for piano lessons; and he still retained until the end "powerful visual memories" of his first visit, sometime between the ages of ten and twelve, to the Metropolitan Museum of Art.

In 1928, the family moved to California, where Peckham's father lectured at the Los Angeles College of Optometry. But a year later, Dr. Peckham began touring the country, lecturing for the Riggs Optical Company, and then came the Stock Market Crash and the Great Depression. And so, with her husband on the road and her older son Robert across the continent at the University of Rochester, Mrs. Peckham decided to save money by taking young Morse along and setting up housekeeping in Rochester with Robert. There, Peckham finished high school. Because there was not enough money to send him away to a college where he could study modern language, as he really wished, Morse Peckham followed his brother to the University of Rochester in 1931 and became an English major.

At Rochester, Peckham achieved the sort of bizarre academic distinction that came to characterize his whole career. After a bad be-

ginning, he did such striking upper-division work in English that he
managed to pull his four-year average "all the way up to B-minus,"
and by so doing convinced a faculty committee that a "B-minus" student was Rochester's most intellectually promising graduate of 1935—
and worthy of election to Phi Beta Kappa!

Still undecided about a career, Peckham followed the suggestion
of a friend, Lewis Whitbeck, and began looking into the possibility of
teaching English. Through the good offices of Professor Edward
Hubler (later a well-known Princeton Shakespearian), Peckham became the first Rochester graduate to be accepted for graduate study
in English at Princeton. Peckham was thus placed in an intimidating
situation. Princeton accepted only ten graduate students in English
per year, and he found that he was two years younger, on the average,
than the nine others who entered with him in 1935. Moreover, though
its graduate students had to be *examined* on nineteenth- and twentieth-century literature, Princeton then *taught* no graduate courses in
any centuries more recent than the eighteenth. But through his friendships with graduate students in art history, like Erving Olsen and
Frederick Hartt, Peckham nurtured an early interest in classical architecture and picked up fascinating tidbits, secondhand, from the
great Erwin Panofsky. But there was no possibility of his earning academic credit for working with Panofsky himself, and when he turned
out an interdisciplinary essay on "The Baroque," Professor Hoyt Hud-
son told him not to waste his time on that sort of thing.

After doing two years of coursework and seeing that the older,
more experienced graduate students were having trouble doing their
dissertations, Peckham felt he was not yet up to this final task. As his
parents had moved to Detroit, Peckham moved there in 1937, on a
year's leave from Princeton, to prepare himself to finish his doctorate.
But then, in 1938, after a year at home, he decided that his parents
had sacrificed enough to put their sons through graduate school, and
he resolved to teach, save, and pay his own way back to Princeton.
He found an instructorship at The Citadel, the Military College of
South Carolina, in Charleston. He was there for three years—a civilian
in uniform, teaching eighteen hours a week, mostly to freshmen and
sophomores, training his public presence in amateur theatricals at the
Dock Street Theater—and, as always, reading. The Citadel gave Peckham the golden chance to teach a one-year upper-division course in
Romanticism. And it also prepared him to "soldier" in earnest. On 15
September 1941, Peckham was about to reenter Princeton when he
was drafted into the Army. Examining his conscience, he decided to
make a go of the service, since the art Hitler found "decadent" was
the only thing in the world that had real meaning for him. He entered

what he came to call his "War-Is-Hell Period," ironically observing that World War II provided him with his only interim of adult peace from university life.

Then, in the fall of 1943, Peckham was shipped to England, commissioned, and assigned to write the official history of the Ninth Bomber Command. This assignment, he said, was one of the most fascinating things he had ever done. Here, shuttling among endless files of Air Corps papers, without Princeton's guidance, Morse Peckham learned that history is not "about the *past*," but "about *documents*." As he found and assembled into narratives more than a million filed shreds of information, he learned that he had an advantage most academic historians and critics of literature do not enjoy. Unlike them, when *he* could not interpret a document, he could generally go elsewhere on the base and ask the document's author, face to face, what it meant. Peckham was able to use the Cambridge University Library, on his days off from the Ninth Bomber Command, to begin his dissertation on Philip James Bailey's *Festus*, a popular Victorian poem that had been totally neglected in his youth because *all* of "Victorianism" had been proscribed by uncomprehending "Moderns." He had already decided that he must work on the Victorians because they "haunted" him. In our interview, this was his only mention of his parents: *They* were Victorians, and Victorianism haunted him because he was their son.

When the Germans surrendered, Peckham was in Belgium. He fondly remembers getting drunk in the company of another soldier with scholarly interests, on whose subsequent work he has since frequently drawn. This was Thomas S. Kuhn, author of *The Structure of Scientific Revolutions*, arguably the most influential work of this century on the history and theory of science.

At the war's end, Peckham returned to Princeton, where he found a champion in Willard Thorpe and finished his degree. Thorpe got Peckham interested in American literature and launched his career by landing him a job at Rutgers. In 1947, he began two "boring" years there of teaching freshmen composition and the sophomore survey of literature. He took his resultant *ennui* back to Thorpe, who represented him to Robert Spiller as a potential asset to the study of American literature at Penn. After an interview with A. C. Baugh, Penn's formidable chairman of English, Peckham went to Philadelphia in 1949, undertaking an extraordinary range of intellectual and administrative projects and establishing the directions his career followed for all the rest of his life.

In 1950, he read "Toward a Theory of Romanticism" at the annual meeting of the Modern Language Association of America. With this paper, published the next year in *PMLA*, Peckham began to have a professional reputation. He proposed not merely to list the "tendencies" of English literary Romanticism, in the manner of Ernest Bernbaum, but to explain a "general European literary movement which had its correspondences in the music, the painting, the architecture, the philosophy, the theology, and the science of the eighteenth and early nineteenth centuries" (*The Triumph of Romanticism* 4). He gave up looking for a "Spirit of the Age" in the nineteenth and twentieth centuries. Instead of a sequence of "periods," each exhibiting a broad ideological unity, Peckham saw different and incompatible "cultural levels" laid down one on top of the other through time (*The Triumph of Romanticism* 25). From Carlyle's "Everlasting No," Peckham coined the term "Negative Romanticism," which he saw exemplified also in Coleridge and Wordsworth. Of the three, only Wordsworth and Carlyle escape to "Positive Romanticism," and Peckham has some pragmatic doubts about the cultural usefulness of these escapes. He concluded that it may be useful to approach the texts of the late eighteenth and early nineteenth centuries with the general thematic expectation that Romanticism "is the revolution of the European mind against thinking in terms of static mechanism and the redirection of the mind to thinking in terms of dynamic organicism" (*The Triumph of Romanticism* 14).

Teaching Victorian literature in the fifties provided Peckham with more strong reasons for transcending the traditional methods of the American English Department. For one thing, the Victorian canon, unlike the canons for other periods of English literature at that time, forced "nonliterary" texts upon its students, demanding that they become "interdisciplinary." Isaac Newton, for instance, who now appears in the *Norton Anthology of English Literature*, was in fact not "literature" for students of the seventeenth century in the fifties; but T. H. Huxley, a nineteenth-century writer in a discipline comparable to Newton's, *was* literature for students of the Victorian period. To understand Huxley, one had to understand Darwin. And so it was that Morse Peckham, trained to edit poetry, decided that he should produce a variorum edition of Darwin's *Origin of Species*, and he soon found himself reading biology in order to come to grips with Victorianism. It rapidly became clear to everybody at Penn that he was an English professor with unusually "broad" interests, though some found him correspondingly "shallow." In 1952, however, those who mattered found him "deep" enough, and he got tenure.

That same year, Peckham was appointed Director of the University of Pennsylvania Press. And he was also asked to organize something called an "Institute of Humanistic Study for Business Executives," sponsored by AT&T. Directing the institute furthered his lifelong empathy with both the "Real World" bourgeois pathos of business and the enforcement of behavior. He understood fully why Wallace Stevens—poet, lawyer, and insurance man—refused his invitation to address the farewell dinner of one of the Institute's classes of telephone executives. "I have never believed," Stevens wrote to Peckham, "that it took a great deal to be both a poet and something else, and to lend myself to the opposite belief, as if to illustrate it and even expound it, would be difficult. . . . I am still active at the office and think that I should leave this sort of thing to other people. . . ." (Stevens 814–815). Peckham gave up running the Press and the Institute in 1954. Far more important, he also gave up alcohol, which had become a problem.

For the next eight years, until the appearance of his first major book in 1962, Peckham published relatively little. Instead, he read philosophy and the social sciences, "laying in a scholar's capital," as he later put it. (Still, in 1961, he became the youngest person yet promoted to "full" Professor in Penn's English Department.) He had some qualms about all his "outside" reading, though he could rationalize some of it as pertinent to the Darwin variorum, which had appeared in 1959. He was especially influenced during this period by George Barnett's *Innovation*, by Richard Von Mies's *Logical Positivism*, and by Charles Morris's *Signs, Language, and Behavior*. He also profited from A. J. Ayer and the late Wittgenstein. And he stood in awe of Penn's Carlton Koon, who seemed to be the only anthropologist whose work offered not just a grab bag of the funny things different peoples do, but a plausible theory of human conduct. Still, he was looking for what he termed "a *real* epistemology" and not finding it. It only dawned on him gradually that his failure to find one was not *his* fault—the fault of a dilettante willfully abandoning the formal schooling he had mastered—but the "fault" of the human condition itself.

His dissatisfaction with conventional literary studies grew; he could not see a credibly self-contained "field" anywhere in the university. After eight years of relative silence on Peckham's part (during which he had, however, published *Word, Meaning, Poem*, a textbook, with Seymour Chatman), Robert Ockene, a former student become a friend, and an employee of the Book Find Club, insisted that Peckham shed his guilt and write the book he had in him on the nineteenth century. Peckham signed a contract to write *Beyond the Tragic Vision: The Quest for Identity in the Nineteenth Century*, which appeared in 1962. Perhaps to stay convinced that he was making sense as he wrote this book in the summer of 1961, Peckham invited four of his graduate students to drop by in the evenings and read the day's output of typed, yellow sheets. The flattered and enthusiastic four were E. Anthony James, Howard L. Koonce, David L. Powell, and myself.

Beyond the Tragic Vision abandons the terminology, but carries on the project proposed in "Toward a Theory of Romanticism." Touching upon forty-odd canonized painters, composers, poets, novelists, philosophers, and critics, Peckham predicts that readers and art perceivers interested in Western high culture from about 1770 until about 1910 can expect to see not "Negative" and "Positive Romanticism," but "analogism," "transcendentalism," "objectism," and "stylism." In 1964, Peckham provided a sort of abstract of *Beyond the Tragic Vision* in "The Dilemma of a Century: The Four Stages of Romanticism" (*The Triumph of Romanticism* 36–57). But in his later lectures and final publications on the intellectual history of the nineteenth and twentieth centuries, these four new terms would themselves go the way of "Negative" and "Positive Romanticism." To Peckham, his work was never revisable or reparable, but always to be begun anew as teaching duties or the requests of friends called for his thoughts.

What Peckham loved was the excitement of *taking* a position on canonized works of art and philosophy that he either had not studied at all or had not studied in a long time. *Holding* that position—casuistically applying it to monuments of nineteenth- and twentieth-century high culture that he had not discussed in staking it out—made him very uneasy. Whether from boredom or anxiety, he was incapable of working cumulatively, piling up documentation for an old thesis and tinkering with it to accommodate works of art and philosophy whose meanings he had failed to anticipate. Nor did he take the pains prescribed by the rhetoric of scholarship to defend his ideas in the academic marketplace. Though he devoured historical and biographical scholarship, he never took reading notes and seldom cited his sources of fact or argued specifically with rival interpreters. The pattern of Peckham's career reflected a constitutional inability to feel that his own learning ever really amounted to "knowledge." Late in his life he said that it took more *chutzpah* than conviction to write *Beyond the Tragic Vision*.

Even so, the book, which was selected for the Book Find Club, became a popular success and led Braziller to ask Peckham for two other books. The first of these was *Romanticism: The Culture of the Nineteenth Century* (1965), which was the seventh volume of the firm's *Cultures of Mankind* series. Although it is only an edited book, it is arguably the best anthology of Romantic writing ever to appear, and its choices (of illustrations as well as of documents), introductions, and annotations are brilliant. It is a lamentably neglected sourcebook for students. The second requested book, however, was to be another original work of theory. When the resultant typescript Peckham produced was returned to him for revision, he—always incapable of tinkering—simply wrote another book from scratch. Braziller read it and backed down. Eventually, in 1965, with the help of a friend who was an editor there, the formidable new book was brought out in Philadelphia by the Chilton Company (primarily known until then as a publisher of automobile manuals). This was *Man's Rage for Chaos: Biology, Behavior, and the Arts,* and it marks Peckham's emergence as a new kind of aesthetician, one capable of repudiating the quasi-religious attitude of ordinary aestheticism. The book became an underground classic on the New York art scene of the late sixties. It also caught the eye of Peckham's famous Penn colleague in sociology, Philip Rieff (who saw to it that *Man's Rage for Chaos* was reprinted by Schocken Books when Chilton went under not long after publishing it). To his students, at least as early as 1960, Peckham had been saying that "discontinuity"—not the "organic unity" or "significant form" of traditional aesthetics—is what emergent works of art offer their perceivers. In other words, art more or less violates our perceptual, cognitive, and ideological expectations—especially the art that Western intellectuals have canonized. In his earlier work, Peckham insisted from his studies of the first Romantics that "Nature"—the sensed field in itself—is not the active source of a passively perceived order by which man must live if he is to survive. *Man's Rage for Chaos* further insists that the supposedly passive perception of "Art" leads no more to the necessary sense of order than does looking at "Nature." Drawing upon psychology and anthropology to confirm what he had first picked up from Wordsworth and Kant, Peckham says that "not art but perception is ordered" (*Man's Rage for Chaos* 33). Moreover, the perceiver's "rage for order" actively interposes itself between him and much of the sensed field (whether of nature or of art) that is potentially there to be seen—and which it may be vitally important *to* see.

For Peckham, then, acculturated, habitual perception's active "rage for order" may not be a blessing, and is often in fact a maladaptive curse. "The desire for death," Peckham notes, "is merely the desire for the most perfect order we can imagine, for total insulation from all perceptual disparities." He goes on: "If art is the satisfaction of the rage for order, then there is no reason why a healthy mind should pay any attention to it and every reason why it should not" (*Man's Rage for Chaos* 34). But if perception's endemic "rage for order" is potentially maladaptive, how come mankind is still here? What keeps the "rage for order" from realizing its maladaptive potential, cutting us off from our environment in a world of pure logic and thus rendering our species extinct? These are the Darwinian questions from which Peckham goes on to explain the ubiquity of art in all known human cultures.

The book's discussion of "signs" did not satisfy Peckham, and he often spoke of doing a second edition which would have incorporated the revisions of his semiotics theory that appeared in his writings of the late 1970s and 1980s. Meanwhile, however, he produced several after-the-fact "abstracts" of *Man's Rage for Chaos* that are revisions of it as well, reflecting his dissatisfaction with the formulations at which his struggle to write the book had arrived when Chilton first published it. First, in "Art and Disorder" (1966), he confessed that he needed to be able to extend his notion of "discontinuity" to fiction (*The Triumph of Romanticism* 271). Then, in 1967, he tried to remedy this omission in two essays—"Order and Disorder in Fiction" and "Discontinuity in Fiction: Persona, Narrator, Scribe." Ten years later, he published yet another such abstract, in which, among other things, he modified his book's treatment of signs on the basis of his intervening work, and this piece he titled "Perceptual and Semiotic Discontinuity in Art." Here, he eliminates the concept of the "natural sign" on the ground that all external stimuli are transformed and categorized in being perceived. What is left are "verbal and nonverbal signs." Among nonverbal signs are what Peckham had called "primary signs" in *Man's Rage for Chaos*—"configurations such as verticality, horizontality, color, scale, light, shadow, line, solidity, hollowness, axial depth, pitch in music and linguistic intonations, gesture, volume, speed, vowel euphony and consonantal alliteration in poetry, and so on (281). These Peckham began calling "regulatory signs"—"regulatory" in that they "regulate the level of behavior, that is, of aggression" (see his collection of essays *Romanticism and Ideology* 284). When we say that a work of art or a person is "expressive" or "inhibited," we are responding to a package of regulatory signs. In addition to nonverbal regulatory signs are "performatory signs," which may be either nonverbal or verbal, and which "elicit a performance in individuals who have learned the appropriate performance response to that sign or set of signs . . ." (*Romanticism and Ideology* 282). He also softened the boundary he had drawn in *Man's Rage for Chaos* between art's formal and semantic aspects, recognizing (for example) that an art perceiver, especially a reader of fiction, can experience "semantic discontinuity" as well as the "formal discontinuity" he had earlier acknowledged (*Romanticism and Ideology* 279–80).

Finally, Peckham's most penetrating discussion of semantic discontinuity appears in "Philosophy and Art as Related and Unrelated Modes of Behavior," a lecture delivered in November of 1973 at the State University of New York in Albany but not published until 1985. Here, Peckham fully realizes the implications of the distinction between "exemplification" and "explanation" that he had first drawn in "Order and Disorder in Fiction" (1967). Art and philosophy are at once both related and unrelated: Related because art can be used to exemplify philosophy's explanations; unrelated because serious art's intended exemplifications of philosophy inevitably "introduce categorial attributes which confuse [the intended explanation] or even subvert it" (*Romanticism and Ideology* 200–201).

After publishing *Man's Rage for Chaos*, Peckham had no major project in mind, and agreed to edit and annotate some Robert Browning for the critical edition of that poet's works that Ohio University was proposing to publish. But in September of 1966, John C. Guilds, Head of the English Department at the University of South Carolina, happened to be in the audience at a conference in Massachusetts, where Peckham read the paper "Hawthorne and Melville as European Authors" (published in *The Triumph of Romanticism* 153–175). So impressed was Guilds with this paper that Peckham became his choice for the Distinguished Professorship of English and Comparative Literature to be established in his department at South Carolina.

Guilds felt Peckham would be the theoretical heavyweight that the department needed to counterpoise its new preponderance of nationally known bibliographers and textual critics. Guilds offered him a substantial salary increase and a minimal teaching load. He would have thirteen years until retirement; hence, if he wished, he could each year take as his seminar's subject one decade of European cultural history in "his period" (that is, from 1790 until 1920). He could thus add, perhaps, an unprecedented weight of data from literature, philosophy, music, and the plastic arts to his evolving sense of Romanticism. President Thomas F. Jones added to Guilds' enticements by telling Peckham that he could expect the University as a whole to turn to him as its "idea man." Peckham has always claimed to possess "the Soul of Pollyanna," and it was this optimism that finally led him to accept South Carolina as a place where he would be more useful than he had come to feel at Penn. And so, in July of 1967, Morse Peckham moved to South Carolina—where, as he told his friend Leo Daugherty in the 1980s, he had "from earliest memory had some kind of postcardish dream of retiring anyway."

Shortly thereafter, in "The Intentional? Fallacy?"—first delivered as an invited lecture at the University of Kentucky in 1968—Peckham tackled the question of interpretation, which has since emerged at the heart of postmodern critical theory. As his strange title implies, Peckham had doubts about one of the sacred texts of the New Criticism, "The Intentional Fallacy," by Monroe C. Beardsley and William K. Wimsatt (1946). He had further doubts about E. D. Hirsch's *Validity in Interpretation* (1967), an influential early attack on the Beardsley-Wimsatt position that "the poem is embodied in language, the peculiar possession of the public, and it is about the human being, an object of public knowledge." Amusingly, Peckham remarks that "The notion of something suprasensible [the poem] being embodied in something sensible [language]" is "structurally identical with the [Christian] theory of transubstantiation" (*The Triumph of Romanticism* 427). Peckham simply could not swallow the idea that the meaning of the poem is "in" its language, and that the poem's words—or any words—"refer" directly to objects in an external world. He analyzed the referential theory of meaning and arrived at the following conclusion, which became the basis for all of his subsequent, frequently apocalyptic thinking about human history:

> Words are said to have reference. But when I say, 'Look at the ceiling,' you look at the ceiling, the sentence does not. . . . Human beings . . . refer; words do not. Words are signs to which, on interpretation, we respond by various modes of behavior, verbal and nonverbal. The meaning of a bit of language is the behavior which is consequent upon responding to it. Therefore, *any* response to a discourse is a meaning of that discourse. . . . [A]ll the generator of an utterance can do is to present a set of instructions for behavior, either his own or another's; and all the responder to an utterance can do is follow those instructions, or not follow them. That is, if he knows how to interpret those instructions he can, if he so decides, behave in accordance with what in that situation is the conventionalized appropriate responsible behavior. . . . We may discern, then, three kinds of response to any utterance: inappropriate response, partially appropriate response, appropriate response. These are the meanings of an utterance. (*The Triumph of Romanticism* 430–421)

Peckham called the idea that meaning is response his "radical theory of meaning," and it derived in part from his study of the American Pragmatist George Herbert Mead, as well as from "symbolic interactionist" sociology and social psychology, which traces its ancestry to Mead.

At about this same time, at the request of John H. Gagnon of the Institute for Sex Research at Indiana University—the so-called "Kinsey Institute"—Peckham undertook to write *Art and Pornography: An Experiment in Explanation* (1969). Here, he began to explore the apocalyptic implications of the theory of meaning he had developed:

We find [in giving meaning to words] the irreconcilable interests of stability and innovation; and the disturbing thought arises that the ultimate function of social power is to control meanings, and that they can be controlled only by naked, brute force, applied to the very limit of dealing out death. One advantage of this scandalous proposal that the meaning of a term is all possible responses to it is that I know of no proposition that so strongly urges compassion for mankind, sweating to stabilize meanings and sweating just as heavily to innovate meanings when the received meanings no longer serve its interests. (*Art and Pornography* 137–139)

He concludes this discussion of meaning with an appalling witticism: "The only final way to prove that [your philosophical antagonist] is indeed mistaken is to kill him. Throughout human history it has been a very popular mode of defeating an opponent in arguments about meaning. Certainly it has an almost irresistible charm" (*Art and Pornography* 141). Later, in "Philosophy and Art as Related and Unrelated Modes of Behavior" [1973], he put the idea more soberly: "No philosophy can effectively channel behavior unless it is backed up by power, as the history of Christianity, Communism, Confucianism, and the American mode of the Enlightenment all show equally well . . ." (*Romanticism and Ideology* 197).

Peckham's friend Robert L. Stewart, a sociologist at the University of South Carolina, saw clearly that this new theory of meaning implied an entire theory of human behavior, and he urged Peckham to write it. This became *Explanation and Power: The Control of Human Behavior* (1979). It was the most difficult of all Peckham's books to write—he worked on it for six years—and it is certainly his most difficult book to read, though it may someday be regarded as his most important work. The book's theory rests upon the observation that "if bees and ants are properly categorized as social animals, then human beings are not" (242). In the human brain, evolution has made a device with "the capacity to produce random responses" (166). This biologically inescapable randomness is the condition of all our knowledge, and hence, of all our actions; yet our behavioral performances, in spite of the big brain, are broadly predictable—not random at all.

Why? Because behavior is controlled by explanation backed by power. In brief, Peckham said that "The structure of [human] 'knowledge' [and action] is the structure of semiotic transformation, of culture which maintains that semiotic behavior, of redundancy systems which maintain culture, and of social institutions which maintain redundancies" (191). We must constantly rehearse the appropriate responses and must constantly ("redundantly") be reminded of them. And we must be punished if we deviate through forgetfulness, perversity—or even through "creativity," which Peckham both jokingly

and seriously called "socially validated error." "Economic deprivation, imprisonment, the infliction of pain, and killing are the ultimate
sanctions for the validation of any semiotic link between sign and
meaning, and obviously the validation of the first three is to be found
in the fourth" (169). "Civilization [itself]," as Peckham elsewhere put
it, is no more than "the multiplication and complication of strategies
for postponing the use of force, always uncertain in its outcome" (*Romanticism and Ideology* 196). Language, then, is our way of dealing with
the brain's randomness, but because our responses to words, ultimately, can only be stabilized by murder, language, too, is often
dysfunctional.

Peckham's impact on the University of South Carolina was not the
one envisioned by those who hired him. When, in the spring of 1970,
Guilds took leave from his post at the head of South Carolina's English
Department to prepare himself for an imminent administrative promotion, he appointed Peckham acting chair in his absence. And when
it was announced that Guilds would not be returning as chair, Peckham was perceived as a possible—even likely—successor. Suddenly,
Peckham, who had never dreamed of doing anything but reading,
writing, and teaching one term a year in South Carolina, found himself tempted by the possibility of actually redirecting an academic institution. And when President Jones and Dean Bruce Nelson offered
him the position, he made up his mind what he would do in office
before accepting, and he circulated a memorandum proposing a new
faculty policy for the department to see how his colleagues responded
to it.

Under the policy Peckham proposed, candidates for tenure or promotion in English would have to show their colleagues that they were
still trying to learn something new—anything new—for which they
were willing to be held accountable. Candidates could do this through
scholarly publication, as before; but from now on publication would
not be the only allowable evidence of continuing intellectual vitality.
Working up courses outside one's prior specialties in English, or taking graduate courses in other fields, would also count toward tenure
and promotion for those who might feel unfulfilled, as Peckham had
felt, by traditional English studies.

Not long after Peckham circulated this memo, President Jones apol-
ogized to him and asked him to withdraw from consideration as
Guilds' prospective successor. Though a majority of the English De-

partment supported the proposed policy, five of the department's other pretenders to national reputation had protested the new proposals. And so Peckham went back to his reading, writing, and teaching, somewhat relieved.

In his "Cultural Stagnation in American Universities and Colleges" (1972), Peckham made public the faculty policy he had proposed to his South Carolina colleagues, along with a justifying rationale (grounded, as always, in the Romantic tradition). He never recanted his opposition to publication as the sole criterion for promotion and tenure; indeed, he repeated it at the close of his last lecture upon retiring from teaching in May of 1980. And in "Three Notions about Criticism" (1979), he affirmed it in print:

Publish-or-perish should be recognized as a policy of *publish-and-perish*, intellectually and morally. It is a policy responsible for a moral and intellectual corruption unparalleled even in the higher education establishment of this country. The enormous expansion of that establishment dependent as it has been on the massive exploitation of graduate students for freshman and sophomore instruction, has meant a corresponding decline in the overall or average quality of undergraduate instruction and a similar decline in the quality of graduate students. . . . (*Romanticism and Ideology* 314)

Early in the 1970s (shortly after the publication of Peckham's *Victorian Revolutionaries: Speculations on Some Heroes of a Culture Crisis* [1970]), Carolyn Burrows Matalene persuaded Peckham to change his annual course from a seminar in which students read papers into a course of lectures he himself would give. These lectures were attended not only by the graduate students enrolled for credit, but by colleagues from as far afield as the Law School. Since the music of one or another nineteenth-century decade was always part of his subject, Peckham ran Sunday listening sessions for his students at his home, where the course had also met on a weeknight when it was a seminar. These evenings of recorded music evolved, when the course became lectures, into Sunday open houses for graduate students and young faculty. For members of the English Department appalled at the careerism of their colleagues and looking more for intellectual friends than for political allies, Peckham's Sunday afternoons were a very lucky find. Moreover, in a university beset, after the departure of President Jones, first by the torpor, and then by the alleged criminality of its chief officers, Peckham's Sunday afternoons were an oasis in a cultural desert (whose president loudly proclaimed "The U.S.C."). Peckham's Sundays included good food, plenty of drink, and a dip in his pool during the warm months. And they might not end until the wee hours of Monday morning, after the playing of two *entire* nineteenth-century operas on the extraordinary stereo system situated amid the paintings and sculpture in Peckham's living room.

The initiatives for much of Morse Peckham's most noteworthy writing have come not from Peckham himself, but from his dear friends and loving students. *Explanation and Power* is a prime example. Along with its inscription "For Robert L. Stewart," it bears two epigraphs that suggest many of Peckham's doubts about his own participation in the endemic "original sin" of human language, and hence, his reluctance about being the initiator of writing projects. One epigraph, from Robert Browning, says, "I thought of turning honest— what a dream!" The other, from the Viennese critic Karl Kraus, asks, "Why does a man write?" and answers, "Because he does not possess enough character not to write."

Peckham's career as a literary and social theorist spanned five decades. Having begun as an interpreter of Romanticism, he came to work at every level of generality at which the various specialists in literary studies and social theory may spend their entire careers—running the gamut from bibliography and textual criticism to theories of human behavior in general. Both his common sense and his originality have been stunning. In the words of Barbara Herrnstein Smith, Peckham has "put at [our] service his uncanny knack for almost always, ultimately, being right" (*On the Margins of Discourse* xvi).

Morse Peckham died suddenly on 4 September 1993 after struggling against a series of strokes that began late in 1990, temporarily paralyzing his right side, but permanently and tragically impairing his genius for following and articulating great language. It is this genius for which I hope he will be remembered.

Bibliography

This bibliography is a revised and expanded version of the one provided by H. W. Matalene in the 1983 *festschrift Romanticism and Culture: A Tribute to Morse Peckham* (for which, see section VII, below). Essays appearing in any of Peckham's three collections of essays are not listed separately in section IV, but are instead cited below the entries for the collections in which they appear in section II. Texts neither by nor directly about Peckham but cited in this volume's Introduction or Biographical Afterword appear here in section VIII.

—Leo Daugherty

I. Books

"Guilt and Glory: A Study of 1839 *Festus*, a Nineteenth-Century Poem of Synthesis." Ph.D. dissertation, Princeton, 1947.

Humanistic Education for Business Executives: An Essay in General Education. Philadelphia: U Pennsylvania P, 1960.

With Seymour Chatman. *Word, Meaning, Poem.* New York: Thomas Y. Crowell, 1961.

Beyond the Tragic Vision: The Quest for Identity in the Nineteenth Century. New York: Braziller, 1962.

Oltre la Visione Tragica: La Ricerca dell'Identita nel Secolo Diciannovesimo [*Beyond the Tragic Vision*]. Translated by Leda Mussio Sartini. Milano: Lerici, 1965.

Man's Rage for Chaos: Biology, Behavior and the Arts. Philadelphia and New York: Chilton, 1965.

Editor. *Romanticism: The Culture of the Nineteenth Century.* New York: Braziller, 1965.

Art and Pornography: An Experiment in Explanation. New York: Basic Books, 1969.

Victorian Revolutionaries: Speculations on Some Heroes of a Culture Crisis. New York: Braziller, 1970.

With George P. Elliott, Philip McFarland, and Harvey Granite. *Themes in World Literature*. Boston: Houghton Mifflin, 1970.

With Philip McFarland, et al. *Moments in Literature*. Houghton Mifflin Literature Series. Boston: Houghton Mifflin, 1972.

————. *Explorations in Literature*. Houghton Mifflin Literature Series. Boston: Houghton Mifflin, 1972.

————. *Perceptions in Literature*. Houghton Mifflin Literature Series. Boston: Houghton Mifflin, 1972.

————. *Reflections in Literature*. Houghton Mifflin Literature Series. Boston: Houghton Mifflin, 1972.

————. *Themes in American Literature*. Houghton Mifflin Literature Series. Boston: Houghton Mifflin, 1972.

————. *Forms in English Literature*. Houghton Mifflin Literature Series. Boston: Houghton Mifflin, 1972.

Explanation and Power: The Control of Human Behavior. New York: Seabury, 1979; reprt Minneapolis: U Minnesota P, 1988.

The Birth of Romanticism: Cultural Crisis 1790–1815. Greenwood, Florida: Penkevill, 1986.

The Uses of the Unfashionable: The Pre-Raphaelites in the Nineteenth Century. Dallas: Contemporary Research Associates, 1993. (A 46-page monographic reprint of Chapter IV of *Victorian Revolutionaries*.)

II. COLLECTIONS OF ESSAYS

The Triumph of Romanticism: Collected Essays [I]. Columbia: U South Carolina P, 1970. Contents: "Toward a Theory of Romanticism" (1950); "Toward a Theory of Romanticism II: Reconsiderations" (1960); "The Dilemma of a Century: The Four Stages of Romanticism" (1964); "Romanticism: The Present State of Theory" (1965); "The Problem of the Nineteenth Century" (1955); "Constable and Wordsworth" (1952); "The Place of Architecture in Nineteenth-Century Romantic Culture" (1966); "Can 'Victorian' Have a Useful Meaning?" (1966); "Hawthorne and Melville as European Authors" (1966); "Darwin and Darwinisticism" (1959); "Aestheticism to Modernism: Fulfillment or Revolution?" (1967); "What Did Lady Windemere Learn?" (1956); "The Current Crisis in the Arts: Pop, Op, and Mini" (1967); "Art and Disorder" (1966); "Art and Creativity: Proposal for Research" (1966); "Order and Disorder in Fiction" (1966); "Discontinuity in Fiction: Persona, Narrator, Scribe" (1967); "Theory of Criticism" (1967); "Is Poetry Self-Expression?" (1953); "Metaphor: A Little Plain Speaking on a Weary Subject" (1962); "The Intentional? Fallacy?" (1968); "On the Historical Interpretation of Literature" (1969).

Romanticism and Behavior: Collected Essays [II]. Columbia: U South Carolina P, 1976. Contents: "Romanticism and Behavior" (1974); "The Function of History in Nineteeth-Century European Culture" (1971); "Reflections on Historical Modes in the Nineteenth Century" (1971); "Rebellion and Deviance" (1973); "Iconography and Iconology in the Arts of the Nineteenth and Twentieth Centuries" (1973); "Historiography and *The Ring and the Book*" (1967); "An Introduction to Emerson's Essays" (1968);

"Ernest Hemingway: Sexual Themes in His Writing" (1971); "The Place of Sex in the Work of William Faulkner" (1971); "Is the Problem of Literary Realism a Pseudoproblem?" (1969); "Poet and Critic: Or, the Damage Coleridge Has Done" (1969); "The Deplorable Consequences of the Idea of Creativity" (1970); "Literature and Knowledge" (1972); "The Virtues of Superficiality" (1969); "The Corporation's Role in Today's Crisis of Cultural Incoherence" (1971); "Arts for the Cultivation of Radical Sensitivity" (1971); "Cultural Stagnation in American Universities and Colleges" (1971); "The Arts and the Centers of Power" (1971); "Humanism, Politics, and Government in the Nineteenth Century" (1973); "The Cultural Crisis of the 1970s" (1973).

Romanticism and Ideology: Collected Essays [III]. Greenwood, Florida: Penkevill, 1985; reprinted Hanover, N.H.: University Press of New England, 1995 (page references in text are to the 1985 edition). Contents: "Cultural Transcendence: The Task of the Romantics" (1981); "Romanticism, Science, and Gossip" (1971); "Romantic Historicism in Italy: Opera, Painting, Fiction" (1976); "*Frederick the Great*" (1973); "Browning and Romanticism" (1973); "An Explanation of Realism" (1977); "Victorian Counterculture" (1974); "Edgar Saltus and the Heroic Decadence" (1978); "Romanticism, Surrealism, *Terra Nostra*" (1978); "Philosophy and Art as Related and Unrelated Modes of Behavior" (1973); "Man's Use of Nature" (1974); "Two Ways of Using 'Creativity'" (1977); "Truth in Art? Why Not?" (1980); "Psychology and Literature" (1974); "Perceptual and Semiotic Discontinuity in Art" (1971); "'Literature': Disjunction and Redundancy" (1977); "Three Notions About Criticism" (1979); "The Problem of Interpretation" (1978); "Literature and Behavior" (1980).

III. EDITIONS WITH INTRODUCTIONS
AND NOTES

Editor. Darwin, Charles Robert. *The Origin of Species: A Variorum Text.* Philadelphia: U Pennsylvania P, 1959.

Browning, Robert. "Paracelsus." In *The Complete Works of Robert Browning with Variant Readings & Annotations.* Roma A. King, Jr., Gen. Ed. Vol. 1, pp. 58–277, 285–306. Athens: Ohio UP, 1969.

Swinburne, Algernon Charles. *Poems and Ballads, Atalanta in Calydon.* Indianapolis and New York: Bobbs-Merrill, 1970.

Browning, Robert. "Pippa Passes." In *The Complete Works of Robert Browning with Variant Readings & Annotations.* Roma A. King, Jr., Gen. Ed. Vol. 3, 5–82, 343–51. Athens: Ohio UP, 1971.

———. "The Return of the Druses." In *The Complete Works of Robert Browning with Variant Readings & Annotations.* Roma A. King, Jr., Gen. Ed. Vol. 3, 263–341, 387–95. Athens: Ohio UP, 1971.

———. "Luria." In *The Complete Works of Robert Browning with Variant Readings & Annotations.* Roma A. King, Jr., Gen. Ed. Vol. 4, 273–351, 393–400. Athens: Ohio UP, 1973.

———. *Sordello: A Marginally Emended Edition.* Troy, New York: Wittston, 1977.

IV. PUBLISHED ESSAYS AND LECTURES
(UNCOLLECTED)

This section contains a few essays collected by Peckham that also appear in books by, or edited by, other writers.

"A Bailey Collection." *Princeton University Library Chronicle* 7 (June 1946): 149–154.

"American Editions of *Festus*: A Preliminary Survey." *Princeton University Library Chronicle* 8 (June 1947): 177–184.

"Selections from the Letters of Philip James Bailey." *Princeton University Library Chronicle* 9 (February 1948): 79–92.

"English Editions of Philip James Bailey's *Festus*." *Papers of the Bibliographical Society of America* 44 (First Quarter 1950): 55–58.

"Blake, Milton, and Edward Burney." *Princeton University Library Chronicle* 11 (Spring 1950): 107–126.

"*Beitrag zu einer Theorie der Romantik*" ["Toward a Theory of Romanticism"]. Trans. Erna Dehring. In *Begriffstimmung der Romantik*, 349–376. Ed. Helmut Prang. Darmstadt: Wissenschaftliche Buchgesellschaft, 1968.

"Dr. Lardner's *Cabinet Cyclopaedia*." *Papers of the Bibliographic Society of America* 45 (First Quarter 1951): 337–358.

"The Triumph of Romanticism." *Magazine of Arts* 45 (November 1952): 291–299.

"Is Poetry Self-Expression?" *Four Quarters* 2 (May 1953): 1–5.

"Emancipating the Executives." *Chicago Review* 8 (Special Issue 1954): 104–114.

"Gray's 'Epitaph' Revisited." *Modern Language Notes* 71 (June 1956): 409–411.

"The Problem of the Nineteenth Century." In *The Cultural Heritage of* 20th *Century Man*, 43–54. Philadelphia: Pennsylvania Literary Review and Philomathean Society.

"Sign/Symbol in the New Bayreuth." *Connotation* 2 (1963): 70–97.

"The Place of Culture in Nineteenth-Century Romantic Culture." *Yearbook of Comparative and General Literature* 15 (1966): 36–49.

"Literary Interpretation as Conventionalized Verbal Behavior." *Penn State Papers in Art Education* 2 (1967).

"Aestheticism to Modernism: Fulfillment or Revolution?" *Mundus Artium* 1 (Winter 1967): 36–55.

"Hawthorne and Melville as European Authors." In *Melville and Hawthorne in the Berkshires*, 42–62. Ed. Howard P. Vincent. Kent, Ohio: Kent State UP, 1968.

"A Reply [to E. H. Gombrich's review of *Man's Rage for Chaos*, in *New York Review of Books*, 23 June 1966, 3]." *New York Review of Books* 17 (November 1966): 42.

"Semantic Autonomy and Immanent Meaning." *Genre* 1 (July 1968): 190–194.

"An Interdisciplinary Approach to Nineteenth Century Culture: Some Problems." *South Atlantic Bulletin* 34 (January 1969): 8.

"Religion as a Humanizing Force." *Southern Humanities Review* 4 (Summer 1970): 214–222.

"The Collins Review of the Browning Edition." *The Browning Newsletter* 5 (Fall 1970): 3–5.

"On Romanticism: Introduction." *Studies in Romanticism* 9 (Fall 1970): 217–224.

"Foundations of Modern Textual Editing." In *Proof: The Yearbook of American Bibliographical and Textual Studies* I. 122–155. 1971.

"The Current Consequences of Romanticism in the Arts." In *Proceedings of the Seventh National Sculpture Conference*, 53–68. Lawrence, Kansas: National Sculpture Center, 1973.

"Browning and Romanticism." In *Robert Browning*, 47–76. Ed. Isobel Armstrong. London: G. Bell, 1974.

With David R. King. "Editing Nineteenth-Century Texts." In *Language and Texts: The Nature of Linguistic Evidence*, 1123–1146. Ed. Herbert H. Paper. Ann Arbor: Center for the Coordination of Ancient and Modern Studies, U Michigan, 1975.

"A Doctor of Philosophy in the Humanities?" *South Atlantic Bulletin* 40 (January 1975): 29–47.

"Victorian Counterculture." *Victorian Studies* 18 (March 1975): 257–276.

"Notes on Freehaver and the CEAA Additions." *Studies in the Novel* 7 (Fall 1975): 402–404.

"Frederick the Great." In *Carlyle Past and Present: A Collection of New Essays*, 198–215. Eds. K. J. Fielding and Rodger L. Tarr. London: Vision, 1976.

"Psychology and Literature." *Yearbook of Comparative Criticism* 7 (1976): 48–68.

"The Pleasures of the Po." *The Texas Arts Journal* 1 (1977): 1–12.

"Semiotic Interpretation in the Humanities." In *Man in Seven Modes*, 10–18. Southern Humanities Conference. Winston-Salem, N.C.: Wake Forest U Publications Office, 1977.

"Thoughts on Editing Sordello." *Studies in Browning and His Circle* 5 (Spring 1977): 11–18.

"The Infinitude of Pluralism." *Critical Inquiry* 3 (Summer 1977): 803–816.

"Edgar Saltus and the Heroic Decadence." In *Essays in American Literature in Memory of Richard P. Adams*, 61–69. Ed. Donald Pizer. *Tulane Studies in English* 23. 1978.

"Literature: Disjunction and Redundancy." In *What is Literature?* 219–230. Ed. Paul Hernadi. Bloomington: Indiana UP, 1978.

"Romantic Historicism in Italy: Opera, Painting, Fiction." *Concept, The Texas Arts Journal* 1–4 (1978): 73–92.

"The Evaluation of Art." *Arts Exchange* (January/February 1978): 13–15.

"An Explanation of 'Realism.'" *Denver Quarterly* 13 (Summer 1978): 3–10.

"The Problem of Interpretation." *College Literature* (1979): 1–17.

"Three Notions about Criticism." In *What is Criticism?* 38–51. Ed. Paul Hernadi. Bloomington: Indiana UP, 1981.

"Documents." In *Literature and History: Theoretical Problems and Russian Case Studies*, 176–191. Ed. Gary Saul Morson. Stanford: Stanford UP, 1986.

"Valuing." In *Pre/Text* 10 (Fall 1989): 209–216.

V . REVIEWS

The Portable Faulkner, ed. Malcolm Cowley. *Foreground* 1 (1946): 185–187.

The Metaphoric Tradition in Modern Poetry, by Sister Mary Bernetta Quinn. The United States Quarterly Book Review 12 (June 1956): 174.

"A Survey of Romantic Period Textbooks." *College English* 20 (October 1958): 49–53.

Regina vs. Palmerston, by Brian Connell. *Saturday Review* (2 September 1961): 20–21.

The Image, or What Happened to the American Dream, by Daniel J. Boorstin. *Annals of the American Academy of Political and Social Sciences* 344 (November 1962): 183.

The Tangled Bank, by Stanley Edgar Hyman. Victorian Studies 6 (December 1962): 180–182.

The Hero of the Waverley Novels, by Alexander Welsh. *Saturday Review* (15 June 1963): 26.

Mrs. Browning: A Poet's Work and Its Setting, by Alethea Hayter. *Saturday Review* (7 September 1963): 34.

Scrutiny: A Quarterly Review, 1932–53, ed. F. R. Leavis. *Saturday Review* (2 November 1963): 27, 37.

Christina Rossetti, by Lona Mosk Packer. *Saturday Review* (28 December 1963): 41.

"Recent Studies of Nineteenth-Century English Lieterature." *SEL* 3 (Autumn 1963): 595–611.

Erasmus Darwin, by Desmond King-Hele; and *Doctor Darwin*, by Hesketh Pearson. *Saturday Review* (28 March 1964): 44–45.

The Correspondence of Emerson and Carlyle, ed. Joseph Slater. *Saturday Review* (19 December 1964): 34, 39.

Religious Humanism and the Victorian Novel, by U. C. Knoepflmacher. *Saturday Review* (22 May 1965): 78.

The Artifice of Reality, by Karl Kroeber. JEGP 64 (July 1965): 591–593.

The Disappearance of God: Five Nineteenth-Century Writers, by J. Hillis Miller. *Victorian Poetry* 3 (1965): 202–204.

The Life of the Mind in America from the Revolution to the Civil War, by Perry Miller. *Saturday Review* (28 August 1965): 31, 48.

Victorian Minds, by Gertrude Himmelfarb; *Feasting with Panthers*, by Rupert Croft-Cooke; and *Prince Albert and Victorian Taste*, by Winslow Ames. *Saturday Review* (30 March 1968): 29.

The Sense of an Ending, by Frank Kermode. *Modern Philology* 65 (May 1968): 434–435.

Life with Queen Victoria, ed. Victor Mallet. *Saturday Review* 26 October 1968): 50.

"Robert Browning: A Review of the Year's Research." *The Browning Newsletter* 2 (April 1969): 3–9.

Carlyle and the Idea of the Modern, by Albert J. La Valley. *Victorian Studies* 112 (June 1969): 485–486.

English Romantic Poetry, by Albert S. Gerard. The CEA Critic 32 (December 1969): 15.

Music, the Arts, and Ideas, by Leonard B. Meyer. *History and Theory* 9 (March 1970): 127–135.

Poetic Closure, by Barbara Herrnstein Smith. Genre 5 (March 1972): 61–64.

Natural Supernaturalism, by M. H. Abrams; and *Revolution and Romanticism,* by Howard Mumford Jones. Studies in Romanticism 13 (Fall 1974): 359–365.

The Transforming Vision, by Jose A. Arguelles. *Journal of Aesthetics and Art Criticism* 34 (Spring 1976): 3343–3344.

Victorian Conventions, by John R. Reed. *Novel* 9 (Winter 1976): 171–172.

The Romantic Progression, by Colin Martindale. American Literature 48 (May 1976): 249–251.

The Letters of Henry James 1843–1875, ed. Leon Edel. *Resources for American Literary Study* 6 (Spring 1976): 113–116.

The Stranger in Shakespeare, by Leslie A. Fiedler. *Shakespeare Studies* 9 (1976): 320–324.

The Classic, by Frank Kermode. *JEGP* 76 (January 1977): 117–121.

William Morris, by Edward P. Thompson. *The Nation* (9 July 1977): 53–55.

The Romantic Will, by Michael G. Cooke. *Studies in Romanticism* 17 (Winter 1978): 91–93.

Progress in Art, bu Suzi Gablik. Lone Star Book Review (June 1979): 7.

A History of the Oratorio, by Howard E. Smither. *Lone Star Book Review* (July 1979): 9.

Cultural Materialism, by Marvin Harris. *Lone Star Book Review* (January/February 1980): 13.

The Walter Scott Operas, by Jerome Mitchell. *Studies in Scottish Literature* 14 (1979): 277–280.

The Scottish Enlightenment, by Anand Chitnis. *Studies in Scottish Literature* 14 (1979): 299–300.

Critical Understanding, by Wayne C. Booth. *JEGP* 1979 (July 1980): 429–431.

On the Margins of Discourse, by Barbara Herrnstein Smith. *Poetics Today* 2:1a (1980): 191–195.

Carlyle and Tennyson, by Michael Timko. *Nineteenth Century Literature* 44 (March 1990): 4.

VI. UNPUBLISHED ESSAYS AND LECTURES

A History of the Ninth Bomber Command (USAF): 1944–1946.

"The Gothic Novel: Some Observations on an Old Hat." November 1972.

"Humanists, Education, and Society." June 1973.

"The Thematic Studies Program of the John Jay College of Criminal Justice." April 1973.

"Methodology in the Humanities." October 1973.

"Literature, Ideology, and Society." February 1975.

"A Response to M. H. Abrams." August 1977.

"What is Affirmation?" December 1977.

"Why Bother With the Humanities?" Undated. Possibly published in 1980s. One copy in possession of Leo Daugherty (c/o Wesleyan UP).

V I I. Festschriften

Matalene, H. W., Ed. *Romanticism and Culture: A Tribute to Morse Peckham and a Bibliography of His Work.* Studies in English and American Literature, Linguistics, and Culture I. Columbia, S.C.: Camden House, 1983.

V I I I. Other Works Mentioned
in the Introduction or
Biographical Afterword

Baudrillard, Jean. *Baudrillard Live.* Ed. Mike Gane. London: Routledge, 1993.
———. *The Ecstasy of Communication.* New York: Semiotext(e). 1988.
Deleuze, Gilles, and Claire Parnet. *Dialogues.* Trans. Hugh Tomlinson and Barbara Habberjam. New York: Columbia UP, 1987 (rprt of 1977 French ed.).
Haraway, Donna J. *Simians, Cyborgs, and Women: The Reinvention of Nature.* New York: Routledge, 1991.
Rorty, Richard. *Contingency, Irony, and Solidarity.* Cambridge: Cambridge UP, 1989.
Salkie, Raphael. *The Chomsky Update: Linguistics and Politics.* London: Unwin Hyman, 1990.
Smith, Barbara Herrnstein. *On the Margins of Discourse: The Relation of Literature to Language.* Chicago: U of Chicago P, 1978.
Stevens, Wallace. *Letters of Wallace Stevens.* Ed. Holly Stevens. New York: Knopf, 1966.

Index

UNIVERSITY PRESS OF NEW ENGLAND publishes books under its own imprint and is the publisher for Brandeis University Press, Brown University Press, Dartmouth College, Middlebury College Press, University of New Hampshire, University of Rhode Island, Tufts University, University of Vermont, Wesleyan University Press, and Salzburg Seminar.

MORSE PECKHAM was Distinguished Professor of English and Comparative Literature at the University of South Carolina. For four decades he was one of America's most important and interesting writers on Romanticism, literary theory, social theory, and problems in human behavior. He was equally well known for being an extraordinarily inspiring teacher. His previous books include *Beyond the Tragic Vision, Man's Rage for Chaos, Art and Pornography, Victorian Revolutionaries, Explanation and Power: The Control of Human Behavior,* and (as editor) the standard variorum edition of Darwin's *Origin of Species.* He also produced three volumes of collected essays, the most recent of which is *Romanticism and Ideology,* now being reissued by Wesleyan. He died in 1993 in his eightieth year.

LEO DAUGHERTY is Professor of Literature and Linguistics at The Evergreen State College, where he also directs the Center for the Study of Science and Human Values. He has published recent studies of Shakespeare and Cormac McCarthy, and his short fiction has appeared in such places as *Exquisite Corpse* and *Omni.* He is currently completing a book on human rights theory. He was Morse Peckham's friend for over twenty years.

H. W. MATALENE is Professor of English at the University of South Carolina. He describes himself as "a Morse Peckham alumnus who works on the problem of how to make English Literature before Romanticism—the aristocracy's literature of heroism, manners, and sensibility—meaningful to those who will be the corporate and state bureaucrats of the first half of the twenty-first century." He is the editor of *Romanticism and Culture: A Tribute to Morse Peckham and a Bibliography of his Work.*

Library of Congress Cataloging-in-Publication Data
Peckham, Morse.
    The romantic virtuoso / Morse Peckham.
      p. cm.
    "Wesleyan University Press."
    Includes bibliographical references (p.) and index.
    ISBN 0-8195-5280-1
    1. Romanticism. I. Title.
PN751.P43 1995
809'.9145—dc20   94-26406